US AGAINST THEM

An Oral History

US AGAINST THEM

of the Ryder Cup

Robin McMillan

HarperCollins*Publishers*

HarperCollins books may be purchased for educational, business, or sales promotional use. For information, please write: Special Markets Department, HarperCollins Publishers Inc., 10 East 53rd Street, New York, NY 10022.

FIRST EDITION

Designed by Jaime Langione

Printed on acid-free paper

Library of Congress Cataloging-in-Publication Data

McMillan, Robin.
    Us against them : an oral history of the Ryder Cup / Robin McMillan.
       p.   cm.
    ISBN 0-06-019791-9
    1. Ryder Cup—History. 2. Golf—Tournaments—United States—History. 3. Golf—Tournaments—Great Britain—History. I. Title.
GV970.3.R93M36 2004
796.352'66—dc22   2004047402

04 05 06 07 08 ❖/RRD   10 9 8 7 6 5 4 3 2 1

To Gail, Madeleine, and Lily

ACKNOWLEDGMENTS

First of all, of course, a big thanks to all those who were inter-
viewed and to all those who helped set up the conversations.
Whether it was sitting in a Champions Tour locker room with Larry
Nelson or in a hallway of a Holiday Inn at Kennedy Airport with
Billy Casper, it always was interesting.

And special thanks to the ever-amusing madman from Ulster,
David Feherty, and to the two 2002 Ryder Cup captains Curtis
Strange and Sam Torrance—three more gracious human beings you
could not find. Sam told his waitress he'd order breakfast just as soon
as he'd answered a few questions. He didn't order for two hours!

Thanks also to Colin Callander and Mitch Platts on the eastern
side of the pond, to Ward Clayton at the PGA Tour, to Glenn
Greenspan at Augusta National, to my former colleague Mike Bryan,
who encouraged me to proceed with this idea, to Jean Brown for
her transcriptions, to my editor at HarperCollins, Hugh Van Dusen,
who is as addicted to this damn event as much as anyone I know;
his assistant, David Semanki; and to agents (and fellow Morningside
Montessori parents) Brian Defiore and Suzanne Gluck.

And I suppose a thank-you to Sam Ryder and all those who have
supported the Ryder Cup and have kept it going through good and
bad. If there is a better contest in sport, I have yet to find it.

CONTENTS

JUST IN CASE...

MATCH PLAY: Generally speaking, you play golf one of two ways, stroke play or match play. In stroke play you count your strokes, and fewest wins. Most professional golf is played at stroke play. Most amateurs, however, play match play, a head-to-head contest in which the fewer strokes on a hole wins the hole and the golfer or team that wins the most holes wins the match. If you and your opponent take an identical amount of strokes on a hole, then it is "halved." However, unlike other sports, you keep score by counting the difference between your and your opponent's totals. For example, if you win four holes and your opponent wins two, then you are said to be "2 up" (and your opponent is "2 down"). When the difference between your total and your opponent's total is greater than the number of holes remaining, then the match is over.

That weekend group? Nearly always match play. Match play also is attractive because you can play relatively badly and win a hole if your opponent plays even worse. It is a series of little contests that can add up to a far bigger whole.

FOURSOMES: Teams of two players play one ball and alternate shots. One player hits the tee shots on the odd-numbered holes (that would be beginning with number one) and the other player begins the even holes. It is not a format that players are used to, and the pressure of not letting down a teammate on top of not letting down the team—and your country or continent—adds an edge.

FOUR-BALLS: Each of two players per team plays his own ball. Low score wins the hole for the team. The interesting twist in four-balls is that players can play out of turn. Normally farthest from the hole hits (or is "away"). In four-balls, teammates can switch the order. Why? Let's say a player is five feet from the hole and has taken five strokes, but his teammate who is farther from the hole has taken three. The closer player would go first to demonstrate to his teammate the speed and break of the green. It's all about teamwork and strategy.

SINGLES: Each player plays his own ball against a single opponent. Low score wins the hole.

TIED MATCHES: The Ryder Cup goes to the team that wins the most points, with one point at stake in each match. In matches that are tied at the end of eighteen holes, each player wins half a point. In the event that the overall score is tied at the end of the competition, the Ryder Cup is retained by the team that won it last.

US AGAINST THEM

On a cold, snowy Tuesday in the winter of 1982, an Englishman named Colin Snape boarded a train in London and traveled some five hundred miles north to Perth, a small town on the southernmost margins of the Scottish highlands. His mission? To save the Ryder Cup.

Before one wonders why Snape, then the executive director of the British Professional Golfers Association, should have been heading to a place not known for much more than its location on the salmon-rich river Tay, one should really question why the Ryder Cup needed saving in the first place. The biennial match that pits golf professionals from the United States against their counterparts from Europe today draws galleries of up to forty thousand per day—even just for practice rounds—and claims a worldwide television audience of more than 100 million (normal coverage now is twenty-six hours during the three days' play, two ten-hour "blocks" on the first two days, and six hours on the third day!). Each time it is played, the Cup's two governing bodies—the PGA of America and a joint body made up of representatives from the European PGA Tour and the British PGA—ka-ching an estimated $60 million between them.

Not too long ago, however, the Ryder Cup was on life support.

It should not have been, but here is what happened. Since the event's genesis in the 1920s, the United States had come to dominate the results to the extent that television, the print media, and golf fans had lost almost complete interest. Some of the American players had, too, and not without good reason. By the time Tom Weiskopf chose to go hunting rather than represent his country in the 1977 matches in England, the United States had lost only three of twenty-three matches. Two years later, Tom Watson withdrew from the U.S. squad at the Greenbrier resort in West Virginia just three days before the matches were to begin, as though the impending birth of a child had taken him completely by surprise.

But things were changing. After a lopsided affair in 1977, it was decided to expand the British team into a European team and tap into the supply of promising young talent emerging on the Continent. With West Germany's Bernhard Langer and Spain's Severiano Ballesteros in the European fold, no longer would Jack Nicklaus and Lee Trevino and Hale Irwin be able to treat their opponents like the Washington Generals. At last there would be a contest!

Except this new European team lost badly in 1979, then was given a good old-fashioned hiding by the United States at Walton Heath, just outside London, in 1981. When the Ryder Cup should really have been taking hold, it was in worse shape than ever.

COLIN SNAPE: That 1981 side was the best American team there ever was, and they gave us a pasting. It couldn't have been worse. And after 1981 our sponsor, the Sun Alliance Insurance Company, was pulling out. The Ryder Cup was finished. Sun Alliance had been one of the last of the "patrons," as distinct from commercial sponsors. The chairman, Lord Aldington, was a golf nut and a friend of British prime minister Ted Heath, and he felt that sponsoring the Ryder Cup was in Britain's national interest. So Sun Alliance sponsored us from 1973, to '81, but almost every one was tainted. Weiskopf going hunting. Tom Watson's wife, Linda, due a baby, so Tom pulled out. Sun Alliance finally said, "Why do we bother?"

So it was my job to find another sponsor. For months I went door to door like a brush salesman, trying to sell someone—*anyone*—the Ryder Cup. I went to a tile company, to Chemical Bank, the American bank which had just opened in London (it is now called JP Morgan Chase). I even approached the company that managed the careers of Tom Jones and Engelbert Humperdinck!

Eventually we had a meeting of the Ryder Cup committee, and I had to report that in six months the only offer I'd had was £80,000 in cigarette coupons which could be redeemed for cash. Because it was tobacco the offer didn't see the light of day, but it shows how bad things were.

Bernard Gallacher [who played in eight Ryder Cups and captained Europe in three] was on the committee and insisted, "Look, we have to get to America in any shape or form. We'll even pay for our own tickets." How realistic that would have been we'd never know but, again, that shows how bad it was.

Then one day I got a call from a man called Bill Watson, who was on the Ryder Cup commmittee and was a former captain of the Scottish PGA. He said, "I think Raymond Miquel of Bell's Scotch Whisky might be worth an approach."

Now, I was getting these calls all the time but never had any luck with any of them. But I called Raymond and made an appointment and went up to Perth on a bleak day and met Raymond for the first time.

"Ruthless" Raymond Miquel was a hard-nosed Scottish businessman whose specialty was "efficiencies," which is to say he slashed costs and boosted productivity wherever he went. While at Bell's in the 1970s and early 1980s, he increased the blended whisky's sales more than sevenfold and almost single-handedly turned it into the top-selling brand in the United Kingdom. He also had Bell's buy the Gleneagles Hotel, where he still lives, and which will host the 2009 Ryder Cup matches.

COLIN SNAPE: Talk about an autocrat! They had a boardroom table that sat twenty-four, and he had all these minions all around him, and let's just say it wasn't a case of "Well, gentlemen, what do you think?" He drove an Aston Martin Lagonda with the registration "1BEL." He wasn't a shrinking violet by any means.

Raymond explained that he wanted Bell's to sponsor the team when it was in America, which was really unusual, but he wanted to spread his wings into the American market. I did a deal for £300,000 for two cups, the second one back in Britain in 1985, and when you consider the Sun Alliance deal was £75,000, that was phenomenal. So at least we were in business, up and running.

Although I then had to persuade the PGA of America to agree to it, because they were loathe to even think of putting a U.K. sponsor's name on a Ryder Cup in America. During a meeting at the PGA Championship at Southern Hills in Tulsa, Oklahoma in 1982, before I'd met with Raymond, we had been quite frank with them and told them that, if we couldn't swing a sponsor, then the Ryder Cup was on its way out. So they were much more supportive than I would ever have expected, but they wanted to see the matches continue.

There would be other, seismic changes in the Ryder Cup scene. Europe would appoint as captain for the 1983 matches Tony Jacklin, British Open champion in 1969 and U.S. Open champion in 1970, the biggest British golf legend of his time. And with the continental European players beginning to come through, and be joined by an equally promising group of British and Irish players, the Europeans finally shed their inferiority complex and the Ryder Cup finally became a contest.

And what a contest it was! Although the United States would win the 1983 matches—by a single point—the European team won in 1985 and then again in 1987, and suddenly for one long weekend every two years, golf morphed from a relatively placid, whispery sort of sport into a cacaphonic feud for transatlantic bragging rights, continent against continent, between the rich, young land of plenty and a bunch of old empires. Golf fans got it quickly, but even those who would normally rather catch forty winks than watch golf—to

4

*them there's not that much difference—found themselves so affront-
ed by the concept of defeat that they would stand in front of the television yelling "U-S-A! U-S-A!" at people they'd barely heard of.*

COLIN SNAPE: To think that I went up there in December of 1982
and the matches were in September of 1983. With less than a year
to go, we didn't have a sponsor, which shows just how desperate
we'd been. So when history is written, I'd have to say that Raymond
Miquel's drive and initiative was the springboard for everything that
has happened since then.

*Oh, there are many good reasons to go to Scotland for matters
related to golf. But this trip north of the border may have been the
best of all. Army-Navy? McEnroe-Borg? Buckeyes-Wolverines? Ali-
Frazier? Heck, even Yankees–Red Sox doesn't come close.*

*The Ryder Cup is the old world against the new, sport's ultimate
us against them.*

THE BEGINNING

The original sponsor—it amounted to not much more than donating the trophy—was Samuel Ryder, a businessman who'd made his fortune selling herbs and seeds (although his creation of the Ryder Cup was as much out of a love for the game as it was an effort to sell product). Ryder was born in Preston, in the north of England, in 1858. In the 1890s, having moved south to a city outside London called St. Alban's, he and his wife started their own mail-order seed business. They would fill small packets of seeds in their own home, then each Friday would mail the packets along with catalogs from the local post office. Within a decade the Ryders were employing up to ninety people a week.

In 1908, Ryder fell into poor health and, at the urging of a local church minister, decided to take up golf. He began with lessons from a professional who would visit his home, soon graduated to a nine-hole course, and then a year later he joined the Verulam Golf Club in St. Alban's. Two years after that he was appointed club captain.

All this we know from various reports, but how he actually established the Ryder Cup has been the topic of some debate. The matches began in 1927, but a couple of transatlantic team matches came along before it. The first is reported to have taken place at

Gleneagles, Scotland, in 1921, but the U.S. team was assembled not to launch the concept of transatlantic team play, but to increase the number of American professionals competing in the British Open. "The plan is to have the American team make its stand at Gleneagles while the American delegation is over for the British Open," wrote the New York Times in February 1921, "and meet the onslaughts of any and all who care to engage them." As it turned out, after seven singles matches and five foursomes, "any and all" won 9–3.

The next contest came in 1926, when Ryder and his brother James suggested that a team match be set up against American professionals who planned to travel to Britain and try to qualify for that year's British Open. The Wentworth Club, just outside London, was chosen because it was close to Sunningdale, one of the qualifying sites. The British team won the matches by a score of 13$\frac{1}{2}$ to 1$\frac{1}{2}$, but the results did not make it into the record books because the American team included transplanted players born outside the United States—two Scots, two Englishmen, and one Australian. The PGA of America could not possibly have endorsed it (furthermore, it wasn't their idea.)

When the actual cup appeared has been the main source of argument. The utterly quaint official story goes that Sam Ryder was in the gallery at the 1926 matches at Wentworth and became enchanted with the whole concept. He later found himself in the company of several players in the clubhouse and commented, "We must do this again." At the prodding of some players, Ryder agreed to donate a trophy.

Except if this is true, someone forgot to alert the media. In April 1926, six weeks before Ryder allegedly agreed to pony up a trophy, The Times of London reported that "Mr S Ryder, of St Albans, has presented a trophy for annual competition between teams of British and American professionals. The first match for the trophy is to take place at Wentworth on June 4 and 5." Then, when those dates rolled around, the New York Times reported, "Today, two teams of British and American professionals met each other on the Wentworth course in combat for the first time in the Ryder Cup, presented by Samuel Ryder."

But there is also evidence that the cup did not make an appearance that year. In his book The Ryder Cup, *English author Dale Concannon quotes a June 11 issue of British magazine* Golf Illustrated *that maintains the cup was the victim of the general strike that crippled Britain in May of that year. Ryder, the magazine says, was nervous about the economic situation and therefore decided "to withhold the cup." Why one should have affected the other is not explained, but suspicious minds might conclude that Ryder just didn't have it ready in time.*

No matter. When the first real Ryder Cup was held the following year, in Worcester, Massachusetts, the cup was ready and waiting. It was nineteen inches high and fashioned from solid gold. Its hallmark read "1927," and on the very top stood the tiny likeness of Abe Mitchell, one of the top British professionals of the day and the personal swing guru to Sam Ryder.

LET PLAY BEGIN

*I*f the British entertained any thoughts of winning in Worcester— buoyed perhaps by the thrashing they'd administered at Wentworth—it took one day's play to change their minds. Led by captain Walter Hagen, the United States won three of four-hole foursomes. The following day, it won six of eight-hole singles matches and halved another (until 1961 the format was always four-hole foursomes followed by eight 36-hole singles matches). Final score: 9½–2½. The British team could have been forgiven had it expressed regret for having shown up.

Truth be told, they nearly didn't. In accepting the invitation to play, the British PGA didn't take into account the cost of sending a team across the Atlantic. To its rescue came Golf Illustrated, which launched a drive to raise $3,000. Not only did its editor George Philpot use the magazine to tout the value of subsidizing the team, but he also appealed to each of 1,750 British golf clubs. Only 216 responded. After counting in a few corporate gifts and a $100 donation from Sam Ryder, the appeal came up $500 short, and Philpot and his magazine plugged the gap themselves.

Granted, it was only a few years earlier that club professionals had first been allowed inside many clubhouses, but the threadbare *approach to the Ryder Cup would handicap the British sides for decades. The United States, meanwhile, did things with gusto. When the British team docked in New York in May 1927 after a stormy six-day crossing—minus Abe Mitchell, who'd come down with appendicitis—they were greeted by a welcome party made up of PGA of America officials and U.S. captain Walter Hagen. A police escort rushed them across midtown Manhattan to the Biltmore Hotel, where they dropped their luggage before being whisked north to the West-chester Biltmore (which much later became the Westchester Country Club, a longtime stop on the PGA Tour) for a welcome dinner and a floodlit putting tournament! All these arrangements would be quite normal today—except perhaps the putting tournament—but to the British this was another world. Even their garb made them look second class next to the flash Yanks—another trend that would haunt the British for years. As the* New York Times *noted after the first day's play, "There was a time when the British were anything but fashionable in their dress. They have perked up. But they still have a long way to go to catch up with the Americans, who are Beau Brummels plus."*

Same story for the 1929 matches at Moortown, in the north of England. The United States raised a war chest of $10,000 while a second Golf Illustrated *fund-raiser gathered £800 and change. But at least Britian won the cup, erasing a one-point deficit after the foursomes by winning five singles matches and halving a sixth.*

More important, the matches caught the fans' attention, as a trail of cars waiting to park stretched one mile back from the club, and galleries of up to ten thousand stood ten deep trying to get a glimpse of the golf. Reported the Associated Press, "The gallery, which often was entirely out of control of the 200 officials and 50 uniformed policemen, fairly fought to get a close-up of play."

The 1931 matches at Scioto Country Club in Columbus, Ohio, were something of a foregone conclusion when the British had to play without three of their top players. Two were victims of a rule that said team members had not only to be British natives but also residents of Britain.

PETER ALLISS (color commentator for ABC-TV and an eight-time Ryder Cupper): My father, Percy, was picked for the team in 1929 but didn't play. Then in 1931 he wasn't eligible because he was in Berlin. And Aubrey Boomer was in France, so he couldn't play.

Father had gone to Berlin in 1926 or '27, to a new golf club [Wannsee] that was very, very productive. He was making probably $5,000 a year, which in the mid-'20s was an absolute fortune.

I was born in Berlin in 1931, just when Hitler was coming to power. War didn't come for another seven, eight years, but Hitler was already starting his purge on the Jews and closing banks, so in 1932 they decided to get out. But it wasn't so easy. The banks were shut, but we managed to get some money, and Mother stuffed it down her knickers and we got on a train and escaped. But instead of coming here with what then would have been a small fortune, a couple of thousand dollars, we came home with about $300.

Although Henry (later "Sir Henry") Cotton was invited to play, he got into a dispute with the British PGA, who insisted he return to the United Kingdom with the rest of the team when he wanted to stay on and play some exhibition matches, and that every member of the squad would get an equal cut of exhibition-match revenue, when Cotton wanted to conduct his own.

The actual matches ended with a 9–3 victory for the United States, but a meteorological victory for the Brits. Although a brief storm offered temporary respite, the matches were played in Ohio in June, and temperatures approached triple digits.

ALLIS: I've seen a picture of somebody tipping a bucket of cold water over the players' heads; it was so hot.

So hot that the British PGA insisted that, although scheduling the Ryder Cup in June allowed the players to enter the U.S. Open on the same trip, they would no longer play in the height of summer. The Ryder Cup thereafter moved to its familiar autumn dates.

Cotton was the victim of the residents-only rule when the Ryder Cup went to Southport and Ainsdale, on England's northwest coast, in 1933; he'd taken a position in Belgium. Still, the British won by a point, 6½–5½. One hopes they enjoyed their celebration, for they would not see victory again for almost a quarter of a century, as the first long spell of American dominance began. At Ridgwood Country Club in New Jersey in 1935—Byron Nelson was the club professional—the United States won 9–3. (The British team featured three brothers, Charles, Ernest, and Reg Whitcombe). On the return to Southport and Ainsdale in 1937, the United States won 8–4.

PETER ALLISS: My father had a match against Gene Sarazen in 1937 in which Sarazen was rather fortunate. The match was all square at the par-3 15th in the afternoon. Sarazen went through the green. The old man had played a good shot in, and Sarazen went over and his ball was in the lap of a woman sitting behind the green. She got up, went like that [motions her excitedly flapping the ball off her lap] and the ball ran down onto the green and stymied the old man [a stymie is when a ball on the green lay between the opponent's ball and the hole; until 1950 the player could insist on it remaining there, whereas now he must mark it and remove it if asked]. So the old man was 1 down and that's what he lost by.

There followed a ten-year hiatus in play, caused mainly by the outbreak of war in Europe on September 3, 1939, two months before the next Ryder Cup was to have been played at the Ponte Vedra Club in Florida. The PGA of America nevertheless named its team—and the Ponte Vedra Club gave each player life membership—while the British PGA announced the eight players who had qualified thus far. As the war years went on, the PGA continued to name unofficial Ryder Cup teams, to play exhibition matches to raise funds for the war efforts. In one of those matches, at the Detroit Golf Club in August 1941, Walter Hagen skippered the "U.S. Ryder Cup Team" against a team captained by legendary amateur Bobby Jones. In front of galleries of up to ten thousand, Jones and Gene Sarazen lost 8 and 6 to Byron Nelson and Jug McSpaden, while other matches were populated by the likes of Ben Hogan, Jimmy Demaret, Craig Wood, Clayton

Heafner, Paul Runyan, and Sam Snead. If nothing else, that the United States could produce two teams of such high caliber only pointed to the superiority it held, superiority that would become "official" when Ryder Cup play resumed in the Pacific Northwest.

*T*he British were going to do it right when the Ryder Cup began again in November 1947. They would look good, and they would have money in their pockets—although not a lot as World War II had ended but a little more than two years earlier. The British economy was in tatters, and food, clothing, and gasoline rationing was still in place (the United States also had a wartime rationing program, but it was not as severe). The day before the British team boarded the Queen Mary for the transatlantic voyage, the United Press news agency reported,

> The handsome double-breasted blazers, emblazoned with the Ryder Cup crest, were designed to escape that "austere look" and to dress the team as true ambassadors of British golf.
>
> The golfers were permitted by the Government to take the old limit of 75 pounds [$300] out of the country instead of being restricted to the current limit of 35 because the trip was arranged before the new ruling was put into effect.
>
> Tailors and sporting goods manufacturers combined to make the Britons a well-equipped group of emissaries. Enough ration coupons were pooled to give each player several pairs of golf shoes, flannel trousers and nylon umbrellas rainbowed in the Ryder Cup colors of maroon, silver and blue.

Once on board, the British golfers ate as if they'd just got out of jail, demolishing the baskets of fresh fruit in their cabins and gorg-

ing on steaks the size of Ohio. One report had it that several players on the team put on several pounds. Upon arrival in New York they were met by one Robert Hudson, the first wealthy sponsor to save the Ryder Cup from extinction.

Oddly enough, while the PGA in previous years had had little trouble raising financial backing, this time around there were no takers, until in stepped Hudson, founder of the Portland, Oregon–based Hudson House food-packing firm, a member of the PGA of America's Advisory Committee and probably the biggest booster of golf in the Pacific Northwest. Hudson not only agreed to pick up all expenses while the teams were in the United States but accompanied the British on the three-and-a-half-day train ride to Portland.

And of course he was there in the pouring rain when, led by Ben Hogan, the United States handed Britain its biggest defeat in the Ryder Cup thus far: an 11–1 thrashing that would have been a total blowout were it not for a victory by Sam King over Herman Keiser in the very last match of all.

The carnage continued. At Ganton, in the north of England, in 1949, the United States won six of the eight singles matches to come back from a 3–1 first-day deficit to win 7–5. Hogan was the leader again, but on crutches. That February his car had collided with a bus on a misty morning in West Texas, and he'd come perilously close to losing not only his legs but his life. He couldn't play at Ganton, of course, but the American captain's appearance on the holes nearest to the clubhouse was an inspiring presence for his players.

In 1951 at Pinehurst, North Carolina, the United States took a 3–1 lead after the foursomes, whereupon both teams took the day off—despite protests by the Brits—to go to a Tennessee–North Carolina college football game. When they resumed, the United States won the singles by a field goal and a safety for a final tally of 9½–2½. In 1953, it was back to where the Ryder Cup began, albeit unofficially: Wentworth.

PETER ALLISS: I appeared for the first time in 1953. After the old guard got slaughtered in Portland in '47, [Britain's *Daily Telegraph* golf writer] Leonard Crawley led a charge to have some young people brought in. I was seventeen at the time, but then I did my national service from 1949 to '51.

In 1953 I was the youngest ever to have played, and we [Alliss and his father, Percy] were the first father-son combination. Rationing was still on, but Henry Cotton, our team captain, managed to get some steaks. He was a great one for steaks and Perrier water and a glass of red wine and relaxation and practice.

As it turned out, Alliss and another young player, Bernard Hunt, would play a crucial role in determining the result. After losing three of the first day's four foursomes, the British rallied in the second-day singles. Fred Daly beat Ted Kroll, Eric Brown beat Lloyd Mangrum, and Harry Weetman beat Sam Snead. Then Harry Bradshaw beat Fred Haas. (Bradshaw was the first golfer from Eire to play in the Ryder Cup. PGA of America literature, and many other sources, maintain Irish players did not compete until 1973. That's not the case. In 1973 "Ireland" was made an official part of the team name.) Finally it came down to Alliss or Hunt. If they could produce 1½ points between them, in any permutation, Britain would win. Both were ahead in the final stages.

PETER ALLISS: I was playing Jim Turnesa, who was the PGA champion at the time. With three holes to play I was 1 up and hit a good drive up the 16th, but I took a five and it was all square. At the 17th he drove it out of bounds, but I went out of bounds, too! I got a four on the second ball [making six] and he got a five. Now he was 1 up. At the last hole, he hit it sixty yards off into the trees, and I hit a good drive. I then hit a 2-iron and ended up twenty yards left of the green. He pitched up to be on the green in four. I was lying in this damp mossy lie. I duffed a sand iron, and my ball just was off the edge of the green. I chipped it up to to four feet, maybe less. He missed for five. And then somehow I missed mine. We halved it with sixes, and he won 1 up.

Now a win by Hunt over Dave Douglas would mean a tie. The United States would retain the cup, but at least Britain would salvage the sort of respect it hadn't known in the past two decades. Both players were on in three, but far from the hole. Hunt rolled his putt up to about three feet. Douglas made his five, and Hunt stepped up to win the point that Britain craved. As the New York Times *reported, "The crowd of more than 15,000 that surged against the barriers around the 36th green was thrashing about in a fever of excitement."*

And then, just like that, Hunt missed the putt.

PETER ALLISS: If Bernard Hunt hadn't three-putted and I'd halved, we'd have won the Ryder Cup, which would have been huge. *Huge.*

We should have won.

A new player entered the Ryder Cup picture in 1955: real estate. In this case, Thunderbird Country Club in the burgeoning golf oasis called Palm Springs.

TOMMY BOLT [1958 U.S. Open champion, and a fiery player who competed in two Ryder Cups]: I really don't know why Thunderbird was chosen. Money had a lot to do with it, if you know what I mean. Thunderbird was the first country club in Palm Springs, and the members had a lot of money and could kind of manipulate the PGA. It was used as promotion.

I tell you, it was a tough match; it was the best British team they'd ever had.

One of the toughest players was the late Eric Brown, a hot-blooded Scot who eventually would play in four British Ryder Cup teams and captain two.

JOHN JACOBS [who played in one Ryder Cup and captained in two; he later helped create the European PGA Tour and ran a successful chain of golf schools in the United States]: Eric Brown had no fear. Medal or match play, he just went straight at it. Syd Scott partnered Eric in 1955. He was just the opposite of Eric—very safe, kept it in play, good short game, not a big hitter, and so on. Sid told me at the end of the first-day foursomes how they had reached the first green in two, and Syd had putted up from a long, long way away. He left it dead in the middle of the hole, about only three inches short, close enough for an easy par, and Eric hissed at him, "It'll never go in the @#%&$ hole if you don't #%$@#$ . . ." What a lovely partnership that was.

Renton Laidlaw [European golf television commentator and long-time golf journalist]: Eric Brown couldn't really care whether you agreed with him or not. The story I always like about Eric Brown took place at a World Cup, but it might easily have been a Ryder Cup. Sitting in front of me in a bus that was taking players and press back from an official function to our hotel was Joan Fontaine, the actress, who was married at the time to an American golf writer called Alfred Wright. At the back of the bus Eric Brown was leading a singsong, and Joan Fontaine said to her husband, "I wonder if he would sing 'Home on the Range' for we Americans." Wright replied, "I don't think so." But Joan Fontaine got up—remember, she didn't know who Eric Brown was—and said, "Excuse me, do you think you could sing 'Home on the Range' for the Americans in the bus?" And Eric barked, "No' bloody likely! 'Glasgow Belongs to Me' is the next song, and you'll like it or lump it!.'" And she sat down somewhat shocked. Wright turned to her and just said, "I told you."

John Jacobs: Curiously, I'd played at Thunderbird in January of '55, with Peter Alliss and Bernard Hunt. We played on the winter circuit for a few months, but didn't have much success. The Thunderbird tournament was the sort of forerunner of the Bob Hope [a celebrity pro-am event on the PGA Tour], so there were all sorts of people from Hollywood there. I'll never forget listening to Hoagy Carmichael play the piano in the evening, and that lovely girl swimmer—Esther Williams—was there.

Anyway our pro-am team finished third, and they gave me a check for $1,000. That was a huge amount of money to me in those days, and it was a good job because we'd run out of cash and were going to have to come home.

Jacobs played Cary Middlecoff in the singles:

JOHN JACOBS: Cary was the top dog at that time. He won The Masters in 1955 and was U.S. Open champion in '56, but I birdied the first three holes. I was totally relaxed even though Cary was such a great player and everybody had written me off. I thought, I know I can get round here in 70 twice today, so he'll have to play well to beat me. We had a wonderful, wonderful game, and I shot a 65 in the afternoon to win.

I was 1 up on the eighteenth. We both were on the back of the green in 2, and the flag was right down at the front. He hit a wonderful putt first, and I gave it to him for a 4. Then I putted down and left a putt to tie the hole and win the match that was about five feet downhill with a hell of a swing on it. The whole world thought I was going to miss, but I knew I was going to hole it. I was standing there, and all I was thinking was, I must remember to take my cap off when the day ends. You see, I never wore a cap in those days, but I did in that desert heat. I give you my word, that's exactly what I was thinking. And it went straight in.

Then Cary shook hands with me and said, "John, well played. I want you to know you've beaten me on one of my best days." He was an absolute gentleman—and a much better player than I was. We eventually became great friends.

Despite Jacobs's play, the United States proved too strong again, as they added five singles victories to three wins in the foursomes. Now with seven straight wins, the United States could have believed they might never lose. In fact, the U.S. captain came out and just about said that. Upon arrival at Heathrow Airport in September 1957, Jack Burke Jr. spoke of the U.S. victories and noted, "I see no reason to doubt that this match will go the same way." He dismissed a suggestion that the United States would be weakened by the absence of Middlecoff and Sam Snead, and pointed out the American team comprised tournament professionals whereas many of the British players were limited by club duties.

Neither team knew the venue really well. It was Lindrick, a heathland course in the north of England near the town of Sheffield, and it was there only because the Cup's latest sugar daddy was a local industrialist. Sir Stuart Goodwin wasn't a golfer but was enthusiastic about having a big golf event in the area and put up £10,000 in sponsorship money.

JIMMY PATINO [former tin magnate and the owner of Valderrama, in Spain, site of the 1997 Ryder Cup]: The first Ryder Cup I saw was at Lindrick. I was a bit of a playboy, then, and I knew some of the European players, like Peter Alliss and Dai Rees. That year I went to Italy for the Italian Open. In those days they didn't have their own caddies. Rees took an Italian caddie who didn't speak a word of English and didn't get on with him. He was so upset with his caddie that he took the bag away from him. I asked Dai if he wanted me to carry his bags. At end he said, "I don't know what to pay you." I said, "You don't have to pay me."

He said, "I'll tell you what. I'll give you two tickets to the Ryder Cup. I'm captain." So off I went, and they won! Unbelievable. I thought it was fantastic. Wonderful way of getting people together.

DOW FINSTERWALD [who represented the United States in four Ryder Cups as a player and captained in 1977]: Lindrick in 1957 was my first trip to Britain. The opening ceremonies, you know, "God Save the Queen" and "The Star-Spangled Banner," made a very favorable impression. But I was very nervous.

They had pretty good galleries there, which I attribute a lot to the fact that at that point there weren't many U.S. players going to the British Open. It was the one chance that British golf fans had to see the so-called top players in the U.S.

TONY JACKLIN: Lindrick is about sixty miles from where I was born, and I still have memories of it. I was thirteen. I saw players

I'd only read about in magazines. Dick Mayer and Tommy Bolt, Dow Finsterwald, Ted Kroll. It was *unbelievable.*

PETER ALLISS: We weren't allowed to have our wives with us. The Americans brought theirs over, very glamorous in mink coats and diamond rings and all that sort of thing. We were staying in a hotel, and the wives weren't allowed there. But that was another part of the inferiority complex.

Burke's assessment at the airport appeared to be spot on, as the United States took a 3–1 lead after the foursomes.

PETER ALLISS: And the great comment from Jack Burke Jr., who was talking to a writer for the *Daily Mail*, was, "If the British team comes back and wins this, . . . you can bury me under ten tons of compost." It was something like that.

Burke actually played, inserting himself into the lineup when Ted Kroll took ill and had to sit out.

PETER ALLISS: [Burke] played Peter Mills, and Mills beat him easily. Mills was looked upon as possibly a weak link in the team, but he played quite beautifully.

DOW FINSTERWALD: We had a totally different day in the second round. The wind came up hard, and the conditions were very different. Against Christy O'Connor I wasn't capable of coping. We were even after eighteen but then I lost badly, 7 and 6.

This day also saw the first real signs of rancor between players and the galleries. It happened in the first match out, a fiery Eric Brown against an equally tempestuous Tommy "Thunder" Bolt. Not that this was unpredictable. While waiting for them to take to the tee, American TV commentator Jimmy Demaret cracked that Bolt and Brown were last seen standing at fifty paces throwing clubs at each other! When it did get going, Bolt and the galleries went at it with an ugly shouting match.

TOMMY BOLT: Eric and I were both temperamental, and the people might have applauded one of Eric's shots and not applauded mine, or something like that. You know how spectators are sometimes. But I lost control of my emotions I tossed a couple of clubs around. Stuck 'em in the ground or they bounced up in the air, and you can't play when you do that. That's all there is to it. I was 4 down by lunchtime and I couldn't get my concentration back—and golf is a game of concentration.

DOW FINSTERWALD: In fairness to the home team, when a guy misses a putt they could be applauding the fact that that British team had won a hole. It wasn't maybe the missing of a putt and may have been misinterpreted by some of us.

In the biggest Ryder Cup upset thus far, Britain won six of eight singles to win 7$\frac{1}{2}$–4$\frac{1}{2}$.

PETER ALLISS: There were tremendous celebrations. Nothing was as big then as it is today, but everybody got drunk at the dinner, and old journalists, old people, were jumping up and saying a few words and singing and dancing. The American team was like a funeral parlor. The glum faces were just unbelievable. We hadn't won since 1933, and the American team looked on in disbelief that they could have lost to this ragtag outfit.

DOW FINSTERWALD: I was nervous in 1957, and was still nervous in '59 [at Eldorado Country Club, in Palm Springs, California]. I don't recall any "We're going to revenge that loss" sort of thing. I'm not sure that's the spirit those matches should be played in anyway.

PETER ALLISS: Eldorado in 1959 was the last time we went by sea. We crossed the Atlantic and then we went to Atlantic City, played a couple of matches, went to the Burning Tree Club outside Washington D.C. We flew across to Los Angeles, and then we got on the dreaded little DC3 airplane to go to Palm Springs. It was extraordinary.

MIKE SOUCHAK [who played for the United States in 1959 and '61]: They got into some kind of a storm and got bounced around pretty good.

PETER ALLISS: We took off, and the pilot said it was likely to be a bit rough—and it was. It was horrendous! We plunged about four thousand feet. Lots of people were sick, and the smell was bloody awful. Frank Pennink, the writer, and former English amateur champion, was looking out the window at the electrical storm, amazed by the patterns of lightning. When we dropped—there were no bins, just open storage trays—coats and cameras and other things were stuck to the roof by the sheer force. And then suddenly—*bang*! It was as if we'd hit the top of a mountain, and all this stuff dropped down on top of everybody. The pilot came on and said, "I'm very sorry but we can't go any farther, we have to go back again." [It later transpired that the Palm Springs Airport had been closed because of the storm.] Eventually we landed back in Los Angeles. The pilot came out. He'd bashed his head and was bleeding all over the place. I think a stewardess may have broken an ankle.

There was a fellow called Lou Freedman who was a [U.S. PGA] vice president. When he got off the plane, Ron Haeger of the *Daily Express* said to him, "Lou, I nearly shit myself up there," and Lou said, "I've got news for you. *I did*." And he rushed off. Oh, Christ, what a mess.

The next day Ron says, "Congratulations, for the first time golf leads the *Daily Express*." The newspaper had a headline like RYDER CUP TEAM IN DEATH DIVE.

Inside, Haeger's report told how "we were tossed around like a cocktail in a shaker. From our flying height of 13,000 feet we dropped like a stone to 9,000 feet. It was like falling in a giant lift [elevator] when the cable had snapped." It is little wonder, then, that the British team made the trip to Palm Springs by bus. Eventually a shaken group of golfers got play under way.

MIKE SOUCHAK: They put Bobby Rosburg and me in the first match. I was so nervous when they played "God Save the Queen" and "The Star-Spangled Banner." We decided that he would drive on the odd holes and I would drive on the even holes, because of the setup of the par-3's. I was a little longer than Bob, and I could handle the par-3 holes with a shorter iron club. Anyhow, he got the privilege of teeing off at number one, a par-5 in the middle of an orange and grapefruit grove. It had a very narrow fairway and trees on either side. I told Bobby, "Look, I don't care how far you hit it. Just keep it between the trees." When he got up to tee his ball, he couldn't keep the ball on the tee, he was so nervous. The ball fell off two or three times. He finally had to put the ball on the tee with both hands! And I'm standing there just grinning because I was so happy it wasn't me up there on the tee, because I would have been doing the same thing.

Anyhow, he hit a low slice, about two hundred yards. It wasn't very long but it was effective, right in the middle of the fairway. And then I took a 3-wood and just killed it, put it right in front of the green. He pitched it on the green about three feet from the hole. The British team had made a five, and I got over the putt for a four, and I jerked that three-footer so badly. Bobby says, "I'm glad you're so nervous, too." And after that, we played beautifully and beat them pretty badly [5 and 4].

DOW FINSTERWALD: On the first hole of our foursomes match [with Julius Boros against Dai Rees and Ken Bousfield], I drove and Boros put a nice second shot maybe forty to fifty yards short of the green. And I shanked it into a bunker! We got a half, but it's hard to forget the feeling after shanking a ball there from that position.

PETER ALLISS: In the very first match Christy O'Connor and I played, I missed the first green and said, "I'm sorry." He just stopped and said, "Listen, I know you're trying to do the very best you can, so if we're going to play well together we don't want any more apologizing." And that's how we played. He used to encourage me and I used to encourage him, and he played the most wonderful shots. I thought he was crazy at times. I mean downhill, wind left to right, out of bounds on the right, small green. And we were 1 up or 2 up and two to play or something. And he'd say, "They're in trouble. I think I'll just cut a driver in there." He had *no* fear.

DOW FINSTERWALD: Two days before the Cup began, Sam Snead was supposed to do a commercial for Chrysler but for some reason he couldn't do it, so they asked me to do it. And they shot it

behind the eighteenth green at Eldorado. With a lot of filming taking place, there was a lot of downtime in between, so I got to chip
a lot. I was just waiting for them to say go. Anyway, the place I had
been chipping back at the eighteenth green, where we had been
filming, was just about identical to where I ended up after hitting
my second shot over the eighteenth green in my singles match
against Dai Rees. So I was very experienced in that particular chip
and knew how extremely fast it was, so I was able to chip it quite
close. I won 1 up.

*Finsterwald was one of five Americans to win that day, the final
tally being a lopsided 8½–3½. For the first time, the talk of change
became serious. Television was spreading and becoming increasingly influential. For example, it was at television's insistence that
the tee markers be moved up in 1959, the idea being to make the
holes easier. It instead made the players' yardages redundant.
match play was a tough enough format with cover, but 36-hole
matches were Bataan death marches compared with the sort of
action that television wanted. And if the overall result was going to be
a foregone conclusion . . .*

*It was obvious something had to be done. There was talk of
opening the British team up to such players as Gary Player of South
Africa or Peter Thomson of Australia, both of whom enjoyed
remarkably successful careers worldwide. In the end the British
PGA made one compromise for the 1961 matches at Royal Lytham,
in northwest England: the format would change; eight foursomes
the first day, sixteen singles the second. The proponents maintained that, with more points at stake, the Brits had a better chance
of catching up, and that a weaker player was in better shape
against a tough opponent in a shorter match. The cynics merely
suggested that the margins of U.S. victory would simply be twice as
large.*

PETER ALLISS: But the new format was more exciting for the
spectators. They were seeing more games, more matches, more
people playing. I remember big crowds at Lytham.

BILLY CASPER [who played for the United States in eight Ryder Cups and was captain in 1979]: It didn't really bother us because we knew we had our hands full. A lot of the matches were very close.

PETER ALLISS: The matches were much closer than the scores suggest. They weren't all 6 and 5s and 8 and 6s and that sort of thing, as many people thought or imagined or even pretended that's how it was. The matches I had with Casper were special and, still whenever I see him, he says, "I'm 1 or 2 up on you in holes."

DOW FINSTERWALD: I didn't play in the Portland, Oregon, tournament before the Ryder Cup because I hadn't entered the tournament in time. Then I flew to Tokyo for a "Shell's Wonderful World of Golf" match, but a typhoon had come through. There wasn't much rain, but the clouds were such that they couldn't film in color the way they wanted to. And I had this appointment in New York. So I flew out of Tokyo and got to New York. Now we go across [to Royal Lytham] for the matches, and [U.S. captain] Jerry Barber left me out of the first-round matches. So now I've gone twenty, twenty-five thousand miles over a couple of weeks, and I haven't played a competitive hole yet. I wasn't enamored of it. And the worst of it was this little bastard paired me with him in the afternoon. But Jerry was all right. They talk about Dai Rees being a feisty little guy. Jerry was every bit of that.

Jerry was a forgetful little guy, too. The story goes that he deposited the actual Ryder Cup in the vault of the hotel where the team stayed upon arrival in London, and forgot to retrieve it before heading north by rail. Perhaps not.

BILLY CASPER: You really want to know what happened? He left it on a train because of a card game. Barber was playing gin rummy with Arnold Palmer and was down quite a bit. He had to go to the bathroom, and asked me to play for him. When he came back from the bathroom, he was way up, because I was beating the heck out of Palmer and Barber said, "You just keep playing." And when we got to our stop—I don't recall which—we got off the train, but Barber left the trophy on the rack up above his seat. He realized what he'd done only after the train had left. It went to the next stop and the police brought it back.

NEIL COLES [who played in eight Ryder Cups for Great Britain and Ireland]: The night before play began, Dai Rees had told us all that the key to winning the Ryder Cup, in his eyes, was to get a good start in the foursomes. We should get going quickly and make sure that we won the early holes. The next morning I stood on the tee and Mike Souchak hit this 1-iron that just went straight as an arrow to about a foot. "Welcome to the Ryder Cup!"

MIKE SOUCHAK: We [Souchak and Bill Collins] were 1 up in that match on the eighteenth green, which at Lytham backs right up to the clubhouse. My partner drove, I put him on the green, and he put it up about fifteen, sixteen inches short of the hole. They'd made their four, and Neil came up to me and said, "Mike, under any other circumstances I'd give it to you, but it's the match and it's right here at the clubhouse." I said, "Neil, don't worry about it. I'd do the same thing." So I went over and got ready to putt.

People were hanging out of the windows on the second floor of the clubhouse, which was right over the top of us and, on my backswing, this lady, who must have been half drunk, hollered at the top of her voice, "Miss it!" Well, fortunately the ball went in the hole and I just told her, "Sorry, lady, not today." She was half in the bag, I'm sure, and it was only lunchtime! I think she ran and hid.

PETER ALLISS: I had a very good match with Arnold Palmer. He holed out three times from off the green. He chipped in once, holed a putt from ten yards short of the green at the seventh and holed a bunker shot at 15.

We were all square on 18 and I hit into the left rough and couldn't reach the green. He hit a good drive. I was forty yards short of the green in two and he was about twenty feet away in two. I'm like, "Jesus, he's going to beat me." And I looked at the clubhouse and saw my father sitting in the window, looking out. I chipped it up close then Arnold putted up. He missed. His putt was about the same distance as mine. And he picked my coin up. He gave me my putt. And so I'm looking at him and I thought, I've had a good result today and you've had a good result—because he was Jesus then, he was the Almighty—and I said, "Pick it up, Arnold, we'll call it a half." And I was disappointed to hear him say when he was talking to the press how badly he had played. And I thought, Well, that's not very generous—because I'd actually played him off the course!

MIKE SOUCHAK: In the afternoon singles I played Bernard Hunt, who was the best player in England at the time. On the fifteenth hole, a dogleg-right, I took the tee shot right over the dogleg. Bernard hit his straight. He had a wood club to the green and I had an 8-iron. I beat him 2 and 1, shook hands, and we were going into the clubhouse when the British golf writer Leonard Crawley came up behind me and said, "You're a dirty bastard, Mike. You played so well, but you *are* a dirty bastard." And I said, "Leonard, thank you very much, I take that as a compliment." He said, "You should." And we became really good friends.

DOW FINSTERWALD: I do recall a humorous incident about those matches. Two U.S. Air Force priests had come over from Wiesbaden [Germany] with I don't know how many suitcases of alcohol. One of them didn't drink at all, and one did have a drink, but both of them were darned good golfers and they were very interested in golf. A guy named Bill McDonald had gotten a suite for them, and they held a hospitality hour in their suite for all the guys. And so finally the day before the matches started Barber declared the priests' room off limits!

MIKE SOUCHAK: I'll never forget walking up the 18th fairway in the match with Bernard. My wife was there, along with the two priests, and we all walked down the fairway because the match was over, and the huge galleries on both sides of the fairway applauded us all the way from the tee to the green. It was a neat deal.

PETER ALLISS: I had about four or five matches in the Ryder Cup where I played some good stuff. It was the only time I've had that sort of appreciation that you see with [Jack] Nicklaus at St. Andrews, when he's walking up the eighteenth and everyone's cheering. It was a wonderful feeling.

The format would change again in for the matches at East Lake Golf Club in Atlanta in 1963 (and several times more in subsequent years). At the PGA of America's insistence, a third day, of four-balls, was slated between the foursomes and the singles.

NEIL COLES: To get to East Lake in 1963, I sailed to New York on the *Queen Mary* and caught the train down to Atlanta. A few of us went over that way, not players but officials and other followers. It took about a week, start to finish. The last time I flew it was earlier in 1963. It wasn't because of anything specific that had happened; I just got claustrophobic. In 1967, I got to Champions in Houston, Texas, by sailing on the *United States*, and then Jaguar gave me a car to drive. In 1971, to get to Old Warson in St. Louis I took the *Queen Mary* across the Atlantic and drove again.

BILLY CASPER: Arnold Palmer was our captain in 1963, and on the first day he paired rookies with seasoned players and we lost big. So we met after we'd finished playing and I said, "Arnie, we need to pair strength with strength, so you and I play. We played in the afternoon and won and that started the comeback.

JOHNNY POTT [who was picked for three United States Ryder Cup teams]: We did have a lot of Ryder Cup rookies that year, Tony Lema and Billy Maxwell, Dave Ragan and Bob Goalby, and the matches were really nerve-racking. Dave Ragan and I both felt like our golf swings got a little quick and that we really didn't play like we should have.

BILLY CASPER: My first partner, Dave Ragan, was so tight you couldn't have driven a tenpenny nail up his ass with a hammer, but that's just the way the Ryder Cup is. I mean, when they play the music at the opening ceremonies you can hardly breathe.

JOHNNY POTT: 1963 was the first year that I was eligible. Arnold [Palmer] and I were both pilots, and would fly airplanes together. The tournament the week before, which Arnold won, was in Philadelphia, and he invited me to fly with him from Philadelphia by way of his home in Latrobe on down to Atlanta. Sometime during the flight I said to Arnold, "I'm really kind of nervous about this Ryder Cup." And he said, "What are you worried about it for?" I said, "Playing for money is one thing, but playing for that gold cup . . . I don't think anybody wants their name on that cup as losing it." Obviously the Americans' track record had been pretty good up to that point, and we had a feeling of superiority in that we felt like we could win, but we still were really nervous about it. So, anyhow, Arnold said, "Oh, well, if you're nervous I'll just pair you with me." I said, "Godammit, that isn't doing me any good!" But Arnold did.

Back then all the fanfare happened on the first tee. They played the National Anthem and raised all the flags and then said, "Now representing the United States . . ." and Arnold said, "Johnny, you go hit the first ball." I said, "Good God, Arnold, what are you getting me *into* here?"

Well, I got up there and I drove into the left rough, which was probably not too bad a drive considering the pressure I was under. And then he hit the ball up on the green, about forty feet from the hole. And then I planted it up about five feet short. And Arnold grabbed me and said, "Don't you *ever* come up short!" All of a sudden Arnold was fussing at me, and we hadn't even finished the first hole!

BILLY CASPER: But it wasn't difficult playing with different people. We all knew each other. We were really close back in those days—it's not like today. We did things with each other all the time. Our wives, too. One might baby-sit for the other wife, and we'd have birthday parties and dinners together.

JOHNNY POTT: We had ten players, and eight played in each of the matches, but Arnold couldn't keep up with who was playing and, with all those rookies on the team, he didn't know what he had. I wasn't, like I say, at the top of my game. [Brian] Huggett dusted me off in the singles, and I didn't know Brian Huggett, other than that he was a little Welshman who beat my brains out.

Anyhow, I was choking and I told Arnold, "I'm just not playing good. I'm swinging too quick." I think that that was the honest thing to do, since Arnold couldn't see me playing. This was probably the reason that they started having non-playing captains.

BRIAN HUGGETT: You don't forget your first Ryder Cup match. George Will and I were playing Johnny Pott and Arnold Palmer. On the first hole, George Will hit the first tee shot and split the fairway. And then I knocked a 6-iron onto the green. That was us away really. We were very nervous, but we had nothing to lose because we were playing against the King. I mean, everybody watched Arnold, and when he hit the ball in those days, the ground kind of shuddered. So it was a great thing for us. We were the underdogs, but we won 3 and 2, and when we won there was applause from about twelve, fifteen people. They were all the officials from the Great Britain and Ireland Ryder Cup committee. It was amazing. Hardly anybody else clapped!

PETER ALLISS: I had a good singles record at East Lake. I beat Arnold Palmer on his own ground, and then I halved with Tony Lema. I was driving badly in the Palmer match, for some reason hitting small slices. I drove with a 3-wood, just to try and keep it in the fairway, and I was fifty yards behind Arnold every time. But I played my irons well and putted soundly, and found myself 1 up with two to play. I hit my little squirty 3-wood off the seventeenth, then played a 6-iron to ten feet. Arnold played his approach to three feet away, and I holed my putt. So now he's got to hole his for a half, which he made, and then we halved the last hole, and I won. That was a very good day's work.

Not good enough, however. The United States won 23–9.

*T*he 1965 Ryder Cup was remarkable not for the result (a 19½–12½ victory for the United States), nor that a sugar daddy had to step in once more to pay the piper (one Brian Park, a successful local businessman and a former club captain at Royal Birk-*

dale), but more for what Park did behind the scenes. In his role as vice chairman of the British PGA, Park had traveled to the United States to bone up on how big tournaments were run, and jotted down numerous notes and ideas. On his return he hired a management company to stage the Cup, and the result was a constant stream of golf fans met with a tented village complete with dining areas, first aid, a post office, and even an equipment tent. We take such facilities for granted today, but they were groundbreaking in the 1960s. So while Britain lagged well behind the United States in terms of the talent pool, at least the Ryder Cup showed signs of being a self-sustaining commercial venture. If Britain could just fix that nagging habit of losing.

This was a habit made slightly harder to fix two years later at Champions Golf Club, in Houston, Texas. Although Byron Nelson had been no slouch when he skippered the U.S. team in 1965, the '67 captain, Ben Hogan, would prove to be one of the toughest, most competitive captains in Cup history.

JOHNNY POTT: We had a player meeting in the locker room at that year's Colonial Tournament in Fort Worth, Texas, and decided to ask Ben Hogan to be the captain. I think the PGA thought that it would be a nice way to honor their past champions. You had Nelson in 1965, and it just kind of made sense for Hogan to be chosen next. We also had to hope he'd agree to it, but we felt he would because it was at Houston, which is kind of nearby—he lived in Fort Worth—and his friends Jackie Burke [coincidentally, the losing U.S. captain at Lindrick] and Jimmy Demaret owned Champions. I was sitting at the end of the table in the meeting and someone said, "Johnny, go find Ben Hogan and ask him if he'll be the captain!"

I went out and found Ben. The year before, Arnold Palmer had beaten me in an eighteen-hole playoff at the Colonial, but I didn't know if Ben knew me from anybody. I said something like, "Mr. Hogan, I'm Johnny Pott, a member of the current Ryder Cup team." And he said, "Well, hey, John." I said, "The team would like to ask you to be the nonplaying captain." And he said, "When is it?" I said, "It's in October, at Champions." He said, "October, Champions, huh? I'll let you know tomorrow."

So the next day, I'm leaving the locker room—and at Colonial you have to go through the golf shop, through these swinging doors—and we happened to hit the doors at the same time; I'm going out and he's coming in, and he says, "I'll do it." And that was it.

MALCOLM GREGSON [one-time British Ryder Cupper]: We rode in a cavalcade of limos going to the hotel from the airport with the police outriders there, flashing lights—oh, it was great. It might have been typical for America, but it was something very different for us.

We were at a dinner with more than a thousand people in this huge place somewhere in Houston. The two teams were on a long table up on the stage. When it was time to present the teams, [British captain] Dai Rees got up and introduced us one by one, to polite applause.

PETER ALLISS: Dai Rees, bless him, goes, "Gentlemen, this is so and so . . . the runner-up in the Dutch Open . . . and so and so . . . third in the Swiss Open . . . and Peter Alliss, winner of last month's medal competition at his local golf club." And then Hogan just got up, gestured for his team to stand, and he said, "Ladies and gentlemen, the finest players in the world."

MALCOLM GREGSON: He just flicked his hand, and they all got up quickly and then sat down again. Take that! The whole place went berserk.

PETER ALLISS: We were 2 down before we started.

MALCOLM GREGSON: It was quite awesome really, the names that we were looking at. Every time they say "It's the best players in the world," but these really were.

PETER ALLISS: And they all had these beautiful suits on. They looked like a million dollars.

JOHNNY POTT: Ben asked us to show up on Monday, because the functions started Monday evening, but Arnold Palmer didn't get there until Tuesday. And Arnold kind of buzzed the golf course with his jet airplane.

MALCOLM GREGSON: We were in the locker room when we heard his jet going over, and they said, "Oh, there he is." And Hogan gave sort of a cursory grunt. About half an hour later in he walked—Arnold. Hogan turned to talk to somebody else. He really wanted to cut Arnold down to size, because he felt that Arnold might be running the show. He was something else, Arnold was; he really was the King.

JOHNNY POTT: Arnold finally got to the practice tee at about eleven o'clock. He walked out, hitching his pants and whatnot, and said, "Hey, Ben, what ball are we playing?" [In those days, players could opt for the American ball or a slightly smaller British ball.] And Ben said, "Mr. Palmer, when I pair you, I'll let you know."

MALCOLM GREGSON: When we went out to practice, they were on sort of a semicircular driving range. We were at one end, and they were at the other. But after warming up for a while, Dai Rees said, "Hey, look guys!" We all looked over. None of the Americans were practicing. They were standing watching Hogan practice. That was his, "Okay, lads, let's get ready for the Ryder Cup." To get them to watch him practice. It's quite amusing that to get the American team psyched up Hogan had them out there watching him practice. And Arnold was standing at the back, looking toward us, sort of bending down, yawning, you know, as if to say, "*Bo*-ring!"

PETER ALLISS: Arnold also took a couple of our boys up in his plane, and he turned somersaults and made them feel ill.

TONY JACKLIN: Arnold had a new airplane that he took me and [British player] George Will up in. He was like a kid with a new toy and he had his pilot with him, but Arnold took over and we ended up buzzing the bloody course about five hundred feet and scaring the living poop out of everybody. George Will actually peed himself. It was bloody unbelievable. And he [Palmer] got a phone call when we got in from a very irate air-traffic controller in the area. It was only because of Jimmy Demaret and a couple of others writing letters on Arnold's behalf that he didn't lose his license.

JOHNNY POTT: Hogan as a captain? Magnificent. *Magnificent.*

PETER ALLISS: Hogan was something else. He was able to give you an inferiority complex just walking around.

JOHNNY POTT: We had a team meeting and he said, "Boys, there's nothing to being the captain of the Ryder Cup. You guys are all great players. Pairing is real easy. I'm going to pair together you boys who drive crooked, I'm going to pair together you boys who drive straight. And the first ball's going to be hit by Julius Boros 'cause he don't give a shit about anything. So y'all just go play your games.

You got these uniforms here. If you don't like the way they fit or whatnot, don't wear them. I never could play in somebody else's clothes. [Doug] Sanders, if you want to come out here and dress like a peacock, that's fine. Whatever you want. But let me tell you boys one thing. I don't want my name on that trophy as a losing captain." So we went out and played great.

TONY JACKLIN: They were all bloody frightened to death of Hogan. By that stage I knew quite a few of the Americans, like Gay Brewer and Johnny Pott, and was friendly enough with them to chitchat, and they were all saying how petrified they were about Hogan, because he used to ride around in his cart watching them play, but he sort of just watched the swings. You know, he didn't watch the result of the ball, almost as if it was of no interest to him where the ball went.

BILLY CASPER: Hogan put Julius Boros and me off first because both of us were very quick players and he wanted us to get out there and get up so that the other players could see it and it would sort of rub off on them. He wanted to set the tone. Hogan wanted to win *all* the matches. He didn't want to lose a point.

Every morning we had a meeting. He'd designate who the players were that he wanted to play that day. And we had the option of using the small ball or the big ball. I think we used the small ball.

JOHNNY POTT: We played the little ball because it was longer and we were driving over all the fairway bunkers at Champions. It was a little smaller chipping around the green, but what the heck: You didn't miss that many greens.

MALCOLM GREGSON: We'd just had a real bumpy summer, running it in from one hundred yards short of the green with a small ball. So it was a very, very different situation to suddenly get to a watered course in late September, early October. The course was really heavy every morning. On the first day I played in the afternoon with Hugh Boyle against Gardner Dickinson and Palmer. Arnold was on his game. Gardner Dickinson lined up every putt and Arnold holed everything. He was just fantastic.

TONY JACKLIN: In those days, I was full of confidence, so I reveled in the whole thing. I played with Dave Thomas as my foursomes partner. Dave was an awful chipper. I mean a bloody *terrible* chipper. All the par-3's were even holes [fourth, eighth, twelve, and sixteenth], so Dave hit on all the even holes and if he missed the green I got the chip. And as long as my drives were in the fairway on the par-5s—which were all odd numbers [five, nine, and thirteenth]—he'd never have to chip. And that's the way it worked. We had a hell of a record, two wins and a half.

JOHNNY POTT: Bobby Nichols and I, who had a history of hitting deep and sometimes left and right, were teamed together, and we won all our points. Now, with the alternate-shot format, someone like Gene Littler would have no idea how to play from some of the places I hit my ball.

TONY JACKLIN, on losing to Palmer in the singles: I'd played with Arnold in the Masters that year, and beat him in the first round. But it was always difficult playing Arnold in America, because of the following that he got. You're still made to feel in some respects that you're there to make the numbers up. That's just the way it is. But I didn't play particularly well [lost 3 and 2], and I certainly didn't play well against Dickinson in the afternoon [same score]. I just didn't get it together, but you can only do what you can do. It was fun.

BRIAN HUGGETT: I can remember beating Julius Boros because he was the U.S. Open champion at the time and it was a good scalp. I hit a very good second shot to the eighteenth green but left a tricky chip that had to be absolutely precise. I played a really lovely little deft chip from behind the green and beat Julius 1 up.

MALCOLM GREGSON: Toward the end of the Ryder Cup, when we were getting murdered, a few of the older players, like Christy O'Connor, sort of pressured Dai into dropping them. They didn't want to play in the last singles. "Oh, I got a bad back. Oh, I don't want to play." I'd lost every game, but I still wanted to play. Let me go out, I want to go out again. Tony Jacklin was like that as well.

I met Ben Hogan again a few years later when I was captain of the British Caledonian Airways Golfing Lions Team, and we were over at Fort Worth, at Shady Oaks. Hogan used to go and watch his mates play cards every morning. He'd just stand behind them as they played, then go out and hit a few balls, or maybe play a few holes on his own, then come in and go home. Some of our team were Hogan [equipment] players, but they had never met him. I said "Oh, I met him in 1967 when he was captain of the Ryder Cup team." So I went inside and I said, "Excuse me, Mr. Hogan, three of our lads would like to meet you." He says, "I'm not going out there. It's raining." And I said "They are three of your staff players, and they think very, very highly of you." He said, "Oh, well, that's different." So he came out in the rain and shook their hands and the players didn't wash their right hand for about three weeks after that.

1969

The final score in 1967 was 23½–8½ in favor of the United States. In eight four-ball matches, Britain managed to win exactly half a point. Of the sixteen singles matches, Britain won four. Of the eleven Ryder Cups played since the competition has been resumed after World War II, Britain had won exactly once—and that was seen as a bit of a fluke. Going into the 1969 Ryder Cup, back at Royal Birkdale, the British probably had one of their strongest team in years, but for the United States there were two "promising" rookies—they passed the five-year "apprenticeship" called for then by the PGA of America—called Jack Nicklaus and Lee Trevino. For Britain, things could only get worse.

FRANK BEARD [who played for the United States in 1969 and '71]: The Ryder Cup was not an exhibition, but we went there thinking it was. I don't know that the word *exhibition* was used, but the overall feeling was, "This is another walk in the park."

On the other hand, there was no social interaction other than set dinners. You wouldn't see the men having a beer together while other matches finished. This was a very deadly match. Absolutely business, business, business.

BERNARD GALLACHER [who played in eight Ryder Cups for both

Great Britain and Ireland and Europe, and captained the Europeans three times]: Our team in 1969 was very optimistic that we could win. The main reason for the optimism was that Tony Jacklin had won the British Open that year, and British and Irish golf was really on a bit of a high. I was having a particularly good season, the second as a professional. Eric Brown was our captain, a very optimistic captain, a fiery Scot. Eric had a great Ryder Cup record [4-0-0 in singles], and he just made us firmly believe that we were going to win. And that's really what captains do.

TONY JACKLIN: By then I was Open champion and had been playing the American tour full-time. All I remember was that there was a lot of bravado at the British end of things. But nobody other than myself had really done much to justify thinking that we might win. It's as simple as that. On the American tour the purses were so much bigger than ours, and everything about it was managed better. It was a better all-around thing. But when the Ryder Cup came round, no one liked to believe that.

PETER ALLISS: This was my last Ryder Cup. My putting wasn't good. I was doing television then, and I was a bit cowardly. I thought to myself, I'll play in the morning and sort of escape in the afternoon to do some television, which Eric Brown allowed me to do.

But there were silly things going on. "The rough is bad," we were told. "Don't go looking to the Americans' ball in the rough because if you kick it there'll be a penalty." It was nonsense. There were always these sort of undercurrents from somewhere. Whether it was disgruntled wives, disgruntled officials, there was always something.

TONY JACKLIN: Eric Brown told us not to look for the bloody balls if they went into the rough. He had been bold in his own day when they played. But he was sort of famous for being a sort of hard man, and he was trying to portray that image as captain.

RENTON LAIDLAW: Eric was worried that his team might go into the rough, look for the ball, and accidentally step on the American ball and incur some kind of penalty. There was really nothing sinister about it.

TONY JACKLIN: But it wasn't a very nice thing to do, and I think he was trying to intimidate them—that was all we had, if you know what I mean. But we really didn't take any bloody notice of it.

BRIAN BARNES [who played in six Ryder Cups for Britain and Europe]: In all honesty, we felt we were struggling. I didn't play in one Ryder Cup where we had twelve fellows out there to play against the Americans. Instead we had six or seven fellows and the rest were second-raters. So the six or seven had to play all six matches, where the American boys had the opportunity to rest and were fresh and raring to go when it came to the afternoon matches on Sunday. It's a matter of depth.

FRANK BEARD: I look at the meetings today that they have and all the strategies. We had a meeting the day we got there, when [U.S. captain] Sam Snead asked us to write down who we did and didn't want to play with. That was the last meeting we had. He put some pairings up and that was the end of the story. He was a nice man, don't get me wrong. But there were no pep talks.

I played with Billy Casper, but he would not have been my choice. I didn't write his name down. He was just older, and more established, and I had friends, like Kenny Still and Dale Douglass and a few of those guys that I would have preferred to play with, who were more of the same generation. In the '60s they were no better golfers than Billy Casper. I do remember that Billy and I played alternate shot, and I put him up under a tree somewhere and I thought, Oh my God, I can't believe I just did this to Billy Casper. But he was very good about it. He went up, played it out, and we went on.

Links-style golf was not quite as different as I thought it would be. I had grown up on public golf courses in Dallas, Texas, and Louisville, Kentucky, where the courses were hard, so the bounce-up shot was nothing new. And the wind was not new because I played a lot of golf in Florida. The only problems I had were with the small golf ball.

I remember a shot Christy O'Connor hit, on the very first hole.

He'd driven it in the rough, and I looked at his lie, and thought, He's in deep trouble now. And he went in there with some kind of wood, had a very abrupt pickup on the backswing, and the ball flew straight up out and right onto the green. I mean, it had to be in the two-hundred-yard range. I couldn't have gotten a 7-iron in on it, but he did it with the wrist, the abruptness of the angle of attack, and obviously had some experience. I'll never forget that shot.

I have other very specific memories of 1969. First, it was a great honor to play. I welled up with tears when the "Star-Spangled Banner" played. I didn't know that I would, but it was a great feeling. But it was also bittersweet because I was not used to anything that resembled team play. I'd never played team sports, and I didn't like it *at all*. I did *not* enjoy it. I shouldn't say it was too much pressure; it was just a different kind. I much preferred having a six-foot putt for my own well-being or loss, but to have teammates, and to have it mean something for the team, I did not look forward to that. And I don't mean just the alternate-shot matches with teammates. Even in the singles matches, it was still for the team. I found it very, very difficult. Beforehand I was looking forward to it, but it was just an overwhelming feeling of "Whoa, man, this is a whole different pressure I'm not used to having." It was not a fun feeling.

When we'd miss a putt, the gallery would clap and cheer, and that was totally new also. I don't think we expected anybody to be pulling for us, but if you hit a good shot, they would politely recognize it and clap or something, but if you missed a putt or hooked the ball into the gorse or something, they were very, very vocal about it. With Tony Jacklin in particular it was much more of a raucous crowd. They were loud. It was a very antagonistic atmosphere.

I didn't talk to any of my teammates about it because in those days we were men who did not express feelings. We weren't up to date. We just didn't speak.

BERNARD GALLACHER: In the morning foursomes on the first day, [Maurice] Bembridge and I played against Lee Trevino and Ken Still. We won 2 and 1, so we got off to a good start in foursomes.

Maurice was a rookie, remember, and Trevino was the 1968 U.S. Open champion.

FRANK BEARD: The second memory was that we had a couple of fights, Dave Hill and Bernard Gallacher [in the second-day four-balls]. They were on the ground. They had to be separated. At least that was the report to me.

Bernard Gallacher was asked by Dave Hill to spot his ball, which was just off the putting surface. You're supposed to spot it, pick it up with two fingers, and set it down somewhere else, or at least hold it in two fingers where it can be seen. [So it's not cleaned.] There was mud on the ball apparently, and Dave Hill said Gallacher knocked it off with his fingers. The next thing you know they're into it. They were the two most likely to do something like that. I mean very, very hot-blooded young men.

BILLY CASPER: Bernard Gallacher was a good player. A bulldog. I loved to play against those guys.

FRANK BEARD: They had another one but not as physical. But they had to be separated again. There's nobody inside the ropes but the players and the caddies, and it's not like you walk around with security guards at your hip. So it doesn't take much. Also, this was the first time in a long time that the British Ryder Cuppers really had a chance. Jacklin had won the British Open and they had a lot of good young players, Gallacher one of them. And the European tour was beginning to take off and develop a few players, some of whom had come to America.

TONY JACKLIN: The [Johnny] Millers and the [Lee] Trevinos and the [Arnold] Palmers felt that, if you were good, they wanted you in the U.S. They wanted to beat you. But there was a smaller-minded element who, for the most part, didn't play outside America, who weren't worldly. They were unpleasant people to be around—mean-spirited players like Gardner Dickinson and Dan Sikes, and many a time I felt like withdrawing when I saw my name paired with them.

So I felt great when I won the U.S. Open [in 1970] because I knew that those same people must have hated it. I happened to be in the same hotel as Gardner Dickinson that week. My wife and I had to share a ride to the airport with him afterward, and he never said "Well played" or anything. And I'd won the U.S. Open by seven strokes!

BERNARD GALLACHER: Ken Still was a feisty character, and was trying all sorts of gimmicks the whole time. I played him twice. The match where Brian Huggett and I played Dave Hill and Ken Still in the second-day afternoon fourballs was really acrimonious. Brian and I got off to a bad start because Dave Hill kept walking around when Brian was about to putt. He was like a jumping bean around the greens—hypertense, hyperactive. He didn't really do it intentionally, but he was putting us off with the way he was prancing around when we were putting. Brian asked him to stop walking around, and Ken Still took up the mantle.

BRIAN HUGGETT: Ken Still was standing quite near me when I was going to putt. I asked him if he was going to stand that close, could he please stand behind me. He made a "Hmmmmph!" sound.

BERNARD GALLACHER: Something else happened on the third green. Ken Still's caddie was holding the flag for me from about thirty feet. In today's world you'd think it would be unusual for Ken Still's caddie to be holding the flag for me, but in those days it wasn't unusual. The caddie closest to the flag held the flag. Ken Still's caddie, who actually was a British caddie, a local guy, was holding it. I was just about to hit the ball when Ken Still started shouting, "Get your own caddie to hold the flag!"

BRIAN HUGGETT: Bernard would look from the ball to the hole maybe fifteen to twenty times before he actually putted, so after about fourteen looks they decided they'd better move their caddie off. There was plenty of friction there.

BERNARD GALLACHER: I wasn't really rattled, but it was just an ungentlemanly thing to do. It just sort of added fuel to what was already a pretty flammable atmosphere.

Then on the seventh green Dave Hill putted out of turn. He

finished up and Brian said, "Well, I'm sorry, you putted out of turn," and that was a sort of a flashpoint for Ken Still. [Under the Rules of Golf, a player can be made to replay a shot hit out of turn.]

BRIAN HUGGETT: They started measuring this, that, and the other, to determine whether Dave Hill did putt out of turn. Then one of them, either Hill or Still, said, "You can have the bloody hole if you want to." And we said, "Okay, we'll have it. Thanks very much." And we went off to the next tee.

BRIAN HUGGETT: And then there was a lot of trouble going at number eight. We were arguing with one another over the decision on the previous green. It had all boiled over and Lord Derby, the PGA president, and Dai Rees came out onto the fairway to calm things down.

BERNARD GALLACHER: On the eighth green, Dave Hill hit a terrific second shot that landed about five feet above the hole. I was lying about ten feet away. Ken Still was at the back [of the green] and putted down. He ended up inside me but outside Dave Hill and on exactly the same line, lying three. And I thought, Why don't I just give him that putt because, if Still putts, he'll show Hill the line." So I gave him the putt for a four, which meant Dave Hill still had a four-foot putt for a three, and Ken Still went bananas.

He said, "I want to putt it! I want to putt it!" I said, "*I know* you want to putt it. That's why I'm giving you it." I mean, I was only twenty years old, but I knew match-play rules, and I wouldn't call it gamesmanship; it's just doing the right thing, really. I mean, Dave Hill was lying very close for a birdie, but the last thing we wanted was for Ken Still to be putting on the same line and maybe give him some assistance. Still just wasn't familiar with the tactics of match play, and he was getting carried away with the occasion. He thought it was sort of a fight.

Then Dave Hill holed it, but he was really playing out of this world. He was the best player on that side. Ken Still couldn't hit a shot.

BRIAN HUGGETT: Hill played absolutely magnificently through-out the week. He held the team together. He stopped us winning. I mean, he won all his matches. If he'd halved just one of them, we'd have won the Ryder Cup. Ken Still was a good player, too, but just a bit temperamental.

BILLY CASPER: You just have to realize that Ken Still's probably the most avid sport fan there is, and Dave Hill calls it like it is. I think they may have gotten fed up with the way that the galleries treat you over there. They were difficult. They'd clap when you missed a putt. But that just made us stronger.

BERNARD GALLACHER: I was quite young, and we were always under the impression that Americans would try anything to win. Eric [Brown] told us this. He said, "They'll try to put you off. They'll try anything to win." And we just felt it was their tactics to try and put us off. You know, walking around when we're putting and then getting the caddie to stop holding the flag at the last moment. But when they putt out of turn then they've gone too far—and when you don't have a strong referee to calm things down, it gets out of hand. The referees in those days were club pros inside the ropes getting a good look at the action, rather than the professional ref-erees that you have today. That Ryder Cup probably brought on the development of proper refereeing.

TONY JACKLIN: On the afternoon of the second day Neil Coles and I played [Lee] Trevino and Miller Barber. On I think 18, Lee's caddie broke his ankle. They have these little paths through the heather, and some of them had ruts in them and he got turned over, landed on his back, and that was that.

And it was so dark when we had to putt on the last green, they brought bloody cars around it somehow and shone the lights on the green so we could see!

RENTON LAIDLAW: [Eric] Brown didn't play Gallacher in the first series of singles, and Gallacher was very annoyed. Brown had said to him, "I didn't play you this morning because you're going to play this afternoon, and you're going to beat Lee Trevino."

BERNARD GALLACHER: I think he felt that battle against Ken Still and Dave Hill maybe took too much out of us. But he did the right thing in leaving me out [in the first series of singles], because by the afternoon I was anxious to get playing.

RENTON LAIDLAW: And he beat Trevino 4 and 3! That was a terrific scalp to take.

BERNARD GALLACHER: I was on fire, 32 on the front nine and never looked back. I won 4 and 3. Eric just said, "Well done," and off we went to look at the other matches, particularly Billy Casper and Brian Huggett. It looked like the key match.

Despite the hammering in Houston in 1967, the British team had responded magnificently. With two matches left on the course, Casper versus Huggett and Jack Nicklaus versus Tony Jacklin, the score was tied at 15. Huggett and Casper were even on 18, while Jacklin was 1 down to Trevino on 17.

BRIAN HUGGETT: Billy and I had a tremendous game. On 18, I hit a fantastic drive, very long, and had only an 8-iron into the green. I hit it pin-high right, a couple of feet off the green, on the fringe. I can't remember where Billy came up, but I know after two shots he was outside me. He went first and hit it pretty close. I conceded the par putt then hit my own first putt, a right-to-lefter, a little bit too firm, and it went past about four and a half feet. Now I had to hole this putt to halve the match with Billy.

While I was standing over it, I heard an enormous roar from the seventeenth green. *Enormous!* The last time I heard anything— because the scoreboards weren't what they are today—Jacklin was up on Nicklaus. And I thought, That's a winning roar. Jacko's won! So then I thought, Christ, if I hole this now and halve with Billy, we've won the Ryder Cup. And I struck it beautifully and it went straight in the middle of the hole, and I broke down walking off the green.

BILLY CASPER: He thought that Britain had won and just burst out in tears.

TONY JACKLIN: He actually wept with his head in Eric Brown's jacket lapel, thinking he'd won the bloody thing.

BRIAN HUGGETT: But then Eric Brown and Lord Derby told me that we *hadn't* won, that the enormous roar was because Jacko had eagled 17 to get level with Jack Nicklaus. I'm good at mathematics, so then I thought, Well, we can still bloody *lose* it.

FRANK BEARD: And of course the culmination was on the eighteenth green.

TONY JACKLIN: I'd also beaten Jack 4 and 3 in the morning. He wasn't at his best, and I was bloody determined, at the top of my game. I'd that year's British Open under my belt, but had a terrible month after that. Mark McCormack [head of mega-agency International Management Group, he died in 2003] insisted that I come back over to America after the British Open when I really needed to rest and digest what had happened. I missed four straight cuts and what should have been the best time in my life was the worst. But by the time September and the Ryder Cup came around, I was up there again and ready for it.

It really was a big deal beating Jack, but I was playing a lot of golf with him by then, practice rounds and tournaments in America and in Britain, money matches, so I wasn't intimidated. I felt equal to the task.

I didn't know I was going to play him again in the afternoon until lunchtime. In those days the captains usually put the strongish men out at the end. Obviously Snead thought Jack was his anchorman and Eric went to me because I was unbeaten.

I'd lost 16 to a par, to go 1 down, and then on 17 [a par-5] I hit a 2-iron second shot, but pushed it. It hit a bank at the side of the green and came down onto the green, but a long way from the hole. Jack hit a much better drive than I did and a wonderful second shot to about fifteen, twenty feet. I then holed this bloody putt from here to eternity and got back to level. That was the roar Brian Huggett heard when he was on the eighteenth.

Jack missed his putt, so we went to the eighteenth tee all square. Eighteen was plain and short, and they played it as a par-4. Three-woods off the tee for position, both of us. We were walk-

ing off the tee, me ahead, when Jack hollered after me. I waited
for him and when he caught up, he said, "How are you feeling? Are
you nervous?" And I said, "I'm bloody petrified." And he said,
"Well I just thought I'd ask because if it's any consolation I feel
just like you." Which was kind of nice, putting it all in perspec-
tive. You know, it was an unenviable position to be in. It all
depended on us.

I then hit an 8-iron, a good shot, right in line with the pin, and
it ran to the back of the green, about thirty feet away. Then Jack
hit a super shot, to about fifteen feet. I putted up to about twenty
inches to two feet, and marked it.

Jack took a good run at his, because he had it for the match,
and he ran it about four and a half feet by. He holed that and, as
he picked his ball out of the hole, he picked my marker up. He
conceded the putt and we halved our match *and* the overall match.

*It has been termed one of the most sporting moments of all
time—but that was not necessarily the consensus at the time.*

BERNARD GALLACHER: I don't think [U.S. captain] Sam Snead was
pleased, and some of the hard-nosed Americans weren't pleased.
But it was the right thing to do.

FRANK BEARD: Snead didn't like it. I don't think any of us cared
for it. We had the Cup and the tie meant we kept it, but nobody
was thinking about that. We wanted to win.

BILLY CASPER: We were very surprised, because all of us had
worked so hard to get to that position. It was a great thing for the
matches and yet a lot of us really didn't enjoy it too much.

TONY JACKLIN: I was a pretty fierce competitor, and I remember
standing on the green before Jack conceded the putt, thinking,
Now, whatever else happens, get ready. You're going to have to
make this putt. Mentally I knew it wasn't over for me, so it came
as a shock, a surprise anyway, when Jack picked the marker up.
He said at the time, "I don't believe you would have missed this."

BRIAN HUGGETT: I'm sure Jacko would have holed it, because he
was a great putter, but you never know. It was a really nice gesture

for Jack to do that, because they still kept the trophy and we got to halve it. It was good for golf.

FRANK BEARD: Was it the right decision by Nicklaus? Well, why do you play? You play to win, don't you? It would be interesting to see what Tony would have done in the same situation. I wouldn't have given him the putt. But we'll never know if he'd have made it. It's tough. Everything's on your shoulders. But if Tony had holed the putt it would have been a bigger thing for him. It would have been a great boost for him. But then it was a great boost for Nicklaus.

TONY JACKLIN: There were a lot of disgruntled men on Sam's team. But mind you, there were a few mean-spirited people on his team. And Snead himself wasn't Charlie Charm when it came to foreigners playing in the U.S. He was a hard case.

FRANK BEARD: I agree with what Jack did now, but it took me a long time. This was a very antagonistic atmosphere, and we did *not* want to tie it. When Jack gave him that putt, Kenny [Still] looked at me and said, "What did he just do?" And I said, "I think he gave him that putt."

TONY JACKLIN: Jack always played the game in a wonderful spirit. Bobby Jones was his hero, and Jack always approached the game in with that marvelous amateur way that was totally honorable.

FRANK BEARD: Jack Nicklaus was always light-years ahead of us when it came to maturity and thinking. And some way he had figured out that for the good of golf, and for the good of European golf, for the good of the Ryder Cup, a tie was best.

BERNARD GALLACHER: That's exactly it. Jack was ahead of his time.

BRIAN BARNES: Nicklaus conceding Jacklin's putt just showed Nicklaus's mentality. He realized what the situation was, and that for Jacklin to have missed that putt to lose the Ryder Cup could have done European-British golf irreparable harm. I was surprised at the time, but I've come to understand where he was coming from. Jack realized that the Ryder Cup was struggling and needed to have something done to it.

BILLY CASPER: The British team had a big reception that night, sort of a victory party. I'd started playing in Europe so I knew all the players—in fact, I was a member of the British PGA—but I was the only American that went to it.

BRIAN HUGGETT: Some of the bad feeling remained with the players afterward. But of course they were probably a jealous lot as well. "Oh, Jack's going to get all the plaudits for being such a sportsman and this, that, and the other." I'm sure Jack wasn't thinking about that at all. I think he was looking at the game overall.

Afterward we flew to America to play in a tournament in Portland, Oregon, and we were all on the plane together. Dave Hill and I got together and the nastiness of our match was forgotten about. We said we'd have a practice round in Portland, which we did.

TONY JACKLIN: You know, one of the things that was forgotten in the fray was that the Americans made a wonderful gesture of letting us keep the Cup for a year. They didn't have to because, in the event of a tie, the team that won last holds on to it for the whole time. The gesture by the Americans has sort of got lost in history, but I promise you faithfully that it happened.

THE BEGINNING OF "THE END"

O *nward and upward! The British finally had shown they could compete with the Americans—and an American side packed with such superstars as Nicklaus, Trevino, and Casper. Less than a year after the tie in 1969, Tony Jacklin lapped the field to win the U.S. Open in Minnesota by seven strokes.*

But as the 1970s wore on, it all fell apart again. Only the U.S. economy had a worse decade than the British Ryder Cup team (although the British economy wasn't exactly on fire). It not only lost in all five editions, but it did so in embarrassing circumstances. First up was an 18½–13½ drubbing at Old Warson in St. Louis, this despite winning each of the first day's sets of foursomes.

FRANK BEARD: In 1971 at Old Warson we felt more comfortable being at home. And the British never quite got into the match. I don't know why. All of a sudden it was pretty obvious we were going to win. There were some close matches, and it wasn't revenge or anything like that. But there was a feeling that we were going to win. And the crowd of course was on our side.

BRIAN HUGGETT: We didn't really think we could win. Playing them on their own dung heap was a different story in those days, because we never got the chance to go and play in the majors or anything like it. You'd get invited to the Masters and that was about it. So our team was nowhere near strong enough in those days to have any chance of winning in America.

TONY JACKLIN: I was embarrassed at the airport because all the American press were interviewing me about this Ryder Cup and I said, "I'm not the captain. He's over there. You should be asking him these questions." But I was the only one they knew because I was playing and touring. I kept referring these guys to talk to Eric [Brown], but they wanted my opinion on the whole bloody thing. Now, there were two big coaches [buses] at the airport to pick us up, but by the time I'd finished with the press the coaches were full. By then back in England I had a nice blue Rolls-Royce, and there was a fellow there in St. Louis with a Rolls-Royce, just like mine. He brought it to the airport to take me to the hotel. I said to the PGA secretary, "The buses are all full up, and this chap's offered my wife and me a ride." At the hotel, I came down from the room to the lobby and saw Eric Brown, and he said, "I dinna' want you ridin' in Rolls-Royces when we're ridin' in buses." I said, "Point taken, Eric, but there was no room on the bus." But these circumstances were always cropping up because I was the only player on the team that the American media knew.

RENTON LAIDLAW: To get to Old Warson, Neil Coles, who didn't fly, came over on the *Queen Mary*, hired a car, and then drove. It took him longer than a week. He drove into the Old Warson car park just as I was walking across it, and I said, "Hello, Neil, any adventures on your trip?" He said, "No, nothing." He did all this and nothing had happened to him? He hadn't gone the wrong way, hadn't been stopped by an American policeman, hadn't been seasick on the boat or anything? It seemed strange.

BILLY CASPER: I broke my toe on my way to St. Louis. I was in a hotel room in New York and when I got up to go to the bathroom I kicked a chair. [U.S. captain] Jay Hebert didn't play me much. In fact, I lost my first two matches, so he didn't play me anymore. The broken toe didn't bother my playing, but it just made me look awkward on the golf course because I was limping.

DAVE STOCKTON [who played for the U.S. in 1971 and '77 and was captain in 1991]: We had an extremely strong team, but in the morning foursomes I was paired with Jack Nicklaus, and we lost [to Tony Jacklin and Brian Huggett]. That was a lousy pairing because in alternate shot you can't play two people who have completely different games. Nicklaus and I in a better ball would be awesome, because he can be aggressive, and I'm going to do what I have to do. In fact, they sat me out in the afternoon and put J. C. Snead with Nicklaus, and they did fine [they beat Maurice Bembridge and Peter Butler].

But I was mad when I was sat down for the entire second day. It was like they were saying, "If Nicklaus can get beat, then it must have been Stockton's fault." But it was the pairing that caused us to get beat.

FRANK BEARD: Jay Hebert, Gardner Dickinson, and Arnold Palmer would sit in the back corner of the Old Warson clubhouse [discussing pairings], and we always felt like there were three captains. In fact, we felt like Palmer and Dickinson and not Hebert were calling the shots.

PETER OOSTERHUIS [now a CBS television broadcaster, but who played on six British/European teams]: On the first day I was paired in the foursomes with Peter Townsend against Arnold Palmer and Gardner Dickinson. On the first hole Peter put me on the green but a long way from the hole. I walked up to the hole and, while I was studying the line, checking around the cup, a butterfly flew out of the hole, which some people seemed to think was an omen. Then I made this monster putt on the first green—a good way to start a Ryder Cup career.

But Arnold was playing brilliantly—and a bit too well for us. They won 2 up, and then we lost to them again in the afternoon. Arnold was a real force, and we couldn't quite handle him.

BERNARD GALLACHER: Harry Bannerman and I beat Billy Casper and Miller Barber. Then Eric split us up. I played with Peter Oosterhuis and lost to Gardner Dickinson and Arnold Palmer. We were

55

going along quite nicely when we came to a par-3 [seventh hole] with the green on a plateau. Arnold hit his tee shot, and the crowd went crazy. Then I hit.

When we got up on the green we found my ball was two feet away from the hole and Arnold's was at the back of the green. Gardner Dickinson had a talk to the referee and then the next minute the referee asked my caddie, an American caddie given to us by the PGA, if he had said "Great shot, Arnie, what club did you use?"

PETER OOSTERHUIS: Bernard's caddie wasn't trying to find out information to help his partner. He was just a fan who'd just seen a super shot hit by his idol. But the PGA of America official decided that that was seeking advice, and we lost the hole. [The Rules of Golf allow you to ask for advice—defined as "any counsel or suggestion that could influence a player in determining his play, the choice of club or the method of making a stroke"—only from your partner or either of your caddies.]

BERNARD GALLACHER: I asked the caddie if this had happened. He said it had, and that he was prepared to walk in. This was an American guy, a club member, and he was really upset. "It's one of those things," I told him. I mean, it's Arnold Palmer, the greatest sportsman of all time, and this caddie is standing next to his hero and he sees his hero hit this shot. Anyway, the point is that Palmer and Dickinson waited till they got up on the green, to see how well they stood, before they spoke to the referee.

PETER OOSTERHUIS: It was a tough loss. Bernard was very upset about it. Obviously he'd been involved in some touchy matches in the previous Cup, in 1969, so maybe there was a bit of a carryover. The atmosphere wasn't good after that. But I never held anything against Arnold. I think Bernard felt that Arnold condoned the officials' decision. The official made the ruling, and that was the way it was.

In the afternoon we played against Billy Casper and Lee Trevino. I remember a fantastic shot Trevino hit. There was a par-5 on the front nine [sixth hole], and there'd been some work done in the rough on the left-hand side. Beyond that there was out of bounds to the left. The grass hadn't come back where the work was done, and it was just hardpan. And Trevino—he could afford to do this in a four ball—said, "Let's see what I can do here." He aimed his tee shot left, out of bounds, but faded the ball and made it land on this hardpan, making it run about fifty yards farther than it would have done landing anywhere else, and that enabled him to go for the green in two. And I just thought, The cheek of it to attempt that shot! But we beat them 1 up.

PETER OOSTERHUIS: The pairings for the final singles matches in the afternoon were made over lunch. [British captain] Dai Rees told me, "You're playing Arnold Palmer." It was really neat seeing Dai, this wonderful enthusiast of the game, enjoy telling me that I was playing Arnold because he knew I wanted a chance to play Arnold. But after a couple of holes I could tell that Arnold wasn't the force he'd been two days previously. He'd played in all the matches and wasn't playing quite as well. I was just a twenty-three-year-old playing some good golf, and felt early on that I could beat him.

I was a few holes up in the middle of the back nine. The overall match had already been decided, and it had started to rain. Arnold said to me, "You know, the match is over—why don't we walk in?" And I said, "Are you conceding?" And he said, "No!" So we carried on playing. That might have been a veteran just messing with a kid, just to see what reaction he could get. I won 3 and 2.

A *similar defeat was inflicted at Muirfield, just east of Edin-burgh, in 1973, when the Ryder Cup made its first and as yet only visit to Scotland. Once again, the British side collapsed after taking a first-day lead, in this case a not inconsiderable three points.*

There also had been another change to the format, one that brought us closer to the current setup. Instead of two sets of four-somes on the first day followed by two sets of four-balls on the sec-

ond, each of the first two days had one set of each. The reason? Two four-balls matches in one day took too long and tired the players.

Returning in charge of the U.S. team was Jack Burke Jr., the losing captain at Lindrick in 1957. Before play began, the diminutive Texan expressed concern that if he were to captain another losing side he might be denied passage back to America. He needn't have worried.

COLIN SNAPE: I was responsible for the complete organization of the matches. We all stayed at the Marine Hotel, in North Berwick, and Arnold Palmer came in with a haggis for the victory dinner, and Ted Heath, the British prime minister, was the guest of honor. The banter and the repartee was something. If you captured it in a film and showed it, people would wonder, Did that actually happen? But that was the camaraderie and the spirit that existed back then.

CHI CHI RODRIGUEZ [who made one U.S. Ryder Cup appearance]: I played in 1973 but actually qualified for two Ryder Cup teams, but they didn't let me play in the first one. I think it was 1965. The PGA claimed I was not born an American. I was born in the Commonwealth of Puerto Rico, and I served in the United States Army from 1955 to 1957, but still they kept me out. I could fight for my country but couldn't play golf for it!

Senator William Fulbright [of Arkansas] was a good friend of mine, and when we were playing golf together down in Puerto Rico, I told him what had happened. I said, "Senator, you know, I qualified for the Ryder Cup team and they won't let me play." He said, "You have control of whether they'll play those matches or not. If you want me to stop them from playing them, I will go to Washington and they'll either let you play or there will be no matches." And I said, "No, if they don't want me on the team, I don't want to be part of it anyway."

TONY JACKLIN: I played with Oosterhuis against Weiskopf and Casper and we were miles under par after nine holes. It was unbelievable golf. On the tenth hole, Billy Casper said to me, "I hope you're enjoying this." I said, "I bloody well am—very much. Thank you." He was pissed, but we weren't gloating. We were just doing our best, and everything was going our way.

BRIAN BARNES: They found a winning combination in Bernie [Gallacher] and myself. He was a very good chipper, and I was a very good driver. He knew damn well that if he knocked me in the rough I was going to get him out on the fairway. So that is why we managed to dovetail very, very well. But then all of a sudden Bernie went down with food poisoning on the Friday night.

BERNARD GALLACHER: I ate some fish in the hotel and was up all night. We were due to play Jack Nicklaus and Tom Weiskopf on the second day, and I was looking forward to that, but I couldn't play. I was asked to play in the singles on the last day, but I really shouldn't have. I played Weiskopf in the morning, lost to him, and I lost badly in the afternoon [to Gay Brewer, 6 and 5]. I felt so disappointed. We were going so well the first day. We were in the lead [5½ to 2½] and off to a good start, but my illness seemed to affect the team. The world came crashing down.

BRIAN BARNES: Bernie was one of our major players, and of course we were in a situation where by the time the singles came around, especially the afternoon singles, your concentration is going. Six rounds of pressurized golf takes its toll.

PETER OOSTERHUIS: In my singles against Lee Trevino, he was chatting away on the first tee, but I birdied the first 2 holes, and he went from chatting to saying nothing—right away. He realized he'd better get down to business or I might embarrass him. He finally got back to all square when I three-putted the fourteenth—and then he started talking again! It was like night and day.

On the seventeenth, he drove into a pot bunker off the tee, and I drove down the fairway. All he could do was chip out so I had my chance, but for some reason I tried to hit a driver off the fairway, went into a bunker, so now all I could do was chip out. And we halved the hole with sixes. And then we halved the last. Lee later wrote that he had me beaten and let the match slip away, but that is totally not the case.

In my last singles match I beat Arnold Palmer. It was a cold, damp day, and Arnold's great big gnarled, workmanlike hands that controlled the club were just too cold. It didn't look as if he could play the way he wanted to.

BILLY CASPER: Nicklaus played against Maurice Bembridge a lot at Muirfield [twice on the first day and twice in singles on the third day]. While we were having lunch one day, he said, "I can't get up for this little shit." He said, "I'm not a team player." Nicklaus would make statements like that. And so after we finished our matches, we went to look for Bembridge to beat Nicklaus. It dated back to the giving of the putt at Birkdale in 1969, Nicklaus not being a team player. It was sort of interesting how some of us felt. Nicklaus and I have become extremely good friends, but it was interesting in those days.

Embarrassments weren't confined to the British, however. When the Ryder Cup went to Laurel Valley in Ligonier, Pennsylvania, with Arnold Palmer as American captain, in 1975, the Americans chipped in their share of red faces.

COLIN SNAPE: Political expediency set in during the 1970s, and when we went to Laurel Valley in '75 it was the first time "Ireland" was part of the title of the British team. There had always been Irish players on the team, people like Christy O'Connor and Harry Bradshaw, but until then it had been the "British" team with the Union Jack as the sole flag and only the British anthem played at the opening ceremonies. And the organization was considered the British PGA, as it always had been.

The band that was to play at the opening ceremonies was from a local high school, and they didn't know how to play the Irish national anthem, which is "The Soldier's Song." But they were busily rehearsing a Protestant Loyalist song from Northern Ireland. There would have been bombs going off in the grandstand if that had been played. So the day before the ceremony I went to them and whistled the [correct] tune to them several times, while their music teacher busily wrote it all down. They put on a very creditable performance the following day.

But the biggest cock-up of all had to do with it being televised. They used to have the opening ceremonies before play on the first day, and, believe it or not, it all started in the dark. It was absolutely pitch-black. That really set the stage for one fiasco after another.

Women weren't allowed in the clubhouse at Laurel Valley, and that included the wives of players. On the first night we always had a team meeting with the respective teams, just to go through the rules and all the rest of it. I'll never forget Jack Nicklaus coming in all steely-eyed and saying, "Never mind the rules and all that crap, Arnold. If my wife is not sitting down to have lunch with me tomorrow, I'm going home." There was a deathly silence. Such consternation. So a compromise was effected whereby the wives of the players—and *only* the wives of the players—were allowed in the clubhouse between twelve and two to consume lunch with their husbands. As Murphy's Law would have it, there was a rain out when play started, so by the time Jack got in it was twenty minutes to two. So Barbara was allowed to have the soup before she was ejected with everybody else.

The climax to this—and this almost became an international incident—involved Walter Annenberg, who was retiring American ambassador to Britain at the time. The British ambassador Sir Peter Ramsbottom was representing Queen Elizabeth at the event. They rolled up in the cavalcade, Lord Derby as the president of the British PGA, and Annenberg there to meet them. Sir Peter came out, Walter greeted him, and so on. Lady Ramsbottom came out, and all of a sudden a big heavy appeared from inside the front door of the clubhouse and barred her entrance. "Sorry, ma'am, no women in the clubhouse."

Well, Annenberg and Lord Derby had a sort of negotiation going on right there on the doorstep, but the club was quite adamant. Lady Ramsbottom, Mrs. Annenberg, et al., had to head off up a hill into a special pavilion that had been erected purely for women!

To spark some interest in what was becoming a yawner of a con-

test, the PGA of America "themed" the 1975 Ryder Cup around its star player.

COLIN SNAPE: Arnold Palmer was captain, and it was Arnold's home area. His hometown of Latrobe was just down the road.

JIM JENNETT [producer, ABC television]: In 1975, the Ryder Cup was minor status as far as a television event was concerned. The U.S. always won, and nobody knew the British players. So we sort of built the Laurel Valley telecast around Arnold Palmer's image; in fact, he could have been one of the reasons that we covered it. Roone Arledge, who was my boss at the time, was very close to Arnold, and Arnold was a big player in another pioneering effort we did, which was bringing the British Open to the U.S. audience.

HALE IRWIN [three-time U.S. Open champion who played on five U.S. Ryder Cup teams]: Arnie was a no-nonsense kind of captain. He said, "You know, guys, we're going to go out, and as far as I'm concerned, I hope they don't win a point. Let's beat 'em."

Arnie was right for a while. The United States won every point in the first morning's foursomes and took two and a half points out of four in the afternoon four-balls to hit their pillows with a five-point lead. Day two wasn't much better for the Brits. Slogging through rain that made the Laurel Valley course play longer than its already daunting 7,045 yards, they managed two points out of a possible eight. On the third day, after winning four morning singles and halving two other morning matches, the U.S. players could sit down and enjoy a victory lunch. The British team was beaten and exhausted, and there was nothing else left to play for. Except a couple of rounds that have gone down in golf history.

HALE IRWIN: I'll never forget it. Barnesy went out and beat him again. Barnesy was a real stalwart against arguably the best player on the team.

Barnesy is, of course, Brian Barnes, the pipe-smoking, Bermuda shorts–wearing, alcoholic (since reformed) Englishman, while "arguably the best player" on the U.S team was none other than Jack Nicklaus. Barnes whupped him twice in one day.

BRIAN BARNES: They've made so much of the particular matches that it bowls me over. I'd played with Jack a fair amount of times, and our captain Bernard Hunt felt I was not going to be quite as much in awe of him as some players might have been. All we did through the thirty-six holes was talk about fishing.

HALE IRWIN: Of all the players I've played against in some sort of match-play format, Brian was the least impressed about the player that he was playing, his record, or what he had done before. Barnesy looked upon it as just another game, and he was not impressed by a name. It was a great attitude. And if he got a bit nervous, out came the pipe.

BRIAN BARNES: I won in the morning, 4 and 2, and at lunchtime Jack and I were both asked questions by the press. Then Jack buggered off. I was asked some more questions, and one of the last was, "How would you like to have the opportunity of taking on the Golden Bear again this afternoon?" I remember distinctly saying, "Lightning doesn't strike twice in the same place."

Now, unbeknownst to me, Jack had gone to Arnold and said, "Look, we've won the cup. The only thing that's going to keep the interest going is if I take on Barnesy again this afternoon." So the draw was changed—the only time in the history of the Ryder Cup that the draw was changed.

After the match [which Barnes won 2 and 1], Jack just congratulated me and went to the separate side of the locker room. That was it. He took defeat as you would expect the greatest golfer in the world would. He took it like a gentleman.

Those who felt the British situation had reached rock bottom clearly had no idea what the two PGAs had planned for Royal Lytham in 1977: another format change, from thirty-two matches in three days to twenty in the same amount of time: five foursomes, five four-balls, and ten singles. With twelve players on each team, there would be a lot of sitting out to do. A lot not happening.

DOW FINSTERWALD [U.S. team captain in 1977]: There was a feeling among the guys, which I shared, that it was a long way to go to play perhaps only thirty-six holes. They wanted to play more golf.

BERNARD GALLACHER: Having been beaten so badly at Laurel Valley, I think they wanted to have fewer points to win. They thought it might be closer. No one would be outright winners until the middle of the singles.

RENTON LAIDLAW: At this stage Britain had gone twenty years without winning. They thought if there were fewer points maybe they had a better chance.

BRIAN HUGGETT [British team captain]: I thought that if we could have got away to a flyer, we had a chance of winning. Over the years, we'd often got away to a flyer but weren't good enough to hang on for another two and a half days. But at Lytham, we didn't. We were behind all the way.

PETER OOSTERHUIS: And there were forty- or forty-five-minute intervals between groups, as the matches were spread out during the day to make the spectators feel they had a full day's golf. But you were scattered all over the place, so you didn't have the feeling of being a part of a team.

RENTON LAIDLAW: There was no atmosphere at all. It was a total disaster.

Not for everyone. At least it started in style.

COLIN SNAPE: The 1977 match was the fiftieth anniversary of the Ryder Cup, so we brought together all the surviving members of the first matches. We brought in three American players—Gene Sarazen, Johnny Farrell, and Wild Bill Mehlhorn, who came in his Stetson! It also was Queen Elizabeth's silver jubilee—her coronation had been in 1952—so we had special plates made that commemorated both jubilees and presented them to the previous players and the 1977 teams. It was an open-air presentation by the eighteenth green, and it really was very impressive. We had the bands and the flags and all the rest of it. It was a super occasion. The match really was an anticlimax.

DOW FINSTERWALD: At the Opening Ceremonies, after acknowledging the presidents—or her Royal Highness, the princess of something—I noted, "It is said that in brevity there is virtue and at least for this afternoon I shall be virtuous." [USGA president] Joe Dey came to me and said, "Dow, that's the finest captain's speech I have ever heard." Then when the matches began, I got Lanny and Hale Irwin out first. They both were fast players.

HALE IRWIN: The first hole at Lytham is a par-3. Now, this was my first opportunity to play with Lanny Wadkins, who's sort of an aggressive, go-get-'em kind of guy. I said, "Lanny, you're up first". I remember him teeing the ball. I thought, Hey, this is pretty cool. The first player out, hitting the first ball on the first hole of the 1977 Ryder Cup."

But sometimes I felt like I was trying to brake the train, because Lanny has a tendency to play aggressively all the time, which can be a little counterproductive in foursomes. I'd say to my partner, "Okay, where would you like me to try and leave this shot for you?" But Lanny was up there just firing away all the time. I tried to adjust my thinking to be a little more aggressive but there were times where I'd say, "Lanny, *no*—that's not a driver. Hit a 2-iron."

But on the forth hole, which runs alongside a railroad, he was going to hit driver, and I said, "Lanny, hold off. There are bunkers out there. Let's just lay up. And he laid it up out of bounds. I should have just gone ahead and let him hit it!"

DOW FINSTERWALD: At that point Nicklaus and Watson were one-two in the world, and Don Padgett [PGA president] said, "Don't get those guys out there in four-balls; they may start playing against each other." I kept that in mind, but I thought they'd make a great team playing alternate shot. Another thing: Don't take a guy like Nicklaus or Watson who is obviously playing quite well and put him with somebody who is not playing well. In other words, in foursomes Nicklaus can't do much if he has to chip out of the gorse or something like that. It takes away the advantage. And if a guy's a scrambler and isn't playing well, maybe playing with another scrambler is good, because he's used to being out there. I didn't believe in watering down a team.

One of the things I said to them beforehand was, "I want you guys to do whatever you do normally the night before you play. If you drink a bottle of whiskey, drink a bottle of whiskey. If you don't drink at all, don't drink at all. Just keep your norm. You got here by playing well and on your own schedule of what time you go to bed." I always remember about the guy who was playing in the club championship and he normally stayed out late or did something. And the night before the championship at the club he went to bed real early but he didn't sleep. So I just wanted them to do whatever they normally do.

The day before the matches began we put the pairings out to play four or five holes. I caught up with Hubert Green and Jack who were playing, I think, a skins games. They let me play the last three holes with them. We got to the last hole, and I think Hubert had it about six or seven feet away, and Jack was about ten. I was thirty-five feet away, but I made the putt. Jack was about to putt, and I said, "Jack, just a minute. If you make this, you're not playing in the first round." Well, he left it short. Now Hubert got ready. I said, "Hubert, if you make this, you're not playing." And he drilled it in. So when I left him out of the first round, he said, "I didn't know you'd do that."

DAVE STOCKTON: I had one great experience with Dow Finsterwald. I told him flat out I was not playing well. He'd paired me with Jerry McGee in the alternate shot, and I didn't hit a fairway through the first fourteen holes. We were 2 down on the sixteenth hole, and I told Jerry, "Just put it anywhere on the green and I'll make it." He knocked it to around twenty feet and I made the putt, so we were 1 down. On the seventeenth he drove it in a bunker in the center of the fairway, and I had to play it out sideways, and after that we still were away. Jerry knocked it to the back of the green, maybe forty feet away. They knocked it over and chipped on. I holed it and they missed for four, so we were even. On 18, I finally hit the fairway—and you can't see that fairway for all the little bunkers—and they double-bogeyed. We won the last three holes to win.

But I was driving the ball so badly that poor Jerry McGee's pants were in shreds from being in all those low rosebushes they have there. He looked like a cat had attacked him. So Finsterwald just said to me, "I'm not going to play you anymore." And I said, "I don't blame you." I had so much respect for how he handled it because it was so different than what had happened with [U.S. captain] Jay Hebert in 1971. So I didn't play the singles, but at least I got asked, you know?

PETER OOSTERHUIS: We were walking down the fifteenth fairway, and the Americans had hit a poor shot and there was a cheer from the gallery, which the players didn't like. I remember walking down the next fairway and Jack Nicklaus saying, "I love playing golf in Great Britain except in the Ryder Cup."

BRIAN BARNES: We didn't have the greatest captain. Brian Huggett wanted to do it his own way and wouldn't listen to any of the players. I suppose you can't fault the guy if he wanted to make his own bloody mistakes, but decisions were made that meant there was no chance of our winning. He dropped Tony Jacklin from the singles on the last day.

PETER OOSTERHUIS: He didn't play Tony Jacklin in the singles on the course where Tony had won the Open Championship. Brian Huggett was a feisty character, and was going to show Tony who was boss.

TONY JACKLIN: I got left out because I told Huggett what I bloody thought of him. Basically Brian went through an acute personality change as soon as we got to the bloody golf course. He set himself apart from the players, sat and ate only with his wife in the evenings; and we asked him to join us on a couple of occasions. He'd taken this thing on, but he wasn't creating much team spirit. Then after [twenty-three-year-old Irishman] Eamonn Darcy and I were beaten in one of the early matches we went back out on the course to support the match that was behind us. Huggett came up to us and said, "Why aren't you out practicing?" Bloody cheeky bastard, telling grown fellows who are out there giving it our best shot that that wasn't good enough. I've never been one to think that practice can create instant success anyway, and if I thought I needed to practice for the afternoon I would have been practicing. I was old enough to know what my own game was.

So I just I took him to the other side of the fairway and told him in no uncertain terms that this wasn't Crystal Palace Football Club—his football [soccer] team—and to mind his own goddamn business. So he dropped me from the singles.

COLIN SNAPE: In terms of crowd appeal and whatnot, leaving Tony Jacklin out was a complete and utter disaster.

TONY JACKLIN: Brian didn't say much to me, because I would have knocked his freaking head off. And I didn't speak to him for a few years after that. He's a tenacious little sod on the golf course, and I would have imagined he would have been like that as a captain. But he sort of reacted in a very, very odd way. I thought he did a bloody terrible job.

BERNARD GALLACHER: On the first day, I was paired with Brian Barnes against Lanny Wadkins and Hale Irwin. We were 2 up with about five to play but lost. I got dropped after that, but I just practiced and waited for the singles. Which turned out to be against Jack Nicklaus. I got to the first tee and counted my clubs—thirteen. My putter had been stolen! Probably a drunken caddie. I had to go to the pro shop and buy another putter. But the putter that was stolen wasn't going great anyway. I was actually quite pleased to see the back of it.

Jack started bogey, bogey, bogey, and I went 3 up. Then I birdied the fourth and was 4 up. But then Jack whittled it down and we were all square on the seventeenth when I holed an eighty-foot putt to go 1 up, and I was just trying to get it close. We halved 18, and that was it. I won.

TONY JACKLIN: This was the year that Tom Weiskopf got chosen for the American team but buggered off hunting and didn't play. Now we really knew something had to be done if we wanted the best players in the world to keep coming over to participate.

DOW FINSTERWALD: I kind of like the way Tom has handled it since. He said he didn't know when he'd ever get a chance to do it [hunting] again. He wanted to go, and we didn't even discuss it. To my knowledge nobody on the team dwelt on it. But he did come out later and say, "I was wrong, I should have played."

PETER OOSTERHUIS: I read an article in which Weiskopf said his justification for going hunting was that all of a sudden the Ryder Cup was like this big affair. It wasn't a golf match. You were getting carted around in the buses and kind of put on show. Maybe he was using it as a convenient excuse, but I remember that in 1975 at Laurel Valley we were trying to play golf and here we were sitting on a bus and getting carted into town to this gigantic dinner party just to be put on show and listen to some speeches.

NEIL COLES: Weiskopf going hunting was the last straw, from Jack Nicklaus's point of view. It was time to change.

COLIN SNAPE: It might have been fine if the matches had been ding-dong contests and the results hung in the balance. But on the first day foursomes, Nicklaus and Watson were playing Mark James and Tommy Horton, who spent half an hour considering every putt. It was a cold afternoon, and Jack got completely brassed off. And that really set the stage.

After that Jack put forward his thoughts to Lord Derby. There wasn't a formal meeting as such; it was purely an informal chat where Jack said to Lord Derby, "John"—he was on Christian names terms with him—"really, this just can't carry on." Weiskopf had gone big-game hunting. From the American point of view, it was becoming more than just a fad, to have to go through all this ritual, and there was no pay, no nothing; it was for the honor.

BERNARD GALLACHER: Jack was always ahead of his time, always had his ear close to the ground. He wanted the Ryder Cup to continue, but it wasn't going to continue if we were going to be beaten all the time. He had this vision. And he told Lord Derby and said, "You're going to have to make it European. There's a couple of good Europeans coming along."

69

Nicklaus's own account, as told much later to the Boston Globe, *"I sat down one night with Lord John Derby, the head of the PGA of Great Britain. I said, 'John, you know that for everyone on the American Team it's a great honor to make the team and it's a great honor to play in these matches. But frankly, when the matches start, there isn't much competition. We win every year. And I don't think that's right.'*

"I said, 'You've got a European Tour that really you're part of, and I think if you included the European players and made it Europe versus the United States, I think you'd have some really great matches that would really add to the Ryder Cup.'

"So John agreed with me and he said he'd take care of it from his end, which he did. I suppose the most difficult aspect was getting the British PGA to include Europe. So he got it through and then the Americans went along with it."

COLIN SNAPE: As far as we were concerned, it was a done deal. What could we do? With no Ryder Cup, the finances of the PGA would have been extremely perilous.

BRIAN HUGGETT: I was British PGA captain at the time, and in 1978 flew to Augusta National with Lord Derby and Peter Butler, who was a member of the board of the British PGA. We weren't there to play in the Masters; we were only there for discussions with the PGA. We'd heard rumors that some of the Americans were thinking it should be America versus the rest of the world. We had to knock that idea on the head; keep it European. It would lose its identity if it started going to Cape Town, Tokyo, Australia, and places like that. But something had to be done because it was a very bad match in America, and we needed the money.

COLIN SNAPE: Expanding it beyond Europe, making the team Great Britain and the rest of the world, was certainly mentioned. But there was a group of die-hards like Peter Alliss who were dead against even extending it to Europe, so the thought of expanding it to the rest of the world never stood a chance.

DAVE STOCKTON: It was an awesome move. Basically expanding

to Europe saved the Ryder Cup. Now if they play over here, we ought to be the favorites, and when we go over there, they ought to be the favorites, and that's the way it should be.

BRIAN BARNES: I was supportive of the move. Oh, there's no doubt the matches had been closer than the final scores reflected. And I think that it was very noticeable that the Americans were far better at holing that crucial putt over the last couple of holes than the Europeans were. They were tougher. Their tour was far tougher than it was in the U.K. Far less tournaments were played in the U.K. in relation to America. But today you notice a big difference in the way that the Europeans now manage to hole those putts. And this was why the Ryder Cup has become a far tighter thing.

DOW FINSTERWALD: When I heard they were considering the change, I said I didn't think the Europeans should be included. Regardless of the number of matches the U.S. had won, winning wasn't what the matches were about. They were about the game of golf, about sportsmanship, and there was enough tradition and history that they were going to be successful regardless. I also said, "I don't give a damn if they include the rest of the world; we're still going to beat them."

TONY JACKLIN: So you know it made sense to do it. It just didn't show itself for the first couple of years.

DOW FINSTERWALD: We won in '79 at the Greenbrier, and in '81 and '83. So there was several years when it didn't change who won. In that respect I was somewhat correct. But now I'm in total agreement the move was the right one.

HALE IRWIN: The move was to get Seve Ballesteros on the team more than anything else, and I think that was a good move. It added a great dimension to the Ryder Cup.

TONY JACKLIN: The PGAs knew that by then we had a few Spaniards coming on the European Tour, and that might make a difference. We'd become the European Tour by then. It established itself in the early '70s really. John Jacobs was running it, and I was playing in tournaments in Germany and Sweden and other new countries to try and get the thing started. And by then Seve and Nick Faldo and some other guys had come on the scene.

JOHN JACOBS: I stopped playing in 1963 and became managing director of a company devoted to building golf centers: driving ranges, par-3's golf courses. That eventually failed, but at about the same time I also was teaching virtually every national team in Europe: the French, Italians, Spanish, Germans, Scots. They each had squads of sixteen to twenty young people, and in no time at all these boys started to win. The first year I went to work with the Spanish, which would have been around 1973 or '74, they had José María Canizares and Manuel Piñero. They were caddies. And I saw Seve in those days. He was about seventeen. I remember thinking I had seen genius, but told him, "You'll get back trouble, young fellow, if you go on swinging like that."

In 1971 the British PGA asked me to take on the British circuit, but I really didn't want to because I'd been on the British PGA's executive committee, and it was thirty people who were all about ninety years old, and you couldn't get a flippin' thing done. But suddenly I realized that I really ought to do it because I knew all the golf authorities on the continent through teaching their squads, and although it was the British PGA that had asked me to do it, I knew that it would have to be a European Tour if we were going to make it substantial, because Britain's too small. So I said, "I'll do it only if I have a free hand."

In a short time I went to all the continental countries, whose amateur bodies were all already running open championships, and said, "Hang on. Your opens are sponsored." So putting them all together was the beginning of the European PGA Tour. I was the first honorary life member of the tour, and then about six months before the 1979 matches they asked me to be Ryder Cup captain. I was thrilled.

With the change to Europe in place, there remained another task to be completed. The job fell to Snape.

COLIN SNAPE: I had to write a manual of rules and regulations, not just about the order of play and number of teams, but also about everybody getting at least a game. Back in '73 John Garner made the team for Britain but never played, and then Jacklin was left out on the last day in '77, which was a disaster. It was decided then that the format would change and that everybody would play singles on the last day. But then typically, because pro golfers are so good at this—good God, if they were in the Senate or Parliament no legislation would ever be passed, because deep down they're all protecting their own self-interest—the debate came up asking, "What happens if somebody is ill?" So we had to have this formula under which, before play began, the captains would put a name in an envelope, hand it to the chief referee, and in the event of somebody not being available, the two names in the envelope would step down and call it half. Each team would get half a point.

Simple really, but it was a rule that would become quite controversial as the 1979 Ryder Cup unfolded at the Greenbrier resort in West Virginia.

BABY STEPS

So the deed was done. The door to Europe had been opened and would not likely be closed again. The promise was just too irresistible. Seve Ballesteros had won the British Open in 1976, and in 1977 he topped the European Tour's money list. The European Tour was taking shape, which could only further growth and the standard of golf on the continent. The planets were lining up nicely— although the realists in the crowd could see that the United States was improving, too.

LARRY NELSON [on the U.S. team in 1979, '81, and '87]: We all thought that opening up to Europe would make the matches more competitive, and that it was the beginning of something. But none of us thought it would make much difference that year [in 1979].

HALE IRWIN: You had the dynamics of newer, younger American players entering the scene: Tom Kite, Fuzzy Zoeller, Jerry Pate. At the same time, the Hale Irwins were starting to assert some of their games and their personalities, and I think that made the Lee Trevinos and Jack Nicklauses, the stalwarts of the game, bear down even more. So the U.S. team became very competitive all around. What I recall most about 1979 was that it wasn't so much the attitude of "Were we going to win or lose?" because we *knew* we were going to win. It was more "Who's going to be on the team?"

BILLY CASPER [U.S. captain in 1979]: I tried to unite the players by making a list of what clothing they should wear to what functions we had. So I had it all set for them. All they had to do was check their papers and see what to wear. Then on Wednesday night we had a dinner, just the players and their wives, and my wife. We tried to get this closeness established, and only one player fouled up. One day Trevino wore royal blue pants instead of navy blue. And I said, "Well that's typical for Trevino. He's always talking and not listening." Or reading, in that instance.

So you have your twelve players and you start watching them very closely toward the end of the season. I had Hubert Green on our team, and he wasn't playing that well, and Gil Morgan slipped and fell on a tennis court at the Greenbrier after one of the practice rounds and hurt his shoulder. So I had to use them very sparingly. Then Tom Watson left for home on Wednesday evening because his wife went into labor, so Mark Hayes filled in for him. I had planned on pairing Watson and Lanny Wadkins together, and was going to tee them off first. Then I decided for some reason to put Larry Nelson and Wadkins together in a practice run on Thursday, and they went out and shot 59, so I paired them in the alternate shot as well as the four-balls. Nelson wound up playing in all five of the matches and won 5 points. Wadkins won 4½ points in the matches he played in, so that pairing was a great find.

LARRY NELSON: I hadn't played any match play until then, so they put me with Lanny because he was probably the most experienced in match play. Kind of guide me around, help me out.

BILLY CASPER: It was a blind draw, and Seve Ballesteros always seemed to wined up playing Larry Nelson [four of five matches]. Ballesteros kept saying, "Larry Nelson's very lucky." But Nelson just kept dusting him off every day.

LARRY NELSON: Seve was just a brash young man, very full of himself. But he had all the reason in the world to be.

BILLY CASPER: We so dominated that year. You'd just pair the guys and show up periodically and hit 'em on the rump. Encourage them. That's all you could do. Encourage them.

But I had a good team. I mean, I had [Tom] Kite, Irwin, [Andy] Bean, Trevino, and [Fuzzy] Zoeller. I put Fuzzy and Trevino together because I thought they could talk their way into winning a match. But it didn't work out that way.

The Trevino-Zoeller pairing indeed lost, 3 and 2, to Brian Barnes and Bernard Gallacher in the second day's afternoon four-balls. But in the morning four-balls on the first day they won 3 and 2 over Mark James and Ken Brown, the latter a duo that caused inummerable problems for the European squad, and even before they'd boarded their flight to the U.S.

COLIN SNAPE: When we were due to set off from Heathrow Airport in those days security wasn't what it is today—Mark James turned up with half an hour to go. Our captain John Jacobs and all the rest of the team were all in their blazers and uniforms, but James wobbled up in tracksuit bottoms [sweatpants], pumps [sneakers], the scruffiest operation you've ever seen. I said, "What's this, Mark? Where's your uniform?" He said, "It's in the bag somewhere." I said, "Well put it on. *Put it on.*" So that set the tone.

JOHN JACOBS: I'd written to everyone and told them that the only thing I wanted from them was for them to be on time if I called a meeting and to dress as per the agreed dress code. It was not a bombastic letter. James and Brown arrived looking like tramps. Somebody—Peter Alliss, I think—wrote that I should have sent them straight home. But it's very easy to say that. Suddenly you're stuck. You're heading for America and you think, well, surely we can get them in order a bit.

COLIN SNAPE: We got to the Greenbrier, and James literally took to his bed. He started ordering room service and stuffing himself with double cheeseburgers. It was pouring rain when the opening ceremony was held the following day, so it was held in a huge hangar that housed the resort's indoor tennis and other recreational facilities, about a mile from the Greenbrier. With twenty minutes to go, everybody was lined up, the bands and everything, but guess who's missing—James. We rang the hotel and finally got through to his room. "No, I'm not bothering to come," James.

By now Brian Barnes is furious, so I said, "Come on, we'll go and fetch him." Barnes and I got a golf buggy and rode to the hotel in the pouring rain. We knew what room he was in, and we hammered on the door. "No, I'm not coming!" James replied. That was when Barnes literally went through the door!

We found James lying on the bed and, well, persuaded him that it would really, *really* be in his interest right there and then to get dressed and come down to the opening ceremony. Whether he bounced once or twice on the bed I can't quite remember, if you know what I mean, but let's just say James was "intimidated" by Mr. Barnes. So James came down and waddled his way through, disinterested and so on. He played in the foursomes and didn't take any further part in the matches, complaining of a bad back.

JOHN JACOBS: The flag raising was being televised, and I could see the pictures on television. I'm introducing my team to the great American public, and I'm going down the line, but I can see on television these two, James and Brown, are chatting away, and when the national anthems were being played and the flags were going up, they were still just chatting. It was absolutely abhorrent.

When I introduced them, they sort of just raised off their seats a bit. It was pathetic. And at a big dinner we had, they wouldn't let photographers take pictures of them. They kept putting their hands in front of their faces.

What was so annoying was that they were two of our strongest players. Both had been playing and practicing well. On the first day they lost a close four-balls match, and Mark reckoned he'd pulled a muscle. We'll never know whether he had or not, but he couldn't play in the afternoon. I put Ken with Des Smyth. Ken hit a couple of bad shots early on and didn't try a lick for the rest of the round.

RENTON LAIDLAW: Ken seemed to be very upset that he didn't get the opportunity to play with Mark in the afternoon, so he never spoke to Des. In fact, he walked on the other side of the fairway from him—and he knew Des Smyth very well!

TONY JACKLIN: Ken Brown didn't look for his partner's ball in the foursomes. His own partner's! No question: I'd have sent them both home.

JOHN JACOBS: They lost 7 and 6 to Hale Irwin and Tom Kite. I saw Hale afterward and apologized for our players' behavior. He said, "Oh, not to worry, John. It was easy for us."

HALE IRWIN: The European team was in turmoil. They were dysfunctional. Brown and Des Smyth didn't say two words to one another, and it was almost as if they were just going through the motions to get it over with and get in early.

JOHN JACOBS: In that evening's team meeting, I humbled Ken Brown in front of everybody. I said I made a mistake when I asked him to play in the afternoon, that he was a baby—and I apologized to Des Smyth for his first Ryder Cup match having been in that situation.

Mark James couldn't play with this pulled muscle, and I couldn't play Ken at all in a partnership, so now I had to play other guys over and over again, which was the last thing I wanted to do.

BERNARD GALLACHER: Mark James and Ken Brown made John Jacobs' job very difficult. They were immature, and they disrupted the team spirit. There's a certain discipline that goes with playing in the Ryder Cup, and they weren't prepared to accept it. I think Tony Jacklin had a few words with them and tried to calm them down.

TONY JACKLIN: They behaved like a couple of buffoons. James was a sorry case who took it upon himself to sabotage any chance we had at all of winning.

John Jacobs is a gentleman and we were all more or less apologizing to him on their behalf. "Never mind, John. Don't worry. Don't let them get you down."

RENTON LAIDLAW: John Jacobs called all the [European] press into the interview room, and said, "You may have heard that there is some trouble." Well, of course we had heard. John said, "I do not want any of this to be in any of the papers. I don't want the team in any way upset. If anybody writes about this, they will be responsible to me." And nobody wrote about it. Could you imagine that happening now?

BERNARD GALLACHER: In today's world, their behavior would not be accepted. Fortunately they've both learned now, but it's really all about nerves. The Ryder Cup's a big occasion, and these guys lost it. Mark's since become a pillar of the establishment and Ken Brown's a BBC commentator. Nice to see they've calmed down. And Ken was Mark's assistant when Mark was Ryder Cup captain at the Country Club in 1999. *Heavy* irony there.

COLIN SNAPE: Anyhow, we got through the match, and lost. Then we had the victory dinner, which is quite an occasion, a time to say thank-you to sponsors, the host club, and everything. Traditionally one passes around menu cards to get the players' autographs. Brown and James both wrote childish comments. I can't remember the exact words, but they were mildly offensive and viewed with extreme displeasure.

TONY JACKLIN: He signed a priest's program "Mark James," then, when he knew it was for a priest, he put "son-of-a-bitch" underneath it.

COLIN SNAPE: We got to Dulles Airport outside Washington, D.C., to fly home. James was going on to play in a tournament somewhere else. There were these huge trash cans where you literally could sling a suitcase straight down into the bowels of the airport or wherever, and James put all his official uniforms, cashmere sweaters, the whole lot, in a suitcase and just threw them all away down there. He rubbed his hands together, and said, "Well, that's that." And off he went! I've spent a lot of time with him since, and he really is good company. To this day I've never understood why he wanted to make a statement to such a degree and to show himself to be such a peasant.

JOHN JACOBS: And then he went on to be chairman of the tournament players association and a Ryder Cup captain. Poacher turned gamekeeper!

Under these circumstances, it was, of course, easy for the United States to win.

HALE IRWIN: By the second day we had a fairly good lead, and it was a matter of how soon into that third day were we going to win. At that stage the American teams were still flying high with a great deal of confidence. We had a very strong team, and the European side, other than Seve and maybe one or two others, hadn't really contributed to the extent that they would in later years.

BERNARD GALLACHER: I remember the second day's afternoon fourballs against Trevino and Zoeller [which Gallacher and Brain Barnes won 3 and 2]. Brian had five birdies on his own ball. I would tell him how to play a hole, and he did it. One thing about me, I never cared who on our side got the birdies.

In the singles, I was out first against Lanny Wadkins. Lanny hadn't lost a match up until then. So it was an important match. I was a bit apprehensive, but John [Jacobs] wanted me to play against him, and I managed to beat him. I was down the middle, on the green, putting well. I won 3 and 2.

JOHN JACOBS: Lanny had not been beaten at that time. The first three greens at the Greenbrier were lightning fast, which we weren't quite used to, and Bernard knocked his first putt on each, oh, seven, eight feet past, and holed every one coming back.

The Wadkins-Gallacher match was indeed the first out, but it did not contribute the first of that day's points. Those came with half a point each from a match that didn't even take place: With James unable to play, the U.S. captain Billy Casper had to, as noted earlier, submit a name in an envelope, with the player whose name was in the envelope sitting out as well. With Morgan hurting from his earlier tennis mishap, there should have been little mystery as to whose name was in the envelope.

COLIN SNAPE: Before the matches, we explained to both teams how the envelope would work. By the time it came to the singles, it was known that Mark James wasn't going to get out of bed, and that there was something up with Gil Morgan.

JOHN JACOBS: I'd asked Mark James to hit some balls and tell me if he could play. He couldn't, so I had to report that. So they had to put a name in the envelope. And Billy Casper put Lee Trevino's name in, even though Lee was only the best player in the world at the time!

COLIN SNAPE: There was consternation all around. I thought the officers from the PGA of America were going to have apoplexy on the spot.

JOHN JACOBS: Billy and I both knew the rules, but the U.S. PGA came to me early in the evening before the singles and said, "Look, Billy's put the wrong name in the hat. We won't tell you who we put in there, but he wants to change it. Will you let him?" I told them, "I want to speak to my team before I say yes to that."

We had a quick meeting at which I said, "We're one point behind going into the game tomorrow [the score was $8\frac{1}{2}$–$7\frac{1}{2}$ in favor of the United States]. We could win. Tell me what you all feel, but my advice is to let them do it." And they agreed with me. So they changed the name and Gil Morgan didn't play. I really don't know why Billy did that.

COLIN SNAPE: I don't know how can anybody be so barmy as to do something like that, but Billy did.

The final day was disastrous for Europe. Although Gallacher beat Wadkins, Europe lost eight of the final ten matches, Nelson beating Ballesteros to give him a 5–0 record as a Ryder Cup rookie. Surely things would be better back in Europe in 1981.

COLIN SNAPE: The 1981 match had been due to have been played at the Belfry [in the English Midlands]. When I joined the British PGA, our offices were at the Kennington Oval cricket ground in south London, a most incongruous setting for professional golf. [Kennington is a working-class district in the British capital, just south of the Thames, and home to not much more than one of the venues used by the English national cricket team.] One of my early plans was to put forward a proposal suggesting the PGA should have its own headquarters and make it a host for the Ryder Cup—really establish itself in the way that the PGA of America had done so successfully in Palm Beach Gardens, Florida. We moved to new headquarters at the Belfry in 1975.

The Belfry actually opened as a hotel in 1959, and in the 1960s became a popular venue for live music. Among the acts to perform there: Led Zeppelin and the Moody Blues. The first course was built there in 1970, by Dave Thomas, a four-time British Ryder Cupper, and Peter Alliss.

The deal was that we would play two Ryder Cup matches there, 1981 and 1989. By the time 1980 came round, the golf course wasn't up to standard—we had to dig up the soil to remove all the stones that players were complaining about. At the last minute we ended up at Walton Heath, an excellent golf course outside London.

JOHN JACOBS [European captain again]: Dave Marr [U.S. captain] and I met at the Open Championship in 1981, and discussed how we were going to run things. I'd been pretty miserable about the way the teams didn't dine together, and I instituted largish tables with two American players, two European players, a nonplayer, and some of the other people who were involved.

BRUCE LEITZKE [on the U.S. team in 1981 and a captain's assistant in 1999] : We had dinner with the opposing team every night. Every night! It was very social, and I'm afraid it's gotten away from that. I wasn't really close to many of the Europeans because I hadn't played "world" golf. I'd played only one British Open, but I still knew Sam Torrance, Sandy Lyle, Nick Faldo, Peter Oosterhuis.

JOHN JACOBS: We talked through all sorts of details. At one point I said [to Dave Marr], "I've only had two difficult players in my life, and I hope I don't get them again," meaning Mark James and Ken Brown. And Dave said to me, "I only have one difficult one." I said,

"I know who that is. The one who knows everything about every-thing." But I'm a great admirer of Jack Nicklaus. He would be my player of the last century.

RENTON LAIDLAW: The American team that came to Walton Heath in 1981 was the strongest ever. Trevino, Kite, [Ben] Crenshaw, [Bill] Rogers, Nelson, Jerry Pate, Lietzke, [Johnny] Miller, Irwin, Nicklaus, [Raymond] Floyd—you don't get much stronger than that. And that was the last time that the result wasn't close, 17–8.

HALE IRWIN: That was the best team I was ever on. The strength throughout the lineup was very, very good, physically and mental-ly. And the captain, Dave Marr, was a great stabilizing influence. He had the task of taking twelve distinctly strong personalities and coalescing them into something that is manageable, and that's the hardest thing for a captain. Your players are living together for a week and playing golf in a format that they've never played before. Outside the Ryder Cup, you don't spend seven hours with these guys in a week, but now you're spending every moment with them. So I think that the task is to make sure if you have any per-sonality differences, you put those aside and keep your players focused on what they're doing. And Dave was very much the gen-tleman captain. Probably one of the best captains I was ever under.

BRUCE LIETZKE: It was really an impressive crew. And we were still in the days when this was going to be an American victory and the Ryder Cup was truly just a quaint little social gathering of Amer-icans and Europeans. It was just a very quiet event.

SAM TORRANCE [playing in the first of his eight Ryder Cups; he was eventually captain in 2002]: That American team was like a who's who of golf. Really impressive. I just wanted to try and win a point. In my first match, Howard Clark and I were on the last green against Johnny Miller and Tom Kite, and I had a perfect putt to win a point, but it horseshoed out. I couldn't speak. It just broke my heart.

My impression of my first Ryder Cup? Now I'd seen how good these American guys actually were, and I knew I had to improve a hell of a lot to stay on the world stage. They were just a different class.

BEN CRENSHAW [who played for the U.S. in four Ryder Cups and was captain in 1999]: I knew about Walton Heath from golf history because it's where James Braid had played. There also was a club maker from there named James Busson, and I actually got a couple of drivers from him. Nick Faldo told me about him. And he gave me a fairway wood that James Braid had been working on. I still have that.

James Henry Busson actually was called Jack, according to Phil Pruett, author of a recent history of Walton Heath. Busson was club pro at Walton Heath from 1951 to 1977, and then "Resident Club Maker" until his death in 1993. He supplied the entire European Ryder Cup team with drivers.

BEN CRENSHAW: It took me several rounds to figure out the golf course. I'd never played a heathland course, because usually when I'd gone over to Britain it was to the British Open and links courses. But I loved it. You had to keep the ball in play, and if you were off the fairway the rough and gorse was very tough.

But it was a wonderful, wonderful experience. I knew about the history of the Ryder Cup and had read all about it, but Dave Marr kept saying to me, "You don't know what it's like until you've played in it."

LARRY NELSON: I always enjoyed Dave Marr. He was probably the most encouraging, upbeat person I'd ever met. He had some good sayings, good things he'd come up with. He called me "Baby-face Assassin."

BRUCE LIETZKE: Dave Marr was truly unforgettable. He was a good old Texas boy—although I grew up and lived in Texas myself I really wasn't very familiar with him—and I grew to truly love him by the end of the week. He was a very low-key kind of a guy, which is kind of the person I am, so I felt right at home with him.

He immediately threw Bill Rogers and me together for both matches the first day, but there was no strategy involved. Bill and

I were and still are best of friends, but we actually were never very good as partners. We played in the PGA Tour's Disney Championship when it was a team event [1974–81] and never made the cut. We played in college matches and never partnered well together. My game is more on length and distance, and Bill had a great short game. We enjoyed each other's company, but we just weren't very good together.

But Dave sent us out there, two rookies. We were the younger guys on the team, so I can just imagine Jack Nicklaus saying, "Listen, don't put me out there twice. Let's put the young guys out, and let them do all the work." If I remember right, it was the first Ryder Cup for Ben Crenshaw and Jerry Pate, and I think they played both matches on Friday. Anyway, Bill and I proceeded to get trounced [they lost 2 and 1 to Sandy Lyle and Mark James, and then 6 and 5 to Des Smyth and José Maria Canizares].

JOSÉ MARIA CANIZARES: We won even though communication was so difficult. My English now is very bad but at that time it was terrible.

BRUCE LIETZKE: At the end of the day we told Dave, "If you'd like to split us up, please do, because we don't ever play well together."

Hale Irwin partnered Raymond Floyd in a foursomes loss to Des Smyth and Bernard Gallacher in a foursomes match on the first day

HALE IRWIN: Well, Bernie's always been a bit of a terrier, always been out there scrapping and playing hard. Des's personality is pretty stable, and he kind of got sucked up into that more aggressive style that Bernie seemed to play. They were a formidable team. My game is not that similar to Raymond Floyd's, but we have similarly strong personalities. And competitiveness Raymond and I have in spades. But I think that may have been harmful; it may have been better spread out than put into one team.

We played better in the afternoon [they beat Gallacher and Eamonn Darcy 2 and 1]. I think losing that morning got our emotions up a bit—and drawing Bernie again. Even though Bernie had a different partner, he was the target of our efforts simply because he seemed to be the captain of those teams. He was not necessarily the best player, but he was the guy who was sort of in charge.

JOHN JACOBS: We didn't know much about Larry Nelson, but I knew a lot about him when we'd finished at the Greenbrier in 1979 [Nelson finished with a 5–0 record]. Then when he won the 1981 PGA Championship I said to Renton Laidlaw, "That victory probably cost us the Ryder Cup." Nelson wasn't in the '81 team before the PGA, but the winner was automatically on the team at the time, and Larry displaced someone we didn't think was that good.

LARRY NELSON [who won all his 1981 matches as well]: That was probably the strongest Ryder Cup team of all time. I was just fortunate enough to be a part of that. But everybody's so involved in what they're doing individually that I wouldn't know if any of the other players even knew that I was undefeated.

On the second day, Irwin and Floyd lost to Bernhard Langer and Manuel Piñero.

HALE IRWIN: They didn't hit the ball particularly well, but got it up and down from every heather bush, every tree, every out-of-bounds marker. It was unbelievable. Once when it looked like we were going to win a hole, Raymond came up to me; he said something to the effect that, "If they get this up and down, I'll do something to a part of my body." And damned if they didn't get it up and down for a half. And that was typical. They didn't play well, but we didn't play well enough to take advantage of that. They kept themselves in it, and when they had an opportunity to go ahead, they did. I think we lost 2 and 1.

BRUCE LIETZKE: Today either the press or the media or the captain might go into a panic, but Dave had such a great arsenal of players that when we lost he just said, "Well, we'll just send Larry Nelson and Hale Irwin out." And by the singles matches it was an American victory. Saturday was an easy day for the Americans, and Sunday was an easy day, too.

PETER ALLISS: The Europeans got overwhelmed in the singles.

But although the Americans had a great team, they had two or three key people who won all the points. Larry Nelson won every match, and Jerry Pate with Trevino also was sensational. They beat [Nick] Faldo and [Sam] Torrance 7 and 5.

PETER OOSTERHUIS: Pate was a good player but Trevino was the one doing the damage. Trevino was a bit too much for us.

SAM TORRANCE: Jerry never hit one shot which Trevino didn't tell him what to do: "4-iron—hit it; 5-iron—keep it down; 6-iron—hit it soft." And this guy was just a machine. Whatever Trevino said, this guy did.

JOHN JACOBS: The Americans won seven of eight matches on the second day. Eventually I got fed up with hearing the British television commentators run down the European team and told them, "Why can't you say that the American teams today have played wonderfully well and putted extraordinarily well in wet, windy conditions on a huge golf course, and they're all way under par in foursomes, which is a difficult form of golf to play." The Europeans didn't play badly; they were just outplayed."

PETER ALLISS: But because it rained, there was no atmosphere. You're holding umbrellas, and it's very hard to applaud one-handed.

LARRY NELSON: My fondest memory of the Ryder Cup has to do with the celebration after the '81 victory. I hadn't been playing golf very long and didn't have any history in the game. When I came back home from Vietnam, around 1969, I started hitting balls at a driving range in Marietta, Georgia. Then I worked in a pro shop for two years. In 1972 I went to Tampa and qualified for the Tour in '73. I didn't know anything about the history of golf. I knew who Arnold Palmer was, who Gary Player was, but that was it.

So to be celebrating in the locker room in 1981 with the likes of Nicklaus and Floyd and Irwin and Watson and Trevino and Kite—you just go down the list. Being a part of it, feeling part of it—that was probably the biggest honor and the most exciting thing ever. You don't learn a whole lot in only twelve years, but I was smart enough to know that this was a good thing.

BERNARD GALLACHER: They had all these major champions on the team. We were missing Seve, and Seve was the best player in the world at that time [he won the British Open in 1979 and the Masters in 1980]. He was in dispute with the Tour at the time. It had to do with appearance money and all the rest of it. But if you're in dispute with the association and the players all year, it's probably quite difficult to just be put in the side at that last moment and think you're suddenly best pals.

So how had that European debacle happened?

COLIN SNAPE: There had been a great furor throughout 1981, with Seve maintaining that it was wrong that he couldn't have appearance money in Europe as the star player, whereas all these American imports were coming over to play in Europe and line their pockets. John Jacobs and the Tour said, "Those are the rules," so Seve played most of that summer in America. But the two [committee] picks turned out to be Peter Oosterhuis, who hadn't been to Europe at all that year and, lo and behold, Mark James—after all that had gone on with James in the previous match at the Greenbrier. As you can imagine, the press had a field day.

TONY JACKLIN [who also was left off the team, based on his place on the European money list]: Seve was arguably the best player in the world, and they banned him. And I thought, "We don't deserve to win!" Then they invited me to go as an official in 1981, and I told them to stick it in their ear.

JOHN JACOBS: I spoke up for Seve, telling the PGA, "He is the current master golfer and a world figure." I also knew at the time that Lee Trevino and others were getting lots of money from sponsors. But I asked the guys who were already in the team whether they thought Seve should be picked, and all of them, including the Spanish players, said, "No, he wants this appearance money." I think there was probably a degree of jealousy, too, because he was such a great player. He was the one person who changed the whole shape of European golf.

COLIN SNAPE: Seve was vitriolic, and rightly so. For years afterward Jacobs would say, "It wasn't me, Seve." But Seve wouldn't have any of it. He knew full well it was a political decision. And quite inconsistent as Oosterhuis, who was on the team, hadn't played at all in Europe.

What was to follow would change the Ryder Cup forever. With Colin Snape having made his lucrative trip north to Scotland to meet with Raymond Miquel at Bell's Scotch Whisky, the Europeans had money in hand and a group of players who were invigorated by the success of Seve Ballesteros (although it was doubtful that Ballesteros would play in 1983). The Europeans were confident that not only could they compete more closely with the United States but they could actually beat them—and this despite such a heavy defeat on home turf at Walton Heath.

But they were in complete disarray behind the scenes, so to fix it they sought out someone who not only was a legend in the European game but, because of his triumph in the U.S. Open in 1970, also was a familiar name in the American game.

COLIN SNAPE: We discussed informally who was available in terms of the European captaincy. It had been tradition up until then that you were made captain because of long service, like being made the governor of Bermuda if you'd lived there for fifty years. You know, a great favor to wrap up the *curriculum vitae*. But Raymond Miquel of Bell's wanted a high-profile person, and it was generally felt that Tony Jacklin was the right man. He would have to be sounded out.

BERNARD GALLACHER: I was on the [selection] committee and voted for Tony Jacklin. He stood head and shoulders above everybody else in terms of being a Ryder Cup captain, just from his record [seven appearances, thirteen wins, fourteen losses, and eight ties], the U.S. Open champion and British Open champion. So it was an easy decision, more or less unanimous.

TONY JACKLIN: In 1981, I was thirteenth on the order of merit [the European money list], and Mark James, who'd done all that stuff at the Greenbrier, was fifteenth, and they picked James instead of me. After that, I just said, "That'll do me. I'm out of here."

Then they went and were well beaten at Walton Heath. Jacobs said it was probably the greatest American team ever; they'd amassed this, that, and the other. *Any sort of excuse.* But the bottom line was that we'd had two matches with a European team, and it hadn't made a single scrap of difference.

Well, I'd finished with it all because, honestly, I just thought they were shallow. The whole bloody lot of them. Behind the scenes, the organizational end of it was a shambles. And I wanted no part of it. I was finished. I put it out of my life altogether.

RENTON LAIDLAW: Jacklin had said at some point—you know, he's a very emotional fellow—"I'm finished with the Ryder Cup." But [PGA European Tour executive director] Ken Scofield thought differently. He knew Jacklin was the man to be the captain, and he managed to convince him to take the job.

TONY JACKLIN: One day I was hitting balls at a tournament, I think in the summer of 1982, and Scofield and Snape came up to me. They sort of mumbled something to the tune that the lads wanted to know if I'd consider being the Ryder Cup captain.

COLIN SNAPE: Let's just say he was circumspect. Remember, Tony was mad as hell at being left out, then suddenly he was asked to be the captain! But he said he'd think about it.

TONY JACKLIN: Well, you could have knocked me down with a feather. I said, "I can't answer your question right now," because, you know, it was just a complete shock. I said, "I'll have to talk to you tomorrow."

I went back to where my first wife, Vivien, and I were staying with friends, and I chatted it over with her, and then I started to think about it. There was all this bloody resentment and anger in me because of the things that had happened on the one side, but on the other hand I couldn't help but be intrigued by the thought that if we could just get it right . . . what would happen?

So I went back to them the next day—and I was in a good position because I didn't care if I did it or not—and I said, "There's just so much wrong with the way things have been done and that need to be put right." I said, "I will only do it if I have carte blanche to try and put it right."

BERNARD GALLACHER: Tony had been a player when we weren't going first class, but we couldn't afford to at that time. When he said that he wanted the players to go first class, the Tour, now the Volvo European Tour, could afford to accede to his request. And that really was the turning point in the success of the Ryder Cup, when the European side could afford to be on equal terms with the Americans in terms of preparation.

PETER OOSTERHUIS: You always felt that the Americans put much more money into everything they did, whether it was the uniforms or the travel or whatever. Tony made a good point. In some ways we felt we were second-class citizens, and Tony was determined to change that. And, of course, he was in the best position to do it, having won a major in America and having made a real statement at the highest level of the game. And it worked. From that year on, things turned around.

TONY JACKLIN: They just said, "Yes." They must have thought, This is our last chance, because they'd seen two European matches that were supposed to make all the difference go south, and somebody somewhere must have thought that maybe I could make a difference. Otherwise why would they ask me—especially after having pissed me off the year before?

The immediate thing was to stop the players feeling like second-class citizens. I remember during one Cup [footwear company] Stylo had given us shoes to wear, but they were plastic shoes and the bloody sole came off halfway through a round! It was so embarrassing. We were wearing anything anybody would give us, and it was cheap crap. The Americans, meanwhile, were all looking like bloody Adonises—first-class everything, suits, jackets—and they looked the part. We looked like a bloody bunch of—well, that was when it first occurred to me that we should be doing things first class. So I was able to say, I want Concorde and cashmere and leather bags and the best of everything.

I can only assume that Colin Snape nearly pooped his pants because he was the one who was going to get hit with it. They said yes to Concorde, and I'm sure he didn't have a bloody clue how he was going to pay whatever it cost. But they worked it out. Colin was a good man, a damn good man.

COLIN SNAPE: It's often been written that Tony insisted we had to fly Concorde. That wasn't quite the case. I was a consultant to British Airways at the time, wearing my PGA hat. Concorde was flying empty, so I did a promotional deal with them, under which they paid a fee to us and we would use the scheduled Concorde service into New York, and then fly down from JFK to Florida to where the matches were.

TONY JACKLIN: I also said to Lord Derby, "What about Seve?" Because if I was mad, Seve was bloody livid. So I had breakfast with Seve a couple of weeks after I'd accepted. It ended up as a two-hour breakfast because he was ranting and raving, but I just said to him, "Seve, I'd said I'd do it, but I can't do it justice if you don't come on board. But if you come and it turns out the way I believe it can, you'll be embraced by the British public like a hometown boy." Within a week he was on board.

COLIN SNAPE: I'm sure Tony didn't win Seve over the first time he asked. It was a sales job to get Seve to play after the way he'd been treated in '81. But Tony was the only man who had that strength and, in Seve's eyes, the talent to be on a par with him to even speak together.

TONY JACKLIN: So now we were at least equal to the opposition when we stood on the first tee. But beyond that, there was no team spirit. We all went our separate ways until I brought into the equation the "team room." On my insistence, I went to Palm Beach Gardens, Florida, early in 1983 and found a room in the hotel at PGA National that was big enough to have everybody fed in that room. All the team members and their wives and families were able to sit down and have what they wanted, when they wanted it, in that room. That was their sanctuary. That was the place where you had a shoulder to cry on, or you could have a laugh. Whatever. In the past, you'd have a meeting for twenty minutes, and then everybody would go where the hell they wanted, and that seemed to me not conducive in any way, shape, or form to creating any sort of team spirit. Once I'd got that room and the size of it was fine, we went from there.

COLIN SNAPE: I can't speak too highly of Tony as a captain, the way he drove people and inspired them. It really had to be seen to be believed. And his first wife, Viv, and my wife, Sandra, made sure that the [European] wives and the rest were treated properly as well. It wasn't long before that that the wives weren't allowed to go with the players.

TONY JACKLIN: I tried as much as I could to take every aspect of it on board. I became responsible for the clothing that we were going to wear on television and all the rest of it. But the real joy for me was doing the pairings. I'd always believed that matching personalities—or certain personalities—go better together than others, which Lee Trevino never agreed with me on, to his detriment [in 1985]. He figured you could put two guys together and spank 'em on the butt and say, you know, "Go get 'em." But I think there's an emotional issue to winning, and I think it very important that one player can feed off another. The Europeans for the most part are closer knit as a group, always felt like underdogs. But that was an opportunity each time this thing rolled around to prove that, given a level playing field, their talents were good enough to match anything America had. They kept on rising to the occasion year after year and have done ever since.

RENTON LAIDLAW: Jacklin had this idea that the best thing to do would be to ask Ballesteros to be the "father" figure, and take under his wing Paul Way, a young guy who had won his way into the side. And Jacklin, very persuasive and very forcefully said to Seve, "You can make him play and give him the confidence he needs and I believe it'll be a great partnership."

TONY JACKLIN: Way was a young kid, still young enough to think he was going to be better than Ballesteros. He was a cocky little bugger and wasn't intimidated by being put with Seve.

But the interesting part was Seve. On the second day Angel Gallardo [former player, at that time an official] came up to me and said, "I think you better talk to Seve." So I took Seve to one side, and I could see there was something he wanted to get off his chest. I said, "Seve, do we have a problem?"

He said, "Well, you know, this boy Paul Way, I feel like I have to hold his hand all the time. I'm, you know, telling him which club to hit. I feel like his father." I said, "You *are* his father, Seve. You *are*. In *here*." And I pointed to Seve's head. "That's exactly why you're bloody well paired together." I said, "Is that a problem?"

And Seve looked at me. It was like the penny dropped. He said, "No, for me, it is no problem."

RENTON LAIDLAW: Although Seve and Paul Way lost their first match against Tom Kite and Calvin Peete, they beat Floyd and [Curtis] Strange in the four-balls on the first afternoon, halved with Morgan and Jay Haas on the second day four-balls, and beat Bob Gilder and Tom Watson 2 and 1 in the foursomes on the second day. It was a winning partnership.

So the stage was set for a historic Ryder Cup, the still all-conquering Americans against the revitalized Europeans. In an interesting twist, the captains were Jacklin and Nicklaus, the main players involved in the legendary tied Ryder Cup of 1969.

CURTIS STRANGE [playing in the first of his five Ryder Cups; he would be U.S. captain in 2002]: I was very, very nervous, young and full of piss and vinegar, and looking forward to it very much.

BEN CRENSHAW: We knew, even if the rest of America didn't, that we were going to have to play our absolutely best golf if we were going to keep the Cup.

CURTIS STRANGE: Back in 1983 we knew they were going to become a much better team with the involvement of European players, but we didn't know how good. We never anticipated just how good Seve, Sandy Lyle, Ian Woosnam, Bernhard Langer, and Nick Faldo were going to be, and how long they would lead that team. That nucleus lasted for a long, long time. Sure, there were always a couple of new guys, but that was the nucleus that really made the Ryder Cup what it is today.

COLIN SNAPE: Jack was a very good host at PGA National. We went to his house nearby, and he had a whole corridor filled with just about every trophy that he'd ever won. I remember Seve standing there just in complete awe and thinking, This is what I'm going to do. I've never been in Seve's house, but I wouldn't be at all surprised if he has an even longer showcase.

RENTON LAIDLAW: Tom Watson hadn't been playing all that well and said to Jack Nicklaus, "I don't want to play in all the games because I may not be up to it." And Nicklaus said, "Listen, whether you're 70 percent fit or 100 percent, it doesn't make any difference. The intimidation factor is there, and you will step onto that tee in every flight." And eventually it came down to Tom Watson beating Bernard Gallacher to give the Americans victory by 12–11.

SAM TORRANCE: Woosie and I were on the putting green before playing Crenshaw and Calvin Peete in the first day's four-balls; Woosy was a bit jumpy because it was his first Ryder Cup. Of course, it was my second Ryder Cup, so I'm Mr. Experience. And I said, "Come on, Woos, for chrissake, let's go and kill 'em." So we got on the first tee and I hit it straight right—lost ball. Woosie hit a perfect 1-iron, then wedge to three feet, made birdie. After that I played the best round of golf I've ever played in the Ryder Cup. I made birdies on six of the last twelve holes. But Crenshaw and Peete played really well, too. We ended up all square. It was a great match.

Next morning, against Tom Watson and Bob Gilder, on the ninth hole, Watson was over the green, chipping back. I was standing next to Woosie, and I said, "He's got this," and Watson chipped it in. Woosie looked at me and said, "What did you fuckin' say that for?"

BEN CRENSHAW: That was also the Ryder Cup when we saw one of the greatest, most amazing shots we'd ever seen. Seve Ballesteros had hit it in a fairway bunker on the par-5 eighteenth in his singles match that he halved with Fuzzy Zoeller, and when he got down in there he was in a position where you would take a 5-iron or even a 7-iron just to get it out. But here comes this 3-wood. I remember watching it on television. I don't remember exactly who I was with, but I remember we all went, "*What?*" And then Seve took this big cut at the ball, and up it popped and ended up on the green. And none of us could believe what we'd just seen. Absolutely *amazing*.

TONY JACKLIN: I was at the receiving end. It just went off the back of the green. But there was no doubt that at that time Seve was the greatest player in the world. I mean, he was *incredible*. There was nothing he couldn't do.

RENTON LAIDLAW: Believe me, if you saw where the ball was lying in the bunker and you saw where the ball finished on the green, you would have to say there is no way that that can happen. The man is a magician and always has been a magician.

CURTIS STRANGE: If there was ever a guy that I really felt that I had to be at my best to beat, it was Seve. I was always so impressed with him. His short game, his ability to play when he wasn't playing well—and he was a hell of a match-play player. Over four rounds of stroke play, he wasn't as intimidating—well, intimidating is the wrong word; he was a player to be reckoned with. But in match play, eighteen holes, you better go, because I never could figure out how he was going to make a bogey. He was a hell of a player.

And he was guilty of gamesmanship. I had a run-in with him almost every time I ever played with him in the Ryder Cup. And I played him a lot. Me being me, I stood up to him. He would always question things, like who was away when you knew damn well you were away. He'd always come over and question any little drop and whether you were doing it by the book. There was always an official there, but he'd be right there to question it. Just gamesmanship.

On the first hole of one match in 1987, I wanted to fucking *kill* him. I'm playing with Kite. We'd had our rules meeting the day before. Some of that's on sportsmanship and courtesy and playing within the rules. Well, to make a long story short, we'd discussed having a "through line," which means the line of your putt past the hole. You don't want people walking around on your through line as you could be putting on it if you miss the previous putt long. On the first hole Seve had a chip from just off the green. I had a long putt down the hill and putted it past the hole. [José Maria] Olazábal putted, then wanted to putt out, but I said, "Well, wait a minute, wait a minute, you can't do that. You're right on my through line." Seve came charging up. "That bother you?" he said. "That bother you?" I said, "Yes, that *does* bother me."

And so Seve stomped over to his chip and chipped it right into the back of the hole—then walked off the green pumping his fist at me! And I almost had to applaud him. More power to him. God-damn, I was so mad I wanted to kill him.

BERNARD GALLACHER: I didn't play much. I had the flu all week. Sandy Lyle and I played against Tom Watson and Ben Crenshaw on the first day and got really whupped. And I didn't play the rest of the week.

JOSÉ MARIA CANIZARES: In the last match with Lanny Wadkins, I was 3 up with seven to play, and was playing good golf. On the 18th hole, a par-5 with water on the right of the green, I was 1 up and hit a very good drive, and a very good second shot. Nobody had come out to watch me, but suddenly everybody comes out. "Win the match, and we win the Ryder Cup." Seve asked me, "Why didn't you hit the green?" I said, "I have 105 yards or 110 yards left, and that pin position is in a very, very difficult place, in the left corner." I have an easy pitching wedge. And then Seve said, "You are 1 up, you go to the green, you make par." And then that hurt my confidence, and changed my game. Then I hit a sand wedge a little short, in the big grass. Wadkins hit a very good shot [a wedge shot stiff] and made a birdie, just like that. And that evened the match. That is for me very, very angry. Maybe it was my fault, that we did not win, because maybe I lost my concentration. I was very angry.

BERNARD GALLACHER: Although I'd been a bit ill, I had to play in the singles, and I played against Tom Watson, probably their best player. I was 1 down with two to play. We hit our tee shots on the par-3 17th—which I hadn't played all week—and mine went over the green. Tom Watson pushed his tee shot. I got a bad lie, and I was trying to be too cute, and ended up missing a four-foot putt to take him down on the 18th, and that was the point that made the difference. So I was disappointed at the time when I felt I had him on the run.

Tom Watson stood on the green and waited until Lanny Wadkins had chipped it stone dead against Canizares at the last. So before I had to putt, we knew we had lost.

SAM TORRANCE: But now it was a whole new ball game. It came right down to the wire. Bernard's shot over the green when playing [Tom] Watson was the best shot he'd hit in his life, but it was half a club too much and he lost the hole. Then Canizares lost the last. Right up until those two matches we looked like we were going to win it. Maybe it was just too much for us, but we knew we'd come back much stronger because we realized, "Jesus, we should have beaten them."

TONY JACKLIN: It was terribly disappointing to lose because we were so close! During the afternoon it looked like we were going to win—until Wadkins hit that wedge on 18 and Jack Nicklaus bent down and kissed the divot where he'd hit it from.

CURTIS STRANGE: Back then, when you were a rookie on the team, you were to be seen and not heard. You listened and learned. After my match [Strange lost to Paul Way] I didn't know if I was supposed to go back out there to watch. Everything was close, and I remember thinking, I can't believe I'm going to be on the first American team to lose in the U.S. I was disappointed because I didn't feel like I kept up my end of the bargain. Then I was standing right beside Lanny when he hit that great wedge shot that saved all of us. And Nicklaus kissed the turf—that was fun, and that's why we all like to be a part of the Ryder Cup. You see individuals doing things you never ordinarily see them do. The emotion, the antics. Nicklaus kissing the turf!

José Maria Canizares: I remember Jack Nicklaus kissing the ground. Jack Nicklaus is happy. Everybody is very happy. The American team is very happy. I'm very, very disappointed. It's a very rough time for me.

Tony Jacklin: I'll always remember the British press coming back at the end of that day from bloody Disney World. They'd gone because they didn't have to send copy on Sunday. Such was their interest.

We were all very miserable, but it was Seve who said, "Let's look at the big picture. We've done a fantastic thing." Losing by a point in the U.S. was almost like a win. Clearly we used it as a stepping-stone to victory in '85. We just had to keep at it, use that confidence that we'd got from, you know, going so close. And, of course, in 1985 the home crowd would carry us through.

And the concept of the team room went very well. It was clear that this was the way to go, where you could build up the team spirit and work things out together in private. That was bigger than the first-class thing, or getting the clothing and everything else right. Now I doubt whether anybody remembers how the team room even came about.

Colin Snape: So 1983 was the start of the renaissance. But we'd been really finished. If I can put it in football [soccer] terms, we'd always been four-nothing down at half time. Things weren't completely different after 1983. You could say we'd pulled it back to 4–3, but the feeling was like, "What the hell. What have we got to lose? Let's have a go!"

Curtis Strange: I'm not going to say the Ryder Cup changed that day because we still won and we still celebrated. But it certainly changed in time. I'd always said that just because sometimes we don't know these guys on a first-name basis, didn't mean they couldn't play.

COLIN SNAPE: There was a much greater degree of happiness in the camp. Bell's and other sponsors were happy, and it generated a lot of good publicity. In America it was still, "Jesus, what's this Ryder Cup?" There was still very little television.

CURTIS STRANGE: On Sunday afternoon we probably had from five hundred to one thousand people watching, probably closer to five hundred. It just wasn't a big thing. Nobody wanted the Ryder Cup. But I birdied the first hole I played, and that shows how big it was for the players; I remember what I did on the first hole.

JIM JENNETT [ABC-TV]: Television helped the Ryder Cup become what it was, and Palm Beach Gardens was where things gave an inkling of beginning to change, although I don't think our telecast was tremendously well received here. The Ryder Cup was still thought of as a ho-hum golfing event.

One of the problems television had was that it was played during football season. ABC had a big commitment to college football, so Saturday afternoon was pretty much wiped out. At half time of the football game we'd come on with a meaningless scoreboard update or something. But it wasn't really right to do it that way.

COLIN SNAPE: There was another absolute fiasco. We arrived back at Heathrow Airport on Concorde at ten twenty-five at night, to be met by a chap from British Airways at baggage control. "I'm awfully sorry," he said, "but your baggage has been left in New York. Would you mind filling in these forms?" We'd come up from Florida on Eastern Airlines and the baggage door had jammed. Jesus, instead of telling us at the time, they let us fly home and find out afterward. And there's poor Sandy Lyle, being asked to fill in the name of the nearest train station to his home. But what an anticlimax. It leaked out to the degree that on the front page of the *Daily Telegraph*, right across the bottom front, was the headline: "Concorde Flies Empty with Golfers' Baggage." And a man called Gerald Bartlett, who I've never met to this day, quoted me as saying how disappointed we were with British Airways, la di dah di dah. The week before the Ryder Cup I had lunch with Lord King, an irascible man who had just taken over as chairman of British Airways, and he wasn't in the least bit interested in golf and wondered what the hell the airline was doing involved with the Ryder Cup in the first place. Well, the day after the story appeared he rang me and he really ripped into me. I told him I'd never even spoken to the man, and then I complained to the *Telegraph*. They said, "We do very well for you in golf terms. You wouldn't like to see that harmed."

We still didn't get our bags.

ALL CHANGE

*E*uropean *golfers were making their marks in other ways, too. Having won the Masters in 1983, Ballesteros then added the British Open in 1984. Sandy Lyle then won the British Open in 1985—the same year that Bernhard Langer won the Masters, overtaking Curtis Strange in a wild final round.*

CURTIS STRANGE: If my impression of European golf didn't change in 1983, it certainly was changed in the '85 Ryder Cup. Not only did they win, but they beat us good.

Sam Torrance: I wouldn't say we were confident of winning but certainly confident that we would put up a great performance.

The venue was the Belfry, the new home for the European PGA Tour that Colin Snape had created in the English Midlands. The parkland course had its detractors, who insisted the Ryder Cup should remain on more traditional links or even heathland courses. But it certainly had a couple of features perfectly suited to match play. The par-4 10th hole was drivable, but the tee shot had to carry water in front of the green. It was a terrific gambler's hole. And on the finishing hole, golfers had first to carry water and hold a small, angled stretch of fairway, then carry water again en route to a three-tiered green. It is not a finisher for the fainthearted.

CURTIS STRANGE: I always thought it didn't matter where you played the Ryder Cup. The Belfry was a decent golf course, challenging enough when the weather turns sour. It's actually much better now. But it was okay even in 1985, with a tough finishing hole.

RENTON LAIDLAW: I think the players themselves would always have enjoyed playing on a seaside links and thought they had a better chance at a seaside links against the Americans. This was an inland course and maybe that would have suited the Americans more.

SAM TORRANCE: I loved the Belfry from day one. It was a very demanding course where you couldn't get away with anything. Howard Clark, the best partner I ever had in the Ryder Cup, drove the 10th nearly every day in 1985. They used a forward tee, so it was just a 3-wood, and wasn't that tough. But the atmosphere was just electric. The crowd really went bananas if you brought a wood out on the tee.

PETER JACOBSEN [who played on the U.S. team in 1985 and '95]: It was quite a gamble. It was a narrow little green with a water hazard in front of it. The back nine was really good, too. Seventeen was a reachable five, 18 was a very difficult driving hole, a dogleg left around the water, which turned out to be the downfall of three or four of the American players. I don't think the Belfry being an inland course helped the Americans. Americans can win on links courses, too, and besides, the players are so good now and have been for years that they can adapt very quickly.

COLIN SNAPE: And so we came into 1985. This really was what we dreamt about when we created the Belfry. There was a lot of criticism that it was played there, that it was all about commercial greed, that we were playing on a manufactured course when before that we'd played on the quality venues like Lytham, Walton Heath, Muirfield, and Royal Birkdale.

On the Monday night of the week of the matches, the American team flew in to Birmingham Airport by Concorde—the very first Concorde flight into Birmingham. We had the television on in the reception room at the Belfry. It was showing a live broadcast of race riots in the Handsworth section of Birmingham, nine o'clock at night, and it looked as though Birmingham was ablaze. I'm thinking, Christ, do I deserve this? So we brought the Americans in from the airport by motorcade, then turned all the televisions off. Luckily, there was just one night of riots.

CURTIS STRANGE: The weather was kind of crappy, and it was a tough week. Nothing derogatory to say about Lee Trevino as captain; he was fine. And you have to remember that captains back then didn't do as much as they do now. Dow Finsterwald told me after a dinner in Dallas, "The only thing I told my guys was to do what you normally do. If you're used to drinking a fifth of liquor, drink a fifth of liquor. Don't change because of the Ryder Cup." So captains didn't do as much. They dressed you up and said, "Go get 'em, boys." They paired you together properly, and that was it.

Oh, we had meetings every night, but you didn't have all these meetings with all that inspirational bullshit that you have now. All we had was our hotel room and a room to go eat. No Ping-Pong tables, no physios.

PETER JACOBSEN: Making the Ryder Cup team was a big deal, something everybody dreams of. I had never really been close before. In '83 it had changed, and it was now a real competitive situation which all of us were looking forward to. All those guys on the European team were my friends. Howard Clark and Ian Woosnam and Seve and Sandy Lyle and Faldo. Some of them played the tour, all of them played the majors, so now it was just wonderful, a great, great, great celebration of golf.

TONY JACKLIN: In those days they were still messing around with the format. It was always being tweaked, with eight-men teams and then bloody ten-men teams, and there never was a right format. It was twelve men with four resting in each round and everyone playing in the singles when I stopped being captain, and I said, "never let anybody mess with this format." Europe I think is always weaker, because we just don't have the strength in depth of America. But from a point of view of the matches being interesting, it makes it closer. We have the opportunity to choose our best players for foursomes and four-balls. On the last day everybody plays, but the captains can dodge and weave and try and hide their weaker players. They have got that bit absolutely right. It would be a tragedy to change.

Some of the early cups had 36-hole singles matches. I mean, it was bloody silly. And then when we won in '85 there was a big scream from America, "Oh, we have to change the format." But we stuck to our guns, and it wasn't changed. And it's accepted now.

I also changed the selection process. I wanted three [captain's] choices, or was it four? But you had guys like Peter Dobereiner [British golf writer], who was knowledgeable, saying, "Why not let Tony Jacklin choose the whole team? What's he going to do? Pick his brother-in-law?"

I was committed to winning the Ryder Cup. It was what I wanted more than anything else in the world. It was always going to be close, and so to have that extra player was crucial.

So we were pretty confident. Home side, home crowd, home course preparation. I took the rough down around the greens a bit to help our guys, because it's the home captain's prerogative to have the course set up the way he wants. Didn't have the greens too quick because I didn't want to play into their hands. We're going back nearly twenty years, when not many Europeans were playing full-time in America, and didn't have that kind of experience on fast greens.

CURTIS STRANGE: 1985 was also the first time I'd ever played in front of fans that weren't rooting for you real hard. Know what I'm saying? They were rooting like hell for their own team and didn't give a rat's ass about you. So that was an eye-opener, too. I was fine with it, but it was troubling to some of the players on the team.

PETER JACOBSEN: The galleries were pretty hostile, which surprised me. Every year I'd been over for the British Open, and that year was the year I'd tackled a streaker on the seventy second green just in front of Sandy Lyle when Sandy won. That got a big laugh and a huge ovation. In the first round of that British Open, I was eight under after 14, and made a ninth or tenth on 15, and I ran into an old Scottish gentleman who said to me, "Peter, you have to realize that out here there's no such thing as pars, birdies, or bogeys, only numbers." He patted me on the back and said, "You shot a fine score, laddie." It made me feel great.

Then at the Ryder Cup, they were cheering misses and booing and all that. The whole flavor was like, "This is *us against them.*" It rattled me the first day. When I would miss a putt, people would cheer, and I thought, You know, you're not supposed to do that. But Lanny Wadkins said to me, "Get used to it. These people *want* us to lose."

After the first morning, Jacklin shockingly dropped one of his star players in Nick Faldo.

TONY JACKLIN: Nick was going through a divorce at the time. One of the things I was determined to have all the way through my years of captaincy was a great one-on-one with everybody. I had quiet time with every single player, thinking that if there was ever any problem they had, they needed to come to me about it, and we'd try and address it. Nick had played with Langer that morning I think, and didn't look comfortable [the pair lost 3 and 2 to Calvin Peete and Tim Kite]. I just said to him, "What must I do? Do I play José Maria Canizares with Langer this afternoon or you? I need to know for the team's sake." And he said, "Put him in." That told me everything I wanted to know. I admired Nick for that. It was all very much a team effort.

PETER JACOBSEN: Being a rookie on the team I pretty much expected I'd play once a day. The strength of my game is in alternate shot, as I hit it pretty straight and keep it in play, but I was put out in the afternoon of the first day with Andy North in a best-ball competition [against Seve Ballesteros and Manuel Piñero], and we didn't play well, maybe three or four birdies between us, and we got beat.

ANDY NORTH [ESPN announcer and two-time U.S. Open Champion, who was making his sole Ryder Cup appearance]: Neither Peter nor I had played in the Ryder Cup, so we were kind of surprised we got thrown together. I don't think it makes that big a difference to play with a more experienced player. If you're going to play well; you'll play well, if you don't, you don't. We didn't play terribly, we just didn't play great.

PETER JACOBSEN: Seve and Manuel Piñero were very focused and very intense. They're both very good friends of mine, and I guess I was expecting a little bit more camaraderie. There really wasn't much. It was pretty much a dog-eat-dog match from their standpoint.

ANDY NORTH: The whole tone of the entire '85 Ryder Cup was that the European team made some remarkable shots. Chipping in from off the greens and the kind of stuff you have to do to win. Piñero made one in that first match, I believe, from thirty or forty yards off the green to win the sixteenth hole. [The Spaniards would win on the very next hole, by 2 and 1.] It was a tough loss, but at that time Seve was at his best, and it seemed that no matter what Spaniard he played with, he seemed to get that Spaniard to play the best he could possibly play.

PETER JACOBSEN: I didn't realize how intense they were or how intent the Europeans were on winning until that match. I thought, Wow, these guys are really here to play. I'm not a bulldog competitor like a Lanny Wadkins or a Raymond Floyd. I want to win, but I don't want to lose a friendship over a match. But it was a great match. I've been a huge Seve Ballesteros fan ever since I met him. He just got the better of us.

On the following day I didn't play the four-balls but was out in the afternoon with Curtis Strange in the alternate shot. I'm a big admirer of Curtis's golf game and the way he prepares, and he's an intense competitor. Curtis and I were, you know, as close as anybody on the Tour at the time, so we saw eye to eye. He said to me on the first tee, "Let's not screw around; let's have some fun. And let's not worry about anything but winning the match." We went out and romped pretty good [they beat Paul Way and Ian Woosnam 4 and 2], 4 or 5 under par in alternate shot. But we had no input into that pairing. I don't think any of the players really had any input. I think Lee Trevino was just making the pairings on his own.

TONY JACKLIN: The thing that turned it was Craig Stadler's missing the two-footer in the four-ball just before lunchtime on the second day. [Stadler's missed putt gave Europe a half in his match and a share of the points won thus far.] We took that and ran with it.

CURTIS STRANGE: On the second day I was in the four-balls with Stadler against Langer and Lyle, and that was when Stadler missed a short putt on the eighteenth green and changed the tide of the entire match. I don't remember where I was on the hole. All I remember is that Craig had a two-foot putt, maybe three feet, to win the match. I was standing right there on top of him, helping him read it, although there wasn't anything to read. He just missed it, and we halved. At that moment, you don't say anything. You certainly don't say, "That's all right." He might slap you up side the head, because it's *not* all right. You shake hands and go about your business. Recoup in a hurry, because you have to play more golf in a few minutes. But it gave them such momentum. Half a point can mean a great deal, and it just changed the course of the matches. I don't mean anything against Craig, but that's just the way it worked.

SAM TORRANCE: I was in our team room watching it. There was such a roar when that happened, it was unbelievable. We knew then that this was it.

In the afternoon, Europe won three of four foursomes, Strange and Jacobsen providing the only point for the U.S. That meant Europe would enter the final day's singles with a 9–7 lead.

TONY JACKLIN: I shocked Nicklaus in 1983 when I flipped the whole lineup. Historically, the strongest player has always gone out last. But I thought, What the hell's the good of the strength at the end if we've already lost? In West Palm Beach Joe Black, the PGA of America president, was there when we opened the envelope with the line-ups. He said, "What have you done?" Well, I started with Seve and propped the low end up with Canizares, who ended up losing to Lanny Wadkins.

That strategy of tipping it upside down came out of bouncing stuff off Seve. Not off everybody, but off Seve, because if I went to two players I'd get two opinions and that would complicate it. In 1985, I thought we should put the strength in the middle, Seve said, "I agree with you." I went and sat at a table on my own, and wrote Piñero, Woosnam, boom-boom-boom, boom-boom-boom, then gave it to Seve. "That's what I've come up with." And he said, "That's fine." I started off with Piñero, then Woosnam, Way, then Seve, then Sandy Lyle, who was British Open champion at the time, then Langer, who was Masters champion, Sam Torrance, . . .

You wouldn't believe the power and strength of mind that Seve brought to our team. When I saw a player who maybe I felt needed a little bit of encouragement or whatever, Seve was always there. I remember David Gilford walking in a bit disheartened one night, I think in 1991, and I said to Seve, "Just go and sit next to him. Tell him how well you think he played." In those days just a word from him was enough. He was formidable, just *formidable*.

SAM TORRANCE: At the team meeting the night before the singles, Manuel Piñero straight out directly said, "I want Wadkins. I want Wadkins." And we kind of knew Wadkins would be out first. Manuel was a tenacious player, a great match player, so we put him out first. And then the draw comes out half an hour later, and there he is—he's got Wadkins. It was fantastic.

PETER JACOBSEN: We didn't have an intense preparation, I think because in Lee Trevino's years of being on the Ryder Cup team they were so dominant. Lee had just gotten married, and I think his mind was more on his marriage and having a good time. Lee said, "You guys can play. You guys know how to handle this. Go get 'em." But it was kind of a new era and boom!—we were hit with a very competitive team.

Piñero was a marvelous little match player, tenacious little chap. He went out first in the singles because that's the way he was.

CURTIS STRANGE: I think everybody was surprised we were down [two points] going into the singles, because we weren't ever down too many times going into Sundays. I don't think anybody was pushing the panic button, but it was damn close.

PETER JACOBSEN: I played Sandy Lyle in the singles. I thought he was just a masterful player, and a wonderful guy. His length off the tee was Tiger-like, Nicklaus-like: he hit the ball a long way back then. He hit his 1-iron 250 yards off the tee.

He was 2 up on 16, hit it in a very tough spot on the green. I thought I was going to get one back as I had maybe a ten- or twelve-footer for birdie, but he holed a putt from off the fringe to win.

JOSÉ MARIA CANIZARES: I think my match [against Zoeller] is very important point in the Ryder Cup. On 17 we are all square. It is a par-5. I hit a very good second shot and Fuzzy is in the bunker and then I chip it very, very close and Fuzzy's very bad. After this I say, I make 4 on 18 and I win the match because 18 is very, very difficult hole.

CURTIS STRANGE: I was playing last, against Ken Brown. I played last twice at the Belfry, in fact. I don't remember it being that big a deal in '85, but in '89 my teammates stood up at the team meeting and said, "Curtis is going last." And Raymond said, "Okay." That's a huge compliment.

But the '85 match was over before I finished. God, it's a terrible thing, isn't it? I was on the fifteenth green. You can just about see the eighteenth green from there, but I could hear the roaring and the singing.

I'd been 5 up against Ken Brown with five holes to go, and he proceeded to win the next two holes with birdies. And the matches were over! I said, "What the *fuck* are you *doing*? I *am* going to beat you. You *do* know that. So why don't you give this hole to me and let's get on with our lives!" Oh, it was funny.

SAM TORRANCE [on the winning point]: I was kind of lucky because Andy North wasn't playing that well. I played the first ten holes about as badly as I could play against anyone. I was 3 down. But he bogeyed 11 and 15, so when I got to 17, the par-5, I was 1 down, two to play.

I hit a good drive, but Andy drove it through the fairway into the thick stuff. He just chipped out, or maybe he didn't even get out. I hit a bad second shot into the hay on the left, about seventy yards short of the green. Real dodgy lie.

Then Andy hit a 1-iron that just looped all over the place, ran past the hole and just went off the back edge. I hit a fabulous shot under pressure, to six feet. He just missed his putt, so I had to hole this putt, to win the hole. Six-footer, left edge. Silence. I was as nervous as I've ever been because I knew exactly the situation, and everything was moving but the putter. The putt went straight in, and I thought, Okay, let's go. Now we can do it.

Jacklin was right beside me, and had told me on the seventeenth that we needed one more point. "You can do it," he told me. Coming off the green I actually handed the driver to Jacklin and said, "Go on, you do it." He laughed and said, "Don't be daft, son, you can do this." And I hit the drive of my life, enormous—and remember, this was with wooden clubs.

North's drive went straight up in the air, and I knew it was in the water. He couldn't get on the green, and I had no more than an 8-iron. That's when I knew. "I've got this." I was actually crying coming over the bridge over the water. All the American wives were sitting there and there were tears streaming down my face. I just couldn't control it. And the roars along the fairway from the bridge to the green gave me goose bumps like I've never felt before.

I had a 9-iron, not an 8-, and my only thought was, Don't hit it fat. I could hit it thin and it would get there, no problem. I hit a great shot to twenty-five, thirty feet. Andy missed his putt for a five, which meant I had three putts to win. The greens weren't as slick in those days. The putt had probably a six- to eight-inch break, and I had to hit it maybe a foot right, dead weight, which means it's going to swing more. Three feet short of the hole I knew it was in, or not going more than a little past. Then it fell in, and I've never felt as strong, as good, on a golf course in all my life. I gave the ball to some kid. The memory's better than the ball.

ANDY NORTH: That was a horrible day. You looked up at the scoreboard and we had a whole bunch of guys who couldn't get a grasp on any matches where we could get some momentum. My match was a pretty good example. I got off to a really good start and got way up on Sam Torrance. Then he made some birdies on the back nine and before you knew it we came to the last hole even. I knew we were in big trouble at that point. I knew I needed to win the hole, and I popped the drive up just enough that it didn't carry over the water. From that point, it was over. Sam played a good shot and put it up on the green, and you know that was the point that decided the Cup.

It was a great moment for Sam, and, yes, it was a disappointing week. Our captain Lee Trevino didn't say much to me. Didn't say very much at all.

RENTON LAIDLAW: Howard Clark could have won 2 and 1 against Mark O'Meara on 17 to take the Cup before Sam Torrance, but he missed it. But maybe it was all meant to be because it's far better for the game to be won on the last green with all the people all around. Sam rolled it right in, and then stood there with tears rolling down his face. I was commentating for BBC Radio at that time, and was right behind the eigthteenth green. It was a magical moment.

SAM TORRANCE: I was interviewed by Clive Clark from the BBC when there still were tears streaming down my face. I said to him, "You got me at a right moment here, but I don't give a shit." And they edited it out. Everyone thought I said, "I don't give a fuck." But I didn't say that. It was just "shit." I was still a wee bit out of control.

RENTON LAIDLAW: My colleague working with me was a long-time BBC man, John Fenton, and after I chatted away about the moment I felt that it was time for him to come in and say something. And I said, "John, what a moment. In '57 we won at Lindrick and we haven't won since, but we've won the Cup back now. And Sam Torrance has done it with that putt against Andy North." And there was silence. John couldn't speak. He was absolutely taken away.

Then moments later, Concorde came over very low in salute of the European team. And I must say that I choked up a bit as well. So it didn't really matter, because as the plane was going over you wouldn't have heard us anyway!

COLIN SNAPE: To this day remembering that moment brings a lump to my throat. The chief test pilot for Concorde telephoned me on the morning of the final day and said, "I have to come up to Birmingham today to pick the American team up. I could do a low flypast, but what time would you like me?" So I sort of swallowed hard and said, "Let's make it five o'clock." Well, play actually finished about four-twenty, but I was a stickler that for certain occasions the players had to wear certain shirts and jackets and ties. And they all went, "Christ, he's here again," but they went and changed. Then we all lined up and went to the ceremonies. And right on the button at five o'clock Concorde came flying by at a thousand feet, right across the sky. People must have thought, Jesus Christ, how did they arrange to have Concorde fly across? The number of people who stood there literally with tears flowing down their cheeks. It really was a very emotional moment. It was the culmination to a dream.

SAM TORRANCE: Afterward there was the victory dinner, which is a tough one to celebrate at, because the losing team's there as well, and you don't want to gloat. We were all very well behaved, and then right after the dinner, when they'd all gone, we all went in this room and it went on till you dropped. The next morning I had six bottles of champagne for breakfast with [former Ryder Cupper]

John O'Leary. That week I was to go to Spain for the Spanish Open. We had to take a driver. On the way I stopped off at the home of a dear friend of mine, and obviously we celebrated heartily there till God knows what time. Up on the Tuesday and on to London airport [*sic*], then out to Spain. Same thing there. Party all night. At about three o'clock on Wednesday morning I was sitting with a glass of wine or vodka, or gin, whatever it was, and I looked at it, and I said, "Okay, that's it. I can't get any more in." And that was the end of the celebrations. How did I do in the Spanish Open? Didn't care.

TONY JACKLIN: I was around the green everywhere that a match was won. That was the oddest thing because you had to be there to congratulate or commiserate if it was required. But I was certainly there when Sam won, and I can see it now, I can see him stroking the putt, I can see the arms going up, and I can see him crying. He was so emotional. But he was riding an incredible wave of emotion and destiny.

Afterward everybody got me to go to the bloody swimming pool and they slung me in with the best suit that I've ever had at a Ryder Cup. And I walked along the corridor pissing wet through, thinking, What the hell, I must be nuts. And I didn't come out, I just stayed in the room with Vivien and had a whisky. It just was very, very comfortable. The guys went to the team room and partied together. But I just felt, you know, I needed to be quiet with my wife and contemplate where we'd come from. I just needed to reflect.

CURTIS STRANGE: We were disappointed afterward, but it had to happen. You were seeing them win more and more, and not just in the Ryder Cup. We knew we had our work cut out.

COLIN SNAPE: Trevino didn't take it all that well. He was most ungracious at the dinner. He was a very poor loser. That's a pity, because I like Lee. I suppose it came as such a tremendous shock—and he had the unhappy task of leaving the Cup back in Europe.

PETER JACOBSEN: I loved the Ryder Cup. I absolutely relished every moment of it. I went in looking at it the proper way, that it's a celebration of the way you've played in the world of golf. It's a recognition by everybody in the world that you're on a team of twelve representing your country and you should be proud of that.

SAM TORRANCE: Now it's great seeing the players who were on that team. You don't have to say anything. You just look at each other. The respect, the joy—it's there.

ANDY NORTH: I'd looked forward to making the team so much, and had come close to making it a couple of other times. Obviously, it's such a great thrill to represent your country. You can tell people you aren't nervous, but when they play the National Anthem you turn chilly.

But it's tough to concentrate and play at your best. And then not performing like you wanted was really disappointing. It was something that I lived with for a long time. I had to sit and watch the next couple of Ryder Cups by myself. No one would want to be near me.

And it still is very disappointing, because there's not a lot of guys who have played that went 0-for-3. But it's a great event and for the European team to win that year probably was very important. It really changed the way people looked at the Ryder Cup.

*T*he 1987 Ryder Cup was at Muirfield Village, a course designed by Jack Nicklaus just outside his hometown of Columbus, Ohio, and the annual home to the PGA Tour's Memorial Tournament, which Nicklaus hosts. So who else to captain the U.S. team in their effort to retrieve what had been theirs for almost thirty years but Jack Nicklaus?

With the European team emboldened with the addition of a young Spaniard named José Maria Olazábal and the United States rallied by the war cries of a brash young player named Mark Calcavecchia—in its Ryder Cup preview issue Golf Magazine portrayed him as General Patton—the game was on.

SAM TORRANCE: 1985 was the best performance of any of our team matches, but 1987 was the one that made the Ryder Cup. We had a team that was just magnificent.

CURTIS STRANGE: At Muirfield Village the fans finally showed up to watch the Ryder Cup in the U.S., and we sold out every day. And it couldn't have gone to a better venue. Columbus is a great sports town, and it's Jack's town and Jack was the captain, so they showed up, thousands and thousands of people out there every day. We had a match!

BEN CRENSHAW: Going in I remember we thought that we would

have an advantage because of Muirfield Village's greens. They were some of the fastest we'd played, and we thought the Europeans would have trouble with them. But they putted them beautifully, both in terms of pace and line.

RENTON LAIDLAW: I remember asking Jack Nicklaus, "Will you set up Muirfield Village to suit the American team?" He looked shocked and said, "What do you mean, set up the course to suit the Americans?" Jack denied that he would do anything, but I think he made the greens a little faster to try to help the Americans—he might deny that—but at the end of the day the Americans found them more difficult to cope with than the Europeans did.

CURTIS STRANGE: Muirfield Village is a fantastic match-play course, and to play it in the fall, when it's hard and fast, is the best. And they beat us good. Again.

TONY JACKLIN: When we got off the plane, Jack and Barbara [Nicklaus] were at the airport to meet us. A press guy came up to me and said, "Who do you think's going to win?" I said, "Oh, we'll win." Just like that. And the guy said, "How can you say that?" And I said, "Because. Just because."

When I got to the evening meal at our hotel, Nick Faldo came up to me and said, "Because? *Because?*" He'd seen the interview on the news. And that was all there was to it. "Because." We'd won in '85, obviously got close in '83, but I still thought there was a lot to prove. We hadn't won in America, and if we were ever going to do it, Christ, we were primed with those last two matches. It sounds crazy but two years just evaporated, and when we got back together, the same nucleus of players was there—and that was the beauty of it all as well.

SAM TORRANCE: I got engaged on the Concorde flight over [to British dancer/actress Suzanne Danielle]. I was in love and just asked her to marry me. She said yes. I hadn't planned it. For a ring we used the rubber band off the rose that comes with your lunch. And then on Thursday night Tony came up to me and said, "Rest yourself. You're playing first tomorrow."

•

PETER ALLISS: They brought back Jack Nicklaus as a Ryder Cup captain and they played on Jack's course. He was going to be the knight on the white charger who was going to bring back the Cup. On the first day, when I got there for ABC-TV, they were down in all the matches. And they had been joking that this would be over by tomorrow afternoon. You know, we'll put on an old Betty Grable movie.

It was true. While the teams shared the morning foursomes with two wins apiece, Europe won all of the afternoon four-balls to take a 6–2 first-day lead.

RENTON LAIDLAW: Tony Jacklin had the happy knack of choosing good partnerships. Nick Faldo and Ian Woosnam was a very good partnership, as was Ballesteros and Olazábal. Gerald Micklem, a great English official, once said to me, "One of the worst things you can ever do in any team match is play two Scots together. They're liable to fall out." But playing two Spaniards together is obvious.

BEN CRENSHAW, who played the morning foursomes with Payne Stewart against Ballesteros and Olazábal: This was a marvelous pairing, and you could see Seve teaching José as they went around the course, telling him what to do and when. And the great thing was the way José not only understood but responded as well.

TONY JACKLIN [on Faldo and Woosnam pairing]: That was when Faldo was the number-one player in the world, the British Open champion, and Woosy was aspiring to get there. That pairing worked very well for them. After one of the rounds [day two afternoon four-balls, in which they birdied the first five holes, were 10 under par for fourteen holes and eventually won 5 and 4], I said, "I never thought I'd live to see golf played like that." The course was perfect and their golf was matching it. It was incredible.

LARRY NELSON: That was a terrible week. Just a terrible week. I don't know how to explain it. It was, well, confusing. I just felt like that our teams were paired by a flip of the coin, really. It was just really bizarre. We played our practice rounds with guys that we had played matches with before, and were kind of given indications that these were the guys that we were going to be paired with. Then, come the first day, everyone was just split up—which was different than the other Ryder Cups I'd played in.

I thought I would be paired with Lanny Wadkins. Both of us wanted to play together, and we'd had so much success in previous Ryder Cups. [Interestingly, Nelson won his place on the Ryder Cup team by beating Wadkins in a playoff for that year's PGA Championship.] Generally, you are paired with people who are similar to you, or whose games are similar. But we were paired with people who were just the opposite. I never could understand that. The Europeans did it much differently than we did. They pretty much stuck with their pairings. But Payne and I both played so poorly [against Ballesteros and Olazábal] that it wouldn't have mattered if we played against Mickey and Minnie. Finally I was paired with Lanny on the second day. I think we'd fallen so far behind that there was some sanity put back into the pairings. [They lost twice, to Sandy Lyle and Bernhard Langer each time.]

CURTIS STRANGE: It surprised me a little that Jack paired Tom Kite and me together every match. I thought Tom and I were an excellent foursomes pair, but not four-ball. Tom and I played the same type of game, but we didn't make enough birdies for four balls. [They won both their foursomes and lost both their four balls.] But I didn't question it at the time, because I wanted to play. I probably said something to Kite. But we were both playing well so Nicklaus sent us right back out.

But I don't think Nicklaus said much of anything, just like he didn't on Sunday afternoon when we got beat. He said a lot of somewhat derogative things to the press but not to us. And he wasn't used to losing.

TONY JACKLIN: There was so much emotion going in, and you could see our players were ready for it. We'd paved the way, and it was time. One of the things that I remember vividly about '87 was that, by and large, the crowds were the same crowds as went to the Memorial. And they were wonderful—but to the point that they really weren't partisan enough. And I remember Jack going around the clubhouse, in the evening after the first day, saying, "We got to get these galleries a bit more enthusiastic for us."

PETER ALLISS: Jack was annoyed because he didn't see any atmosphere, and he sent his wife, Barbara, out to buy little Stars-and-Stripes flags, to get them all going.

TONY JACKLIN: The wives of the players distributed them. But the American fans were still very subdued and polite, a golfing crowd who appreciated good golf, and they appreciated what we were doing as much as what the Americans were doing.

JIM JENNETT [ABC-TV]: The victory by the Europeans at the Belfry in '85 had a big effect on our coverage in '87. I remember how exciting it was. We were planning to record the action in bits and pieces so we could have some highlights to play at half time on the football game. [They also lobbied for a fourth day's play, but Tony Jacklin vetoed it.] But as it went on, and the BBC was there taking our feed since we were going to have to be there anyway, we really realized how much great sport the American audience was missing [ABC aired Saturday coverage from 12:30 P.M. to 3:30 P.M. and Sunday coverage from 12:30 P.M. to 3:00 P.M.]. And we all sort of vowed that we would never let that happen again, that we would somehow find a way to present the drama of the Ryder Cup.

When the foursomes and four-balls were done, Europe was carrying a 5-point lead into the final day, 10½–5½. All they needed was 3½ points to tie and retain the Cup, or 4 for the outright win. With 12 points up for grabs, and a team playing on form from top to bottom, it should have been routine.

TONY JACKLIN: We were where we wanted to be, but the job hadn't been completed. We knew how strong the U.S. had always been over last day. We were just going to go out there and do the best we could.

BEN CRENSHAW: I three-putted the sixth hole [against Eamonn Darcy] and as I was walking off the green I saw this little nut on the ground; they call them buckeyes. Out of frustration I tapped at this nut as I went by, and the shaft of my putter broke! Oh, no! I'm playing on the final day of the Ryder Cup, and I just broke my putter. So I putted for a few holes with a wedge, then changed to a 1-iron. Much later I saw Eamonn, and he said he thought I'd been putting with a 1-iron to slow the ball down on the fast greens.

On the eighth hole, Jack [Nicklaus] came up to me and said, "How are we doing?" And I said, sort of under my breath, "I just broke my putter." Jack looked at me and didn't say anything at first, then said, "You did *what?*" And I muttered, "I just broke my putter." And he said, "I'm not surprised, the way things are going!"

In truth, for a while things went quite well for the United States. Andy Bean, Mark Calcavecchia, Payne Stewart, and Scott Simpson all prevailed within the first six matches, while Larry Mize halved. It was becoming a long afternoon for Europe, until Larry Nelson and Bernhard Langer came into the final hole tied, with Europe needing half a point.

LARRY NELSON: Bernhard and I had played seventeen really good holes—back and forth, back and forth. On the last green we had the same length of putt, a couple of feet, and we just kind of looked at each other and said, "Good, good?" It was not like they were four-footers. Jack Nicklaus said something to me later about how I should have made Bernhard putt it, but I replied, "Jack, I remember you giving Jacklin a putt on the last hole in 1969. I thought we were out here to have a good time." I don't think there was any comment. [Nicklaus later told the media, "We've had that happen before."]

SAM TORRANCE: I played Larry Mize and that's where it all started for the U.S. I was 1 down playing the last, but he drove in the hazard to the left of the fairway.

BEN CRENSHAW: A few of our players did that. It's a very tough driving hole. It's a tough green to hit so you want to get down there and give yourself a chance, and you don't want to push the ball right because there are bunkers and a tree. When we play the

Memorial at Muirfield Village in spring, it usually is wet. But in September the course was slicker and faster and it was possible to roll through the fairway and into trouble.

SAM TORRANCE: About fifteen, twenty minutes passed before I could hit my second shot because Mize was getting a ruling. It was a strange ruling. He got line of sight in a hazard because there was a sign in front of him, but he had to drop it in the hazard. I was thinking, Jesus, now he's going to get on the green or something. But he didn't. He hit his third shot into a bunker. His fourth went up to the back of the green, miles away from the hole—and then he holed it for five! And I'd hit twelve feet short of the hole and told myself, "I *have* to two-putt this thing." But on those greens, anything can happen, and, honestly, my hands were really shaking. When I connected with the ball, I had no idea whether it was going to end up ten feet past or ten feet short! But it just ran up like that, stone dead. I've never been as relieved in all my life.

The pressure of that situation was where my later putting problems started. Fortunately I found a way out of it by using a long putter, but that match did some harm.

TONY JACKLIN: A lot of the Americans actually fell by the wayside when the real heat was on. That was interesting because through the years we'd always seen the Americans coming through and always holing those putts when they had to hole them. We sort of humanized them that week. All of us suddenly under real pressure, they realized they're human like everybody else. They make mistakes.

RENTON LAIDLAW: It came down to crucial putts on the final day, and the one I'll always remember is Eamonn Darcy's downhill, left-to-right, five-footer, not the kind of putt that any player wants on a fast Muirfield Village green.

SAM TORRANCE: Eamonn was magnificent. I was right there beside the green. What people don't understand is that if that putt didn't go in, it was going to go ten, fifteen feet past the hole. There's no way you can stop it.

When the closing ceremony was held on the last green, Eamonn still had his putter in his hand. "Give me that bloody thing," I said. I threw the ball down where his putt had been and belted one straight into the hole. "What was tough about that?" I said. It was a great moment.

CURTIS STRANGE: My singles match decided it. I knew I was playing Seve when the draw came out Saturday night. That was fine, because I was playing really well [Strange would win the U.S. Open in each of the next two years]. But he chipped in on me on the 1st hole for the second time in that Cup! And you know what he did this time? We were right beside each other, both in a greenside bunker, and he questioned who was away. He started his stuff on the first hole! He knew damn well that he was away, and he knew also that he wanted to go first, but he was just screwing around. And then he made it. So I was 1 down after one.

I didn't play well, and Seve played okay. I got way down, 3 down I think, and came back—and if I'd have made any putts at all, I could have really gotten back into the match. I was 2 down on 17, and we were getting beaten pretty well, so at this point it was a matter of time. I think I lost 2 and 1, and it just so happened that this was the match that decided the points.

Tony Jacklin: Afterward there was a bit of dancing on the 18th green, and Olazábal did a little jig.

PETER ALLISS: Olazábal was the strong man on the team; I don't think he ever got enough credit for it. Seve was Seve, dashing around, upsetting everybody, querying things, just being a bit of a pain really.

BEN CRENSHAW: I can't blame them for dancing. They were the first team to win on U.S. soil and had played really well. I don't think anyone could complain. They'd earned it. We were very dejected, though. We'd been outputted, but we also lost so many matches near the end. Jack kept saying to us, "You have to finish your matches," but we just didn't do it.

CURTIS STRANGE: The dancing was okay. I never took offense to any of that type of stuff after play. They were celebrating. They had all the right in the world to be excited. All you can do is shake their hands and applaud them, because they came over to America and beat us. It was a hell of a win.

LARRY NELSON: There was just no camaraderie, no energy, synergy, whatever, in our team. But that's a very important part of the European team. Losing is bad enough, but losing and then having to watch a celebration is even worse.

TONY JACKLIN: That night I got all the players to go to the hotel where a thousand European supporters were staying. But it was hellish hard to get them to do it. They were all having dinner, and I said, "Guys, this is the last thing I'm going to ask you to do." And when we walked in the bloody roof nearly lifted off of the place. I'd pleaded with the players, "Stay just for five minutes," and after five minutes I said to Seve, "You can go now." He said, "No, I'm very happy here." He didn't want to leave!

I wanted to step down after 1987, always very cognizant of one bridge too far and all that. I'd lost by a point, then went win-win. But Sam and Seve and a bunch of others said, "No, you can't step down." But it's a bit like a drug. It was getting progressively harder, not the pairings and the doing of the pairings and getting all that right—I reveled in that, and still I loved all that golf. But I was trying to keep everybody sweet all the time, and it was becoming progressively more difficult to do that. Players with kids wanting babysitters looking after them in an extra room next to our room and this and that. And I thought, Shit, I don't bring my kids to Ryder Cups. I'd think to myself, Tell him to leave the kids at home! But it's difficult to do that, so you say, I'll do what I can. And Langer saying, "My trousers don't fit." Little niggly things like that started to piss me off a bit. Just little stuff. I felt it was becoming increasingly more difficult to do it the way I wanted it to be done. Anyway, I ended up saying, "Well, okay. I'll do it." Then of course in 1989 we tied, which is perfect. I was involved in the two ties, one as a player in 1969 and one as captain twenty years later!

As Jacklin noted, 1989 was tied, which meant that Europe held on to the Cup. But at least the United States, led by Raymond Floyd, was back on its feet after two resounding losses. More significant, the swing in momentum to Europe had grabbed the attention of the entire sporting world. Dozens of American media representatives flocked across the pond to an event that only half a dozen years earlier—and fifty-something years before that—was all but ignored. The final day's worldwide televison audience was none too conservatively estimated at 200 million. Knocking the United States off its pedestal had turned the Ryder Cup into a spectacle of epic proportions.

MIKE HICKS, who caddied for the late Payne Stewart [who played in four Ryder Cups]: Payne didn't really prepare me for the Ryder Cup other than that to tell me it was just *intense.* Without question it is different from any other event. There's more pressure for caddies, too, especially in the singles matches, because you have to make sure you're right with every answer that you give the guy. When you're doing the four-balls and the foursomes, you're basically just doing your yardages. Players may ask for your opinion on a club or whatnot, but usually the players are doing that for themselves. But the singles matches—that's just you and your player; you know, it's up to you.

I would just go out and just check and make sure that, you know, things were right in the [yardage] book. And then you have to get some things that aren't in the book, such as certain run-outs if the wind changes. A run-out is through the fairway on a certain line, you know, whether it's at a bunker or at a hazard or at a grove of trees.

I don't think anything compares to the pressure that you feel in a Ryder Cup. I'm fortunate enough to have been with Payne when he won three majors [1985 PGA Championship, 1991 U.S. Open, and '99 U.S. Open], and even those don't compare. The pressure comes from what's at stake. I also worked one Presidents Cup [PGA

Tour event that pits a U.S. team against a team from the "rest of the world," excluding Europe], and there's just no comparison. After the Presidents Cup was over, everybody just left, everybody just went their own way. There was no celebration, no champagne. It's just not the same thing.

TONY JACKLIN: 1989 was the first one that my second wife, Astrid, came to with me, as my first wife, Vivien, had died in '88 [his first wife suffered a brain hemorrhage]. I felt it was important for our future for her to understand the kind of emotion that went into all these things, and it was an opportunity to show her a bit more of what my world was like. Astrid got thrown into the bloody deep end, but she did an incredible job.

RENTON LAIDLAW: By this time Jacklin had decided that his team was getting that little bit older, and weren't going to be quite as good. He felt that he should give someone else a chance to captain the side. I think it was he who really selected [Bernard] Gallacher, with Seve supporting Gallacher very, very strongly.

TONY JACKLIN: I did say to [European Tour deputy executive director] George O'Grady when we were at the Belfry in '89, "George, how long am I supposed to do this?" And he said, "As long as you like." I said, "*Shit!*"

Then he said, "Who's going to take over?" And I pointed to Bernard. He'd sat in the car next to me in '85, '87, and '89, knowing what I was doing and what was going on and how I operated and all the rest of it. It would be self-indulgent for me to carry on beyond '89. We'd had a loss, we'd had two wins, and we'd taken the thing to a different level altogether. It was time for me to get on with the rest of my life.

The 1989 matches also saw the introduction of an American player who quickly became part of Ryder Cup lore—not because of any particular shot or result, but because of his intense competitiveness and his willingness to stand up to the sometimes questionable behavior of Seve Ballesteros. He was a tall, reedy Floridian (albeit born in Massachusetts) named Paul Azinger.

Tony Jacklin: Paul Azinger was a tough player—he's a match player for you, tough as nails. He was a hard case, and he and Seve went at it.

Curtis Strange: He and Seve got a little bit of press for having some confrontations on the golf course. By the 1987 matches I'd come to realize that that's what you have to deal with when you play Seve. And so I just didn't mess with it. And that's mainly what I told Paul Azinger when he played him in 1989: "Just don't mess with him." But Paul is even more outspoken than I am. He wasn't any more inspirational or enthusiastic about the Ryder Cup than many players. He was just more vocal.

Jack Whitaker [ABC-TV]: I was at the Belfry in 1989 as an observer, and I was quite amazed by the galleries' behavior. To me, that was the beginning of this terribly fractious cheering from the galleries. It would come to fruition at Kiawah Island [South Carolina] in 1991, but this behavior has a longer history than people think. The galleries at the Belfry were just dreadful. The stuff they were yelling at the Americans was the worst I've ever heard.

Reason, perhaps, for the United States to lose all of the afternoon four-balls on the first day and hand Europe a 5–3 lead. But a 4–4 share of the second day's matches left them only two points behind going into the singles.

Tony Jacklin: All my main men lost in '89. Shit, Seve got beat, Woosy got beat, Faldo got beat. I mean it was a miracle we finished up tied.

That was because two unlikely people came through for Europe: Christy O'Connor [the nephew of the father who'd played in ten Ryder Cups], who was playing Fred Couples, and the old man on the team, José María Cañizares, who was playing Ken Green. And it's just as well for Europe that they did, because the four matches on the golf course behind them all were won by the United States.

Tony Jacklin: I was on the seventeenth hole with Christy and Fred Couples. Couples had about a three- or four-footer to win the hole. I was looking at his hands and he had this reverse overlap grip going, and suddenly his hands made an involuntary movement, and he missed the putt from very, very close range. I just knew that he was overcome, because the Ryder Cup is an incredible pressure cooker, and you have nowhere to hide. I called Christy over and told him, "If you can just get something going on this last hole—*somehow*—something will happen."

Couples hit from the eighteenth tee, and came over the top on his tee shot and he pulled the bloody thing twenty-five yards left of where he wanted it to go. But, of course, he's so long, it flew over the water, and his ball sat there in the middle of the fairway looking like a perfect drive. But I knew he'd pulled it.

Couples had an 8-iron left. Christy hit his drive safely, but he had a 2-iron left! As we walked to the ball, I said, "One more good swing for us, Christy. If you put this ball on the green, I just know something's going to happen." And, of course, he made that wonderful swing, that wonderful shot. I think he hit it to about four feet. And Fred disintegrated. He missed the green completely with the 8-iron, and that was that.

José Maria Canizares: Ken Green at that time was the best putter on the American tour, so everybody thought I would lose that match. But I played very good golf, five or six under par. On the eighteenth, the pin was in the middle of the green, and that green has three tiers. My ball was on the top tier, sixty feet away, so my putt was very difficult. Ken Green hit his second shot short, on the very front of the green. I hit the first putt close. Then Ken Green putted, to maybe six feet. Ken missed his putt. My putt looked nice, left to right, and—boom!—I hit it in the hole.

My half point kept the Cup for Europe. Everyone was very happy, and I was very happy. I was forty-four years old, and everyone looked at me very, very nicely. Seve very happy. Tony said, *"Muy bien, muy bien."*

Curtis Strange: I was 2 down against Ian Woosnam in the last match on the course and birdied the last four holes to beat him 2 up. I birdied 15, par-5, just wedged it on and made about a fifteen-footer. On 16, 7-iron to about three feet. All square. And then on 17, I hit a wedge to about a foot. That took me to 1 up. What made me so happy was that we needed this match, because at that point the best we could have done was half the entire match. And then on 18, I hit a 2-iron to about three feet, and he gave me the putt. I don't know that Ian has ever won a singles match [he hasn't], as good a player as he is. But I was happy that I came through for the team, especially then, as they kind of talked me into going last.

And here's a little bit of trivia that nobody knows, or nobody really cares about. I think I'm the only person ever to play every hole in a Ryder Cup. I went to the eighteenth hole five times that year.

Strange is correct when referring to modern-day players. In the days when the Cup consisted of two rounds, singles and foursomes, Ernest Whitcombe played every hole in 1929, Syd Easterbrook did likewise in 1933, Denny Shute and Gene Sarazen in 1937, John Jacobs in 1955, and both Dow Finsterwald and Dai Rees in 1959.

*T*hings began to get out of hand in 1991. With Europe now hav- ing held on to the Ryder Cup for the last six years, the U.S pas- sion to win it back was growing frantic. This was good because it increased the popularity of the contest, but it also incited the more vocal fans of the sport to new levels of partisan behavior. In January of that year, the United States drove Iraq out of Kuwait in the Gulf War, and by the time the Ryder Cup came to Kiawah Island, just south of Charleston, the media (and the PGA of America) seized on the military mood of the country and dubbed the 1991 Ryder Cup "The War by the Shore."

Both teams were stocked with experience, Ballesteros, Langer, and Faldo, of course, for Europe—along with a rookie named Colin Montgomerie—and Ray Floyd, Lanny Wadkins, and a revitalized Hale Irwin for the United States.

HALE IRWIN: I immediately saw a difference in the attitude of the European team. Almost a swagger. There was the presence of Colin Montgomerie. Whether he was good or bad for the European team I don't know, but I think Monty brought a dynamic to the team that they hadn't had.

When I was on the four previous U.S. teams, our approach had been, "Hey, we're going to win. Who wants to clinch the winning point?" Now it was, "Hey, these guys are good and we have to play well to win." It was a step backward in terms of approach and attitude. But I still had my old attitude of "Let's go out there and let's win this thing now," with the realization that we still had a very formidable team in front of us and they indeed were holding the Cup.

In the mid-1980s I had started thinking a bit about expanding my career into golf course design, and finally pulled that trigger in 1985. I won the Memorial that year, but that was my last sort of swing at any kind of good play. And it just shows what happens when you take just a little bit of the edge off. I really struggled for two or three years. I wasn't thinking about making the Ryder Cup team. I was thinking about survival. But now I felt terrific. I was just so anxious to get back, particularly because, in the interim, the European team had asserted its dominance. And I wanted to be part of the team that tried to break that spell.

This also was the first time in this country that the Ryder Cup had really been recognized as something. It now was on a new course; it was being hyped; it was on television. There was a great deal of, let's say, good old southern-boy hospitality. There was a lot of that rolling out of the marshlands of South Carolina, which was good in the sense that it upped the tempo of things.

Americans tend to make assumptions that they're the best, and then when you lose it you say, "What happened?" And I think that's what happened in the '80s. The other side had some great players, and now suddenly the Cup was not around and people were starting to take notice. And now they're thinking, Maybe there is something here. And that sort of came together in '91, the recognition of "It's not here, so let's get it back. Let's go! Rah-rah! U-S-A!" That kind of stuff.

Leading the U.S. troops into battle would be Dave Stockton, himself a two-time Ryder Cupper.

DAVE STOCKTON: I gave up all my corporate outings, which

came to about sixty a year, because I wanted to promote the Ryder Cup in the U.S. I wanted to explain to people why we get fired up about it and give them some understanding of it. When we'd go over to Britain, everybody was so knowledgeable about the Ryder Cup. But when the Cup was played here, it was just one of a whole bunch of other tournaments. So I had a mission.

In the Ryder Cup you're not playing for yourself, you're playing for your country. How else could a player like Peter Oosterhuis, who won one or two tournaments on our tour, and could be playing badly, all of a sudden just dominate in the Ryder Cup? He had a great record, and that right there says what you get up for. We play thirty tournaments a year for ourselves, and all of a sudden now you're playing for your country.

His counterpart across the pond was Bernard Gallacher, replacing the hugely successful four-time captain Tony Jacklin.

TONY JACKLIN: In some respects it was a tough situation, but in another Bernard was dealing with teams that knew that they were up to their task. I'm just grateful to see that all the matches have maintained their closeness since I got off the pot.

BERNARD GALLACHER: Somebody's got to be captain, and my name was put forward. But it was like a normal evolution. I was Tony's right-hand man, and I'd played in a lot of Ryder Cups. But I was really just a helper with Tony; there were no formal assistant captains in those days. He could speak to me and bounce things off me, and I was quite happy to sort of be his sounding board. But when you become captain, it's all about being optimistic. I mean, if you don't think you're going to win, don't be captain. So think you're going to win, be optimistic, give the players a chance. And then when you get into picking foursomes and four-balls, you really need your players to give you some input. You don't want to put people on the golf course if they don't get on. At the end of the day, the players have got to enjoy your captaincy, and they have to have respect for you. It's all about respect and being optimistic.

SAM TORRANCE: David Feherty, who played in 1991, and I have

children of the same age. When he finally made the team he said, "Well now you can tell me what the Ryder Cup is like?" I said, "It's like having a kid. You can't explain it to someone that hasn't got a kid." And that's exactly what the Ryder Cup's like. You cannot explain it.

DAVID FEHERTY [now a CBS broadcaster but then appearing in his sole Ryder Cup]: Making the Ryder Cup was the culmination of everything I had ever dreamed of as a European player, but I knew absolutely nothing. We flew into Charleston Airport and people were lined up, cars parked in swamps and all sorts of shit around. It was amazing. And I said, "This must be a big event." And Sam says to me, "They're here to see the Concorde, you fucking prick."

RENTON LAIDLAW: When Concorde brought the team over to Kiawah Island, I was at the airport waiting for them. It circled round and round and round, and everyone thought this was just an opportunity for the locals who had never seen the plane to get a good look. It turned out they couldn't get the landing gear down, and the captain had had to come into the main cabin, open a trap door in the aisle, and turn a handle to lower the wheels manually.

DAVID FEHERTY: You should see the official team photograph for 1991. It's fucking hilarious. Everybody's standing there beside their bags or whatever, and Torrance and I are at the back, looking at each other and laughing uncontrollably. And I don't know why.

One big surprise: a last-minute venue change. The original site was to have been PGA West, a new golf complex developed by the Landmark Land Company in California for the PGA of America. But the time difference was too great for the matches to be broadcast live in Europe, so the Ocean Course, designed by Pete Dye, was built from scratch on Kiawah Island. Although in time the Ocean Course would improve its reputation, when the Ryder Cup was played on it it was still young and rough, and the accompanying accommodations were makeshift and temporary.

Mike Hicks [caddie for Payne Stewart]: I got into town on the Sunday before the matches began and saw the course for the first time on Monday. I was very disappointed. Thank God they didn't play it from all the way back; it would have been impossible. It was probably the hardest golf course I've ever caddied on. Then you multiply the pressures of the Ryder Cup, and it just wasn't any fun.

Plus the guys had to use trailers for their locker rooms, and we had a tent set up for us to sit in or have something to eat. The place just wasn't ready. Everyone was in the same frame of mind: "Why are we here?"

JOHNNY POTT [head of the Design and Construction Committee for Landmark Golf and a U.S. Ryder Cupper in 1963 and '67]: We've built other golf courses in less than a year—actually they had a year to build it and almost a year for it to mature. I don't think anybody complained about the condition of the course. It was a great venue.

I actually went to the 1991 Ryder Cup as a photographer. I have a lot of hobbies and ended up getting a press photographer's media badge, and took maybe a couple of thousand images for our company brochures. I was all over the place, but I tried to not be in prominent spots, because I didn't want Raymond Floyd looking at me and saying, "Johnny, what the hell are *you* doing there?"

Right after the '91 Ryder Cup the Landmark Land Company dissolved because of the savings-and-loan crisis. We went in two directions. One group was more real estate–oriented, and our group became Landmark Golf.

DAVE STOCKTON: I actually think the switch to Kiawah favored the Europeans, because it was built on a sand dune; it's a links course. It may not look like normal European courses, but you're elevated and the elements are hitting you, and it's nothing like what we normally play. Some of the guys actually visited three, four, five times to get the feel for the course. I also extended Gallacher the opportunity to have his players come up after the Masters, even though the course wasn't really complete. None of them, to my knowledge, ever went.

DAVID FEHERTY: I saw the golf course when we went out and played on the morning of the first day we were there. They had the golf course set up with the tees far back, and I'm thinking, This can't be happening to me. Why can't I reach the fairways from the tees? It was totally unmanageable. Absolutely the hardest golf course that I'd ever seen. As close to unplayable, unmanageable as I've ever seen.

The weather was okay—not much rain, but it blew. The golf course is built right on the ocean with the greens built up, so you have to have some kind of a high shot to hold the green, but it requires a low shot to keep out of the wind. That's a fundamental design flaw. I heard it was supposed to be like Scottish and Irish golf, but I'd been all over Scotland and Ireland and I'd seen nothing like this.

Then Bernard Gallacher talked to us about the course. He said, "Shut up and play."

HALE IRWIN: I went to Kiawah in the summer of 1991 with my son to look at the golf course. We played with Pete Dye and the design work was typical of Pete's: bizarre, tantalizing, very penal. He had done some things that probably would land anybody else in jail. In fact, he told me that they had the cell next to [former Panamanian dictator Manuel] Noriega waiting for him! It was a little difficult, but it was much like the links courses you might find at the British Open.

RENTON LAIDLAW: It was a brilliant course for the competition, because there were plenty of holes in which there could be drama. Gallacher wandered backward and forward to give advice to team members. He found out exactly which clubs were being used, so when his players came round, he would say, "Just to let you know Faldo used a so-and-so, Feherty used a such-and-such, Colin Montgomerie did so-and-so."

DAVE STOCKTON: I had an awesome team. I really had no weaknesses. My toughest job was making my captain's picks. I told Curtis Strange a year out that he'd be one, but he didn't play well. I was going to make Raymond Floyd a choice and pair him with Freddie Couples, because I didn't feel that Freddie really knew how good he was. And anybody I paired with Raymond would get fired up. Couples and Floyd also gave me a team that could play both ways, meaning best-ball and alternate-shot, which was highly important to me. They both hit the ball about the same. When it came to alternate-shot, there was no way in the world I was going to pair a long hitter and a short hitter because I remembered what had happened when I'd been paired with Nicklaus [at Old Warson in 1971].

The other pick came down to one of three players. I knew Tom Watson would be my captain following me, and gave him a hard look, as I did Tom Kite, who is a very good friend. Right after the PGA Championship I polled my top seven or eight guys by phone to ask who they'd want, because I'm not presumptuous enough to think, Okay, I'm the captain, I get to make all the decisions, and I'm going to stuff somebody down their throats. It turned out most of the guys on the team really wanted Chip Beck. He's a very positive person and a good friend of Paul Azinger, and that gave me another team that could go both ways if I needed it.

DAVE STOCKTON: But my number-one team was Steve Pate and Corey Pavin, and it just killed me when Pate got hurt in a limo wreck. We were driving to Charleston to the Grand Opening dinner. I was up front in the first car, with Bernard Gallacher. The roads were wet, and I think two cars ran into each other at a stoplight.

DAVID FEHERTY: We caused it. Nick Faldo and his ex-wife and me and my ex-wife were in the same limo. My ex-wife asked a really stupid question of the driver at exactly the wrong time, just as we were coming to a red light. She asked, "Why is that policeman standing in the middle of the road?"

The driver saw the red light, but he didn't see the policeman waving us through. We stopped, the car behind us almost hit us, the car behind it almost hit it, and the car behind that one did hit it.

DAVE STOCKTON: Floyd got dinged a little bit but not badly, but Pate got thrown five feet forward and crashed right into the metal [drinks] bar in the limo. He was lucky he didn't break any ribs. He had cut himself right across his stomach, really badly, and had to be taken to hospital.

DAVID FEHERTY: We found out Pate had been injured when we got to the dinner. Steve's one of the all-time great guys who play golf, just a fun guy, and the initial announcement was an awful thing.

DAVE STOCKTON: Pate was playing so well—I don't think he had a practice round higher than 67—and you can't beat Pavin because he's an absolute bulldog. They would have been perfect together. I was absolutely thrown for a tizzy.

I'd worked with a sports psychologist called Deborah Graham, and I knew the personality profiles of every one of my guys. I knew which ones would and wouldn't mesh, and I paired them accordingly. But all of a sudden, Pate goes down, and I haven't practiced Corey with anybody apart from one round with Lanny Wadkins, so it just blew me away.

Deborah Graham and her husband, Jon Stabler, have been studying professional golfers' personalities since 1981. Their "process" involves players taking a questionnaire, whereupon Graham and Stabler analyze the answers and identify certain traits that do or don't need work. Their traits include such personality elements as focus, tough-mindedness, and self-assurance.

DEBORAH GRAHAM: I met Dave Stockton at the 1991 Masters, and we started working together on his own game, preparing for the Senior [Champions] Tour. A little while after that, Dave asked me if I had worked with any of the members of his Ryder Cup team. And as it turned out, I had already tested and talked with several of them. Paul Azinger, Fred Couples, Mark O'Meara, Steve Pate, Raymond Floyd, Chip Beck, and, I think, Mark Calcavecchia. I guess Dave deduced that maybe it would be helpful to him to be able to get them organized as a team and be able to bring out their best skills, their best talents, and maybe be able to match players according to their personalities.

I was there to help Dave create a really strong team atmosphere. I had a conversation with Johnny Pott, who played under two Ryder Cup captains. One was very loose [Arnold Palmer] and the other was very organized [Ben Hogan]. And there's a fine line there because you have to have some kind of structure, you have to have guidance. Yet if you're autocratic, you're going to lose respect. You have to respect the fact that they all have to be pretty self-sufficient, pretty dominant people to be on that team to begin with. But just like the military, you need a leader, and if you're not listening to your team, you're not going to be a very good leader.

Dave had a very organized approach. He planned everything. All their free time was basically together, whether it was having dinners, whether it was talking, whether it was doing something a little bit more social with the wives. All the players were married, and he very much tried to include the wives in some of the activities to make them feel like a group. He got a lot of players feeling part of a team and feeling that group cohesion, even before things started.

Dave did discuss pairings with me before the Ryder Cup, but I had to be a little careful because I didn't have permission from all the players to discuss their personalities. But some of the players said fine, discuss whatever you want. We want this to be the best.

After the Steve Pate incident we discussed how to help the team. Dave especially wanted to get the players' emotions under control. And as at probably all Ryder Cups, emotions are right on the surface.

It was very disappointing for Steve because you know how competitive he is. In some ways it made the players step back a little bit and maybe sort of even want it more. You know—let's pull together, let's make this work.

I'd also worked with Seve Ballesteros. I had gotten to know Seve prior to the Ryder Cup, and the last time I'd seen him he had decided that he wanted to take the questionnaire and get started. I told him I would bring the packet of materials that included the questionnaire to the Ryder Cup and give it to him there.

But I was pretty naive. I was with the U.S. team, and we were riding the elevator in the building where the players were housed to a central area for the U.S. team, where they had physical therapists and such, and a little training area. On the way up, the elevator stopped, and the door opened, and there were some European players on their floor, but the elevator was too crowded for them to get in. I saw Seve there, and he said, "Do you have the materials?" And I said, "Yes, I'll bring them to you."

When the door closed, Dave turned to me, and I'd never seen him with such a serious, stern look on his face. He just said, "You . . . will . . . *not!*"

That's when it really hit me what was going on with the Ryder Cup. And that was only the beginning. I mean it really, really shook me. I loved it—and I hated it.

DAVE STOCKTON: And the dinner in Charleston was the biggest fiasco of the week as far as I was concerned, because the PGA [of America] showed a very distasteful videotape about our side, and there was nothing about the Europeans. I have no idea why they did that.

RENTON LAIDLAW: The videotape made no mention of any European victories. And the padre giving the blessing, you know, hoped that the Americans would win in his prayers and this sort of thing. It was so bad that Nick Faldo considered walking out. But the dinner ended very quickly because of the crash.

DAVE STOCKTON: I have no idea why they called the videotape *The War by the Shore* either. I didn't agree with that at all.

RENTON LAIDLAW: Everybody was talking about war and the desert, because of the Gulf War that was going on. Of course, this wasn't the desert, but it was a neat way to package it.

Then a local radio station found the numbers of the various rooms that the European players were in at their hotel and said, "If you want to wake them up in the middle of the night and cause them some concern, this is what you do." There were a lot of calls in the middle of the night. It was all very unpleasant.

BERNARD GALLACHER: The Americans were desperate to win it back because they hadn't won the Ryder Cup since 1983. And some of the players I think got carried away in the euphoria of the Gulf War and they sort of pretended the Ryder Cup was like Gulf War II. There was no inkling that they would be coming out in the first day wearing battle fatigue hats. It wound up spectators, wound up their side.

DEBORAH GRAHAM: It was not fun. I'm from Texas, and it was like Texas college football, where you're going to kill each other. You're in a war against each other. And that really surfaced with the galleries. They were like a mob. There were even people wearing fatigues. It just felt like a war. It felt like hate. It was loud, and there was snarling and there was heckling. I still have this great impression of Rocco Mediate [U.S. player, albeit not on the team] walking around with U.S. flags sticking out of his hat. And if we showed our patriotism in such a simple way as that, it would be wonderful. But to abuse each other and call each other names?

I wasn't scared, and again, I loved the patriotism. I loved the fact that we're representing our country. I loved the fact that we can come together and challenge each other in sport. But I really disliked the attitudes that came with it. And I didn't feel it had to be that way. I still feel like we should be able to say, "Okay, let the best team win." I would prefer that it not be that antagonistic if we're going to do it.

The players felt a little of that, too, of course. And they were trying to not let emotions come into their play, which wasn't totally easy. Dave was pretty much trying to keep them in the process, trying to get them to stay in the moment, play one shot at a time. Don't let your play be influenced by the position of where you are. Stay with your strategy. Stay with your game plan. And save the emotions for later. I really think he did a good job.

And yes, it's more of a challenge when you have the perception that you're playing for your country. And for your team. If Dave were to build that up too much, he would have been fueling that emotional fire. So he was trying to balance building the team cohesion but still trying to get them to play individually.

DAVE STOCKTON: The one thing I was really proud of is that on the only evening when there wasn't something we had to do—Tuesday or Wednesday—I created this low-country cookout and didn't invite any officials from either side. It was players and family from both teams, beer, Cajun cooking and seafood, or whatever else you wanted. We had a great time.

I read all the stuff written later about the fans, and you'd think there were all these idiots running around, but I didn't see that. The fans on the first tee were awesome. There was one with a Union Jack flag wrapped around him, and another wrapped in the flag of Spain, and they would yell and scream after the Europeans teed off. And when the Americans were announced they'd clap and yell again—which to me is what it's all about.

Tom Watson followed me as captain in 1993, and said he was going to make a gallant effort to cut down on all this stuff, but that puzzled me. I didn't agree with the "War by the Shore" stuff, but I thought the American fans really supported us. And if there had been somebody rude, I'd have found them and thrown them out.

When play began, Irwin found himself paired with his old sparring partner Lanny Wadkins, as they beat newcomer David Gilford and the outspoken Colin Montgomerie 4 and 2.

HALE IRWIN: Dave had gone back and done his research, and knew that Lanny and I were a good team. So it was back to being the captain of the sled. The same formula I had used with Lanny in years past I used again. I just said, "Go to it, Lanny." And I just felt like he was a better player when you kind of let him run.

There had been some reports that, when it had been announced that Steve Pate might not be able to play because of the limo crash, Colin Montgomerie had said, "Too bad it didn't kill him." That's just what somebody said. I was absolutely offended by the statement, and I went to Tony Jacklin, who was sort of a second captain, and I said "Tony, tell me, is this true?" He said, "Oh, absolutely not. He wouldn't do such a thing." Yet that cloud sort of hung over it. So, okay, I wanted Monty. And I got him. And I threw some darts in there that were pretty spectacular. [Irwin/Wadkins won 4 and 2. Montgomerie later commented, "Hale Irwin hit some shots that were godlike."]

DAVID FEHERTY: In the Ryder Cup you spend most of your time trying to look invincible and trying not to show any kind of soft underbelly. I think most people do. It's about controlling the panic. You're thinking, Oh God, no, my head's going to fall off! It's a strange thing. So when I hit my first putt, everything moved but my bowels. It was a fifteen-foot putt, and I left it four feet short, and five feet right. Sam [Torrance] just quietly walked over to me said, "Pull yourself together, or I'm joining them and you're playing the three of us."

I made the next one. And then it was nice to make a couple of putts at the right moments, especially one on the last hole. It was dusk, and all four of us had played the hole as though it was completely fuckin' dark You couldn't see the ball. And it tied the match.

DAVE STOCKTON: Emotions run high. At one point Bernard Gallacher's radio didn't work, and he thought I was sabotaging his radio! But he should know me better than that. In fact, I laugh at these guys now; they've got all these professional assistants. Hell, my assistants were my two sons.

BOB JOYCE: I was on the board of directors of the PGA of America and part of our duties was to select the Ryder Cup captain, and then officiate in one capacity or another. Jimmy Patino and I were observers at the 1991 Ryder Cup. In each match there are two rules officials and two observers. We're out at the tee shot landing areas, at the greens on the par-3's, so if, for instance, a ball enters a hazard, we tell the players exactly where the point of entry was [so they know where to take a penalty drop]. If there is anything that a rules official would not be close enough to observe, it becomes our duty.

Jimmy and I struck up a nice friendship. Our first match was the foursome, José Maria Olazábal and Seve Ballesteros against

Chip Beck and Paul Azinger. I tell you, it started like on the second hole. José María hit a ball into a hazard, and the ball would have been playable, but they couldn't find it. Seve tried to establish a more beneficial point of entry than they were entitled to, but I just said, "No, *this* is the point of entry." Eventually I found the ball and they were able to pitch it out of the hazard. But I could see the intensity of Seve and Paul Azinger. It was so obvious. And then, of course, came the ball incident.

In a foursomes match each side has only one ball in play. Azinger was on a different equipment staff from Chip Beck. I don't know what staffs they were on, but let's say one might have been Titleist, one might have been Maxfli. They started off playing, let's say, the Titleist, and then I guess for some reason Azinger reached in his bag, I think on the seventh hole, and pulled out a Maxfli—I think it was Paul Azinger that took out the wrong ball—and they finished the hole. After the ninth hole Seve brought the issue up to the rules officials. Jimmy and I actually were unaware of this. We were waiting out on the tenth fairway. After twenty minutes, no one had hit a ball. So we got on the walkie-talkie and found out what was happening. It was resolved that there was no penalty because in match play, any objection must be brought up prior to teeing off on the next hole [which would have been the eighth]. Otherwise it's null and void.

BERNARD GALLACHER: It had nothing to do with Seve. Olazábal said that they had changed the ball, which they're not entitled to do. Then I brought it to the attention of the referee, and they denied it. But they admitted doing it at a previous hole. Because we hadn't claimed it before we hit the next tee shot, then we had to forget that one.

DAVE STOCKTON: I don't know why our guys would think they could use two different kind of balls. I have no clue. Do you think that's something a captain has to tell them? I'm going, "Guys, this is something you're supposed to know—you know?" And I don't know why the Europeans didn't report it immediately.

PETER JACOBSEN: I did television for NBC at Kiawah Island and was assigned this match when they got into the little discussion over the ball. When the official said, "If you didn't call the hole before you teed off on the next hole, that hole stood." Seve was pissed. He was irate. And I know from talking to Chip and Paul afterward that they both felt so awful that they had broken the rules and in a sense had gotten away with it.

DEBORAH GRAHAM: The incident really shook me because I hadn't seen such intensity and such emotion and such anger. I had never seen Seve quite that emotional, quite that intense. I'd been around him for a couple of years off and on, and knew him fairly well, but I hadn't tested him, so I didn't know how emotional he might be or how competitive he might be. But I'd never quite seen it surface like that before. And I guess that's probably natural for Seve.

The altercation indeed had an immediate effect, as the European duo won four of the next six holes to take a 1-up lead and eventually won with a birdie on the seventeenth.

BOB JOYCE: When the match was over, they shook hands, but Azinger was just beside himself. He was livid. Even when his wife tried to comfort him, he could not contain himself. He was so upset. That showed how competitive this man was.

BERNARD GALLACHER: At the end of the day the Spaniards won. I was quite pleased about that. It was probably justice.

DAVE STOCKTON: They played each other again in the afternoon four-balls [Europe won 2 and 1 again]. Chip didn't play that well, and Azinger had been emotionally derailed a little bit by what happened. Ballesteros has a knack for getting under your skin if he wants to. He can be tough to deal with. I lucked out the next day because I got Floyd and Couples playing against him, and Ballesteros was much calmer playing against Floyd. I think he could realize that gamesmanship should not be how you win or lose the Ryder Cup. It should be by hitting fantastic shots.

MIKE HICKS: The Spaniards are something. They're real "gamey" out there. They *really*, really work on your head as far as taking too much time. Seve would be eight feet for birdie, and José would have an unbelievable chip from fifty yards over the green for par or something—and he would go play it. They took their time, trying to put us off.

Payne and Fred Couples played Olazábal and Ballesteros in the Saturday afternoon four-balls. It took longer than six hours! It was so dark when we finished that we couldn't have played another shot. And Freddy holed a bunker shot on 15 to halve the hole when Payne was in his pocket. Unbelievable. And against the Spaniards!

Seve also had an uncontrollable cough at the time. I think he still has it. I think that was the first experience with the cough. Not that he did it during your swing or anything, but you're in your pre-shot routine, thirty seconds before you hit the ball, and you're getting into your mental focus, and you hear this *cough!*

Amid the blustery conditions, on the toughest golf course the Ryder Cup had ever seen, in an atmosphere that was rapidly reaching the boiling point, both teams slugged it out for two days until they ended up tied at 8–8, with the singles remaining. The final day that would test the resolve of every player in each team and would become the most intense day in the history of the Ryder Cup.

DAVE STOCKTON: On Sunday, Pate just couldn't go. I mean he wanted to play so bad, so I put him out Saturday afternoon to see if he could go. I wasn't trying to hide anybody; I wanted him to play. He and Pavin got beat 2 and 1, but he just couldn't go. He couldn't move.

BERNARD GALLACHER: Steve Pate's a good player, and Dave Stockton wanted to play him, but we felt his injury was overplayed. And Dave Stockton didn't tell me until the [singles] draw had been made and just before the matches were about to be played. A couple of years later [in 1993] Sam Torrance wasn't well, and his name went in the envelope. I told U.S. captain Tom Watson early on that there was the possibility that one of my players wouldn't play. It just gives the captain a bit more leeway to think about who he puts in the envelope. He can then prepare the player who's in the envelope and give him the reasons why. David Gilford was very upset because I hadn't told him he was in the envelope. If I'd been told that Steve Pate wasn't going to play, I would have prepared him a bit better for it. I would have said, "David, I put your name in the envelope for this reason, that reason." But it came out as if I didn't have any confidence in David Gilford.

After talking to him, I then asked Tony [Jacklin], "Could you go and have a word with David? He might take it a little bit better from you." As it turned out, he didn't.

TONY JACKLIN: That was probably my worst Ryder Cup moment. David was totally gutted. He sat in our room all day. He was devastated.

DAVE STOCKTON: Both teams ought to have an alternate, a thirteenth guy. If every PGA of America official can have the exact Ryder Cup wardrobe, what's the problem of having a thirteenth guy? Nobody wants to be put in the envelope, and no captain wants to have the pressure of putting somebody in the envelope. If somebody can't play, put your alternate in. It's that simple.

RENTON LAIDLAW: Under the rules that meant half a point each, and that half-point proved very valuable at the end of the day to the Americans.

DAVE STOCKTON: One of the intriguing things at Kiawah was that nobody could say who was the key man on our team, because there wasn't one. The team won. The only negative thing that came out of it was Calcavecchia halving with Monty in the singles after being 5 up after nine, but that's sad. I've talked to Calc about it over and over. I put Floyd and Payne Stewart out first. I would have put Lanny out first, but by then Lanny was tired and he wanted to go last or next to last, which surprised me. So Payne and Floyd were getting clobbered by David Feherty and Nick Faldo, but Calcavecchia's 1 up, 2 up, 3 up, 4 up, 5 up. I got to 17, the par-3, just in time to see Calc bomb it into the water twice. He just came completely unglued. But to a man, the players behind him were going,

"Can you see what Calc's doing?" We were losing the first two matches, but they were just so focused on how Calc was just killing them. And they were saying, "If Calc can do it, I can do it."

PETER JACOBSEN: Calc smashing Colin was making a big statement. It's always a huge confidence boost to your team when it looks like a player's going to run out and run away with the match.

DAVID FEHERTY: I saw the shanks by Calc on 17. I said to Calc afterward, "No disrespect; most people would lose the first ten holes on purpose just so they wouldn't have to play the final four holes."

BOB JOYCE: This guy was in tears for a long time. Since when is a grown man in tears over a situation where he has no money to lose? I was so impressed at the competitiveness of those players.

DAVE STOCKTON: So Calc ends up getting half a point, which is not the way he wanted it, obviously. But if anybody was the reason we won that Ryder Cup, it was Calc, because he was carrying the day, and the team was noticing it.

DAVID FEHERTY, who would beat Payne Stewart 2 and 1 in the second match out: Everything settled down on the first tee. I just felt like the ball was going to go where it wanted to go. It was one great shot after another. I went 3 under par through twelve holes— which was unheard of!—and I was 4 up on the fourteenth.

But 15 I bogeyd after a poor tee shot, and on 16 I hit one almost into the ocean. So now I'd lost two holes in a row, and I got to 17, which is the hardest par-3 in the galaxy, where you have to hit a long shot to a green the size of a monkey's nipple. Just the thought of trying to get the ball on the green is nauseating.

MIKE HICKS: There was nowhere to hit it. You couldn't miss it left, because if it went in that bunker, you were dead. If you hit it in the water, obviously you were making five. The green was not set up for the kind of a shot that you had to hit in there. It was sort of a short-iron shot green, but you're back there with a long iron. And some guys even had woods out.

DAVID FEHERTY: We were walking from the sixteenth green to

the seventeenth tee with all this mayhem, this noise, people yelling and screaming, "Go Payne! Go Payne!" And then this huge lady marshal jumped out of nowhere and poked me in the chest, and said, "Where do you think *you're* going?" Of course I would have liked to have told her that I was wearing this uniform because I was a heavily disguised spectator, just trying to sneak my way on. But then Payne's arm came over my shoulder and he put his face right against mine, his right cheek on my left cheek. And he turned my head toward her and said, "Ma'am, I'd love you to hold him right here, but he's playing against me."

MIKE HICKS: On 17 we hit it left, where you couldn't play from, and then conceded David's second putt [giving Feherty the victory 2 and 1]. The match with David was fun because he's such a personality, and Payne and I were both good friends with him. In my mind, and I think in Payne's mind also, it didn't hurt as badly to lose to somebody that you really liked.

DAVID FEHERTY [after safely hitting his tee shot onto the seventeenth green]: I turned around, and Bernard Gallacher was running up the tee waving his arms in the air. Jacklin was facing the other direction, covering his eyes. He had less faith in me than I had!

PETER JACOBSEN: The final match I followed was Seve against Wayne Levi. Seve went out to a 3- up lead at the turn, at which point I speculated that the most important thing Wayne Levi could do for his team right then was to win some holes, certainly to maybe win the match or get half a point, but more than anything to keep Seve occupied and keep him out of the other players' faces. Because Seve's such an emotional and such an inspirational player that once he is done with his match, he can get out on the course and he can get into Mark James and Sam Torrance's mind-set and help them. So Wayne birdied a hole and Seve bogeyed another, and I think Wayne took him all the way to 16. It was looking like a blowout, but then Wayne came creeping back. [Levi lost 3 and 2.]

But the final match, Hale Irwin versus Bernhard Langer, was the one that left everyone who witnessed it out of breath.

DAVE STOCKTON: I wanted to have somebody at the back who had a cool mind and a good putter to come in and finish the job. Hale was it, because anybody who has won three U.S. Opens has to be able to withstand pressure. And every Ryder Cup captain up until that point had always put his best players first or last, and tried to hide his other people in the center. Gallacher did the dead opposite. He had his best players right in the middle, which blew me away.

HALE IRWIN: Dave asked me where would I prefer playing, and I said, "Dave, I can play front, I can play back. I'm comfortable wherever you think it would be best to put me." So he put up the lineup and I saw I was last, and then as the two lineups were put together, I told my wife, "You know, I think it's going to come down to our match."

The next day, the wind was blowing, and I felt the early holes and the finishing holes, which were playing into the wind, were going to play more into Langer's forte than they were mine. I was not hitting the ball real strongly, and Langer, he could play that low hook he hits to keep the ball down. But the middle holes were more to my way of playing. I managed quite well, but the outgoing holes, then when we turned again with the wind, that's where I felt like, "Okay, now I have to make up ground." And that's exactly what happened. I just held my own. I went through the first holes in decent shape. I got to the middle holes and when we sort of made the turn at 14 and started going back to the finish, I had a 2 up lead.

As the day unfolded, I didn't feel like a prophet, but boy, it was getting spooky because as each match ahead of us would finish, you could see the scoreboards and then you'd see the players starting to drop back and follow the remaining matches. Our team had not gone out and asserted itself, the European team was holding its own, and this thing was up for grabs. It became very obvious that this match was going to win or lose it.

This was absolutely a new Ryder Cup experience for me.

Absolutely. The teams I played on were accustomed to dominating. Now it was a fight to the finish. And you talk about a guy that will fight to the finish—Bernhard Langer was that kind of a player.

We made the turn into the 14th hole. It's a par-3 and was playing very long. Langer hit a long iron right at the hole. Boy, it was a fabulous shot. But it hit just on the front edge of the green and then rolled back down the hill. I hit maybe a 3-wood. It landed up on top and rolled down to the right. So here we were, I was 1 up, but it looked like Langer has the upper hand. But he doubled, so I carried a two-hole lead into the fifteenth hole. I drove into the sand and lost that hole. Now I was 1 up playing 16, a par-5. He hit his third shot into the left bunker, and it looked like he had no chance, as he was up against the lip. I was just off the edge. But he hit a miraculous bunker shot to about six feet. And I pitched mine down to about five feet. And even with that wobbly stroke he has he knocked that thing in. Then I made my five-footer to stay 1 up.

On 17, the par-3, he hit one just off the left edge of the green. I was thinking, You can't knock it in the lake, you can't . . . I was thinking of a lot of inappropriate things. Don't do this, don't do that. I should have been focusing, but I was in emotional overload. So I hit mine sort of in the same area [as Langer], but as my ball landed someone threw a ball out onto the green! It turned out to be just somebody in the crowd who thought it would be funny to throw a ball out on the green.

BOB JOYCE: The ball just appeared on the green and everybody went, "Where did *that* come from?" It was just bizarre. There was probably twenty thousand spectators on that hole alone.

HALE IRWIN: So I putted my ball past the hole about eight feet and Langer put his up there within five feet. I missed, he made, and there we were, playing the last hole with no advantage.

SAM TORRANCE: What people forget is what Langer had done to get in that situation. Magnificent up-and-downs at 15, 16, and 17 to keep the match going. I mean, that bunker on 16 is the height of your bloody ceiling, but he hit a wonderful bunker shot and made the putt.

BOB JOYCE: I tried to go to the eighteenth tee, but I went with the crowd, just going and going, and all of a sudden I wound up on the 10th fairway! I couldn't believe it. I just couldn't move anywhere. But I made my way to the 18th fairway and got inside the ropes, then got up to the green.

HALE IRWIN: Langer's drive on 18 was in the fairway. I pulled mine a bit left, and it hit in the gallery. My ball had hit some lady somewhere, but it just sort of fell down back there, so I had to hit a 3-wood for my second shot.

I hit it short and right of the green. That was the safe play; maybe the more courageous play would have been to try to aim it at the hole, but there was a big bunker in there, and I didn't feel like that was the appropriate play. Then Langer hit his just short of the green as well. I pitched up, probably twenty or twenty-five feet short of the hole, and then Langer pitched his six feet left of the hole. My putt again was a poor putt, probably a couple of feet from the hole. Langer conceded it for bogey. Which meant that, if he holed his putt, he would win our match, the overall match would be tied, and Europe would retain the Cup again. I was just absolutely in despair that I had faltered.

DAVE STOCKTON: I was at the front of the green with the rest of the team. We'd walked down the fairway, so we were down below looking up at the green. I was kneeling down to let the people behind see. At that time I was just kind of depressed, for two reasons. One, I was mad that there was a chance we might not win this thing, and, two, if we did win, it would be because Langer missed the putt, and that just didn't seem fair. At the low-country cookout, I'd found out his daughter had a serious illness, which they thought was possibly terminal, and here the poor guy was facing this last putt. I was still thinking about his daughter, and felt so sorry for him.

DAVID FEHERTY: Herman [the German; Langer's nickname] was of course squeezing the fucking life out of his putter. Everything had gone quiet. Even the ocean was fucking silent. I was next to [the late English photographer] Lawrence Levy. Just before Herman hit the putt, Lawrence turned to me and said—and I shall never forget this, "The last time a German was under this kind of pressure, he shot himself in a bunker."

BOB JOYCE: I have never witnessed anything that intense. And the crowd was about to burst. They just had to have something happen.

DEBORAH GRAHAM: I was watching the players and their wives seated around the eighteenth green. I watched their expressions, their emotions—all kinds of emotions about to explode, and it was a magical moment to see that much intensity and passion. I like to say that when you're really working together coherently, the sum is greater than the parts. And in some ways the Ryder Cup felt like that.

HALE IRWIN: I did have a glimmer of hope. In my earlier practice rounds I had hit a putt from the left side of that green to the right side of the green, and I remembered telling the team in one of the team meetings that if you ever had to putt across that green, it breaks more than you think. The grain was stronger; there was something there that pulled the ball more than you anticipated. And that's what I was thinking to myself: If there is local knowledge, I hope that I have it and he doesn't. And that was exactly what happened. He said he read it to be left edge, hit it about where he wanted to—and it missed on the short side. Exactly what I had seen in earlier practice runs.

There's not a whole lot you can say. I told him no one deserves that. With all the pressure coming down I thought he handled it extremely well. I know he was bitterly disappointed, and I must say I was a little disappointed for him.

MIKE HICKS: I was sitting with everybody else, right there by the green. Bernhard's another good friend, a wonderful guy, and you hate to see that happen to anybody. You know, that Ryder Cup would have been fine with me if we'd have just drawn.

PETER ALLISS: I swear to God, if Langer had holed that putt there would have been fisticuffs. Hale Irwin's tee shot might have just hit somebody and or somebody might have pitched it out. Somebody knows. But the whole thing, the last green, the last hole, you couldn't have had a better finish.

JOHNNY POTT: I was right behind Langer, fifteen feet from him, when he missed the final putt. He could have probably putted it fifty times and not made it twice. It was a hard putt.

DAVE STOCKTON: Then when he won the very next week, in Europe, I was never so glad to have somebody win. I mean, what a class individual.

DEBORAH GRAHAM: The best players in the world learn from their most traumatic mistakes. When Bernhard missed that putt, two paths were in front of him. He could have chosen the path of regret, berating himself, being hard on himself. The other path is to say, "Okay, what, if anything, could I have done better?" And he chose that path. He chose to learn from that experience and to get stronger for it, as opposed to letting it weaken him. That's really thinking like a champion.

And then the celebration began. First the winning captain was tossed into the Atlantic.

DAVE STOCKTON: I was mad at first. Hell, they had to carry me quite a ways to chuck me in the water. Calcavecchia and [Mark] O'Meara and Pavin carried me—and Payne Stewart. He was the jokester the whole way. They just ran up behind me and grabbed me and then just started running into the ocean. I fought for a minute, then I realized I wasn't going to win, so I just went with them. The worst part was that that coat was the only one in the whole outfit that I really liked, and it just got trashed.

DAVID FEHERTY: Afterward Sam and I were standing outside our trailer, just looking around. We could hear the Americans celebrating in their trailer. It looked like it was bouncing up and down. Sam said, "Let's go over there." So we knocked on their door, and Payne answered it. "Come on in!" he said. Dan Quayle [then the U.S. vice president] was in there with his wife, Marilyn. Sam and I were just like, "Congratulations, well done, you played great."

DAVE STOCKTON: When we went to closing ceremony, they had two buses. Both teams could fit on one bus except for two people. So Woosy picked up Corey Pavin and carried him down the center of the bus, and we all rode in one. I have to say, the Europeans were very gracious in defeat, much more gracious than we would have been. That probably was a direct result of Bernard Gallacher. But you can't begrudge another team for winning when the competition is so keen and intense.

DAVID FEHERTY: Then it was to the hotel, get changed, have a huge dinner. The dinner was all fall down.

BOB JOYCE: After the whole thing was over, Ian Woosnam and some others partied with everybody. It was in a huge tent, the size of two football fields, set up for the general public, with big television sets. This was late at night. Woosnam was dancing on the tables, and Nick Faldo's caddie, Fanny Sunesson, was doing the jitterbug. After it was all over, it was a lot of fun.

DAVID FEHERTY: Torrance and I ended up in the parking lot, and I barfed.

DAVE STOCKTON: A month later we went to the White House for a dinner, and Lanny—who played on the 1977 team with me when Dow Finsterwald was captain—walked over to me and said, "You know, I never thought I'd say this to anybody, but you did as good a job as Finsterwald. You were a marvelous captain." That meant so much, because I really respected how Dow had handled the team. That made me feel good.

Later I did a debriefing with the PGA. Among the things I said was that we have too many people in the wings to have somebody captain twice. When Payne Stewart was killed it occurred to me that some team was really going to miss having Payne be the captain. He was forever asking me questions.

And I think they should play ten from each team instead of eight during the foursomes and four-balls on the first two days. That was old-time thinking when you would hide some players. But now neither team stronger or weaker. Let the guys play.

After the drama of Kiawah Island, the 1993 Ryder Cup—back at the Belfry—was something of a comedown. It had to be. Not only was there such an outcry that no one wanted a repeat of the unruly crowd behavior, but several steps were put in place—limiting ticket sales, better roping of galleries—to make sure it couldn't be repeated.

Despite all his best efforts, U.S. captain Tom Watson still found himself burdened with controversy. First his players balked at a pre–Ryder Cup invitation to the White House from U.S. President Bill Clinton. Eventually the players, staunch Republicans all, relented. Then Watson himself refused to participate in the long tradition of players and captains autographing the menus at the Opening Dinner. That the menu in question belonged to Sam Torrance, an immensely popular player, didn't help.

As it turned out, Torrance didn't play much in this Ryder Cup because of an infected toe. After partnering Mark James in the Cup's opening foursomes match, and losing to Corey Pavin and Lanny Wadkins, Torrance could play no more. That meant the U.S. would put a name in the envelope for the singles. At his own insistence, it belonged to Wadkins.

There was one scenario under which Torrance might have been pressed into action, however. On Saturday evening, the daughter of English rookie Peter Baker was rushed to a local hospital with a suspected case of meningitis. Off Baker went to be by her side, and for most of the night he was up, awaiting word (U.S. player Davis Love sent the Bakers a note on behalf of the U.S. team). When the girl's illness was diagnosed as a viral infection, only hours before play was due to begin, Baker returned to the Belfry to play Corey Pavin. Had Baker pulled out and had Torrance not played, under the rules of the competition, the Cup would have been awarded to the United States. Instead Baker performed impressively, beating Pavin 2 up.

But the Cup went back stateside as the United States overcame a one-point deficit on the final day to win by two, 15–13. This time the tail of the order came through as late starters Love, Payne Stewart, rookie Jim Gallagher Jr. (he beat Seve Ballesteros, no less), Raymond Floyd, and Tom Kite all came through. The United States dropped only half a point in the last six matches and even that—Paul Azinger halved with Nick Faldo—came after the destiny of the trophy had been determined.

All in all, it was a muted Ryder Cup, but one that restored a degree of sportsmanship. Writing in Links *magazine, Jack Whitaker noted, "Over the last six years the matches were in danger of deteriorating into nationalistic feuds, the last thing Sam Ryder had in mind when he started this exercise. The two captains and their teams should be congratulated for returning civility and grace to this competition in a world where both are in short supply."*

The First Comeback

*T*hankfully, the decorum remained in place in 1995, at Oak Hill
Country Club in Rochester, New York—and the drama
returned. Oak Hill was a solid choice of a site—a classic northeast-
ern U.S. course, which is to say long, tight, and tree-lined—and significant because it was here that in 1989 Curtis Strange became the
first player to win back-to-back U.S. Opens since Ben Hogan had
done likewise in 1951. Strange's victory, it turned out, would
become significant in the outcome of the 1995 Ryder Cup—or at
least to the reaction to it. Lanny Wadkins was given the captain's
task of defending the trophy for the United States while Bernard Gallacher was back to lead the European team.

JIMMY ROBERTS [NBC-TV essayist, formerly with ESPN]: The first
Ryder Cup I actually covered was Oak Hill in 1995. By now I'd
heard all about how it was such a big deal and about the tension
that existed and how it wasn't really like other golf events. I had
done spots on the Ryder Cup before. Because of the stir that
Kiawah caused in 1991, I was dispatched to the Belfry to do a preview for ESPN's SportsCenter, and went there around the time of
the British Open, principally to take a look at the course. I did a
spot on the eighteenth fairway, talking about how Couples had col-

lapsed in his singles match with Christy O'Connor, and how O'Connor had hit that marvelous approach shot. But it was the oddity of the 10th hole that made the impact. Now, SportsCenter was meat-and-potatoes American sports. Football, baseball, basketball, hockey. But if it was going to pay attention to a single golf hole, then clearly things had changed in terms of the public consciousness of the Ryder Cup.

BRAD FAXON [who played for the U.S. in 1995 and '97]: I qualified for the U.S. team at the last possible opportunity. Everybody knows the PGA Championship, in August, is the last qualifying event. And you have to finish in the top ten to get points, and major championships earn double points, so the pressure was on. I'd played three so-so rounds and was in twentieth or twenty-first place, maybe five under par. On Saturday evening, Bob Rotella, the sports psychologist, and I went for a walk at a friend's house in Pacific Palisades [the PGA was held in 1995 at the nearby Riviera Country Club] through these beautiful gardens overlooking the sea, and we talked about what it meant to play on the Ryder Cup team.

I'd had a chance to make the team in 1993, in a similar situation: a good last round in the PGA and I make the team. I thought about the Ryder Cup the whole time I played and didn't make it. This time I said, "Let's go out and see how immersed I can get in the process," as we call it. And everything went perfectly. I shot 28 on the front nine, which was a major championship record, and 63 for 18, which tied the major championship record, and finished fifth. Lanny Wadkins was standing next to Davis Love when I made a big birdie putt on 18, and he was really pumped—and I'll never forget the roar from the crowd. I think most of them knew what was on the line. It was an unbelievable way to make the Ryder Cup team.

PETER JACOBSEN: Lanny was a tremendous captain. People don't really see the human side of Lanny because he's such a competitor. They see him inside the ropes as a real intense player, and he is. But boy, from an organizational standpoint, from a captain's standpoint, he was absolutely tremendous. From the clothing to the shoes to the dinners to the rooms to the functions to the scheduling—everything was done for us.

And he was very inspirational. You looked at Lanny's eyes and you heard him talk and he got emotional talking about the Ryder Cup and about the United States of America, representing your country. You could just see Lanny wanted to win. Some of the greatest memories were our team dinners, where all the players and their wives sat around a big circular table. Lanny always had a theme to talk about. What does the Ryder Cup mean to you? What does your family mean to you? What was the greatest victory you ever had? We just went around the table and talked about those things, and Lanny was trying to get all the players to open up and get to know each other personally. We already knew each other well enough, but it really enhanced the experience.

There were no joint dinners, but we were all on the same floor of our hotel, so after dinner we'd invariably walk from the west wing to the east wing and we'd be playing cards in the European team room or they'd be shooting the breeze in our room. And our wives would be talking with each other. It was great.

From the beginning, the weather was very, very wet, which made the course play very, very long. The wind was blowing, and it was chilly, and when the media asked me what I thought about the conditions, I said, "I'm an Oregonian with Norwegian blood. I can handle it."

BRAD FAXON: The first match of all was Corey Pavin and Tom Lehman against Colin Montgomerie and Nick Faldo in the foursomes, and that was a very big win for us. At that time Corey was our silent leader. "The Bulldog" was his nickname, which is great in match play. He was such a tough competitor.

TOM LEHMAN [playing in his first Ryder Cup]: I was really nervous. It was a big match, because we were playing their best team—at least on paper. But at the time Corey was U.S. Open champion. I hit the first shot. I hit a 3-wood about 320. With all the adrenaline and the excitement and the nerves, I just corked one. I think the first hole was 450 yards, and Corey had an 8-iron for our second shot.

One hole later, Lehman and Faldo exchanged words, confirming the old adage that the U.S. and Britain are two countries separated by a common language.

TOM LEHMAN: I wouldn't say I had a run-in. Neither Corey nor I could understand what Faldo was saying. We had a two-footer for a par, and we thought he was conceding it, but I didn't understand what he said and neither did Corey, and so I asked him again. He said it again, and I still didn't understand what he was saying, and neither did Corey. And then he said it again with a kind of, you know, a gesture, so I told him that if he could speak in a way that I could understand it wouldn't be a problem. It was the beginning of the match and guys were on edge. Corey was like, "Hey, this is not a big deal. He's not trying to be a jerk and neither are you, Tom. Everything's fine." So everything was fine.

But Corey was a great partner. He gave me the best piece of advice I've ever gotten in golf. We were on the seventeenth hole, the match was tied, and I said to him, "I'm so nervous I can hardly swing the club." The situation was just so new to me. And he just said, "Tom, it's really simple. Just get committed and swing. Get committed and swing." And so the idea was, you know, commitment. Then on the eighteenth hole I hit the best shot I've ever hit under pressure. In my *life*. It was a 5-iron from 205, crossing wind, raining sideways. I just said to myself, "Get committed and swing." And I hit it on the front part of the green forty feet short of the hole. We two-putted to win.

BRAD FAXON: I played with Peter Jacobsen in the afternoon four-balls. Peter and I knew that Lanny was trying to pair us up as we'd played three practices together. We played Seve and David Gilford. None of the American people really knew who Gilford was, and Seve's game was going south, but in four-balls he was still somebody who could contend and make a difference. But Peter and I never really got it going.

PETER JACOBSEN: Brad was nervous; it was his first Ryder Cup, and it was only my second, so I could relate to what he was feeling. But I felt good because I loved playing against Seve.

Then one of the craziest things in my life happened on the seventh hole. I took all the blame for it. On the sixth hole, David Gilford's birdie putt leveled the match after I had birdied the second and fourth holes.

BRAD FAXON: It was kind of rainy. Peter drove it down the middle. Seve and I drove it way to the right, into trees.

PETER JACOBSEN: Brad laughed when the ball was flying off to the right, heading toward deep, deep willows. He turned to me, and said, "Play hard, partner; looks like it's your hole."

The strength of my game is control and keeping the ball in play, so I smashed a good drive down the middle. Brad and his caddie went over with Seve and Seve's caddie to look for their balls. My caddie, Mike Cowan, said, "Brad's out of it. Forget about Brad. Let's just make birdie on our own."

BRAD FAXON: What we didn't know was that there was a creek over in the trees, and I had hit mine in the creek. I had to [take a penalty] drop, and I was behind these big trees. Peter couldn't see me from the fairway, I guess, although I didn't know that at the time. I just figured he knew I was in the creek. But he was standing up by his ball. Well, I hit this punch shot out there right in front of the green, lying three.

PETER JACOBSEN: We got to the balls that were in the fairway. I was fine. David Gilford was fine. Gilford hit his second shot over the green. I had about 155 yards, a bit uphill. The ball had a little mud on it. We couldn't even see Brad and Seve over in the willows. Seve just put the ball in his pocket, and came over and jumped on Gilford's back like he did all day. Just started riding him to the finish line.

All of a sudden I heard a ball being hit. I heard it hit a few limbs and, boom, the ball came up about fifteen yards short of the green. I thought, Wow, what a tremendous shot. So my caddie and

I said, "Well, gosh, he's there in two, so let's go ahead and let's just hit a good shot, keep it below the hole." I hit an 8-iron, right at the hole, and the ball came up on the front fringe, plugged, probably twenty-five feet short of the hole.

Brad had walked up ahead of me, so at that point I didn't have a chance to have any verbal contact with him. Before I'd even got up to him, he took a 9-iron or a pitching wedge and pitched it about fifteen feet short of the hole, right on my line. He marked his ball. Gilford then chipped down to about eight feet. He was lying three. Seve wasn't playing.

I was over my shot, getting ready to bump an 8-iron up the hill, when Brad said to me, "Why don't you let me putt and show you the line?" Good idea. So he putted. It broke from right to left, and he drained it, then gave the fist pump into the air. The crowd went crazy! So I took my 8-iron and chipped my ball probably two and a half, three feet by the hole, and marked it.

Now, Seve and Gilford are looking over their putt. They're looking, and looking, and they're taking an awful lot of time. I was looking at my coin thinking, I'd like to putt out even though Brad's already made four. And I'm waiting, I'm waiting, I'm waiting, I'm waiting. I looked back down to the fairway, and there were Jeff Maggert, Loren Roberts, Sam Torrance, and Costantino Rocca, the match behind us. It was starting to rain, and their umbrellas were up, and I thought, Shit, we're already taking too much time. I just walked over and picked up my coin. I thought that if I holed it, my four tied Brad's and we were out of there. You know, let's go, make the other guy putt to tie the hole.

Meanwhile, Brad's off to the side talking to Lanny Wadkins and Lanny's brother Bobby. I walked over and gave Brad a high five. I said, "Great four." And he went, "That was a *five*." I said, "*Five*? One, two out short, three on, in four. That's four." He said, "No, there's a hazard over there. I had to drop a ball." I said, "Brad, I just picked up my ball." He said, "You did *what*?"

Well, before Gilford putted, Seve walked all the way across to the green to me and said, "Did you pick your coin up?" And I said, "Yes." He said to me, "I'm sorry, but I didn't give that to you." I said, "I know that, Seve. I was mistaken. I thought Brad had made a four."

He walked back over, and Gilford made his putt. Seve then walked back up to me specifically and said, "I'm sorry, we don't want to win a hole that way." I looked at him and said, "I understand and I appreciate that. I made a mistake."

I should have checked with Brad. But then, why didn't Brad come over to me? If he can't see me, then I can't see him drop. And why didn't the caddies communicate? I'm not blaming Brad. And Brad doesn't blame me. It was just—it was raining, it was wet, it was sloppy, we're dealing with umbrellas, towels, whatever. We just never got together, if you see what I'm saying.

BRAD FAXON: It's easy to laugh at it now because it was so stupid, but it was a very easy mistake to make. We were totally embarrassed by it.

PETER JACOBSEN: At the end of the match, boy, we were just hounded by the press. Brad didn't want to talk to the press. He couldn't talk to the press. And he did not talk to the press. I stood in there alone and took the heat, and got a majority of the blame for it. But I'm a big boy, and I made a mistake. In my mind, he hit a wild drive, he whacked it out short, chipped it, putted it—hey, great four. It really shook us up.

To Lanny's credit, he laughed it off. He said, "Don't worry about it. What the hell. You're 1 down. Go ahead and win." But I had never felt so bad in my life. It just deflated us. [The Europeans won 4 and 3.]

BRAD FAXON: Seve was past his prime by this time. He wasn't the intimidating and swashbuckling Seve that we all watched. I think he hit three fairways the whole day. But he never let Gilford out of his sight. He talked to him the whole time. He was doing everything for him. He'd take his practice swings for him. On the long thirteenth, Peter and I both had birdie putts. Gilford was just off the green with his second shot, and Seve pointed to where on the green he should hit his ball. He hit it and it rolled round and round and round and round—and into the hole! That was the swing point there.

I didn't play in the foursomes the next day, but I played in the four-balls in the afternoon with [Fred] Couples. Peter had played in the morning in alternate shot. He drives it so straight that he wanted to play alternate shot. Freddie was the kind of the guy that had only a few guys that he wanted to play with. We'd won the Shark Shootout [an unofficial event on the PGA Tour], we'd played together a lot, and our caddies were buddies. It made sense that we play together. And I'm comfortable playing with Freddie. We were paired against Sam Torrance and Colin Montgomerie, which was a big team. Torrance was playing great at the time, and Monty was their number-one player.

It was a great day of golf for me. I played fantastic, did everything well. I remember making a big putt for a two on the third, and also on 10 and 11. Freddy chipped in on 14. That was one of the most exciting moments I've ever been part of, and the loudest roar I've ever heard, louder than the roar when Tiger made that hole-in-one on 16 at the Phoenix Open in Scottsdale.

We were 2 up at the time. Fourteen is a par-5 that's unreachable in 2. They had both hit their third shots to within a foot, two beautiful shots. I hit my third way past the pin, to thirty-five, forty feet, and Freddy hit a good shot but it spun off the front of the green. So now here we are, desperate. We needed to tie this hole, because we didn't want to go back to 1 up. I think Freddie was away, and my caddie and I had just walked to the back of the green. I was talking about how I was going to make this putt. We kind of turned around to watch Freddy chip it, and it went right in the hole! The place was electric, because it was an amphitheater-type green, right by the clubhouse, and was packed. Freddie is not the most emotional person out there, but he went nuts. And the crowd were like animals. It was unbelievable.

SAM TORRANCE: I'd *never* heard a roar like it in all my life. It was deafening.

BRAD FAXON: After we walked off the green, Freddie did a fist-pump again and the place just roared again. Walking onto the next tee Torrance just kind of smiled and said something under his breath to Freddie. Typical Sam.

SAM TORRANCE: I sauntered up beside him and whispered in his ear, "Fuck you." He looked at me and laughed.

For all the heroics by Couples and screwups by Faxon and Jacobsen, things looked bleak for the Europeans by the time the singles arrived. They were down 9–7 with a lineup that had a couple of gaping holes, one called Ballesteros and two others called David Gilford and Philip Walton. Gilford had actually played at Kiawah Island—it was he who sat out the last day when Steve Pate withdrew—but on paper no one gave Gilford or Walton a chance. Further, in the entire history of the Ryder Cup only four teams had won after having been behind when the singles began, the last time in 1993 but before that all the way back in 1957.

BERNARD GALLACHER: Oak Hill was tremendous because we suddenly did well in singles. Why we didn't do well in singles before was always beyond me because we had good players. I thought it was coincidental. But this time the players were fired up. We were disappointed we were two points behind on Saturday night, but I didn't really tell them to do anything; they were playing well. They just went out there and went for it.

TOM LEHMAN: We had a two-point lead, a huge lead really, and everybody was feeling pretty confident. I was up first, and I think Lanny felt comfortable with that. They were probably going to put a strong player up first, so I took it as a compliment. But I got Ballesteros. I think that Lanny was expecting, you know, Faldo or Montgomerie or someone like that. I don't think he expected Ballesteros to be put first. Seve wasn't playing his best.

BRAD FAXON: They were absolutely hoping that Ballesteros could steal a point, but they also wanted him to be able to walk around and talk to his teammates when his match was finished. He showed up at my match with Gilford at about the 14th or 15th hole.

TOM LEHMAN: Seve and I had a good match. He showed a lot of heart in the way he hit it all over the park but managed to stay in the match for a long time. His short game was phenomenal. It was a pretty amazing performance.

Lehman was 2 up on the twelfth hole when again he ran into a language barrier.

TOM LEHMAN: It was a classic case of being a little misunderstood. I was putting first and rolled it up to about maybe ten inches from the hole. I looked up, and said, "Good?" He said, "No, it's not." I tapped it in, so now I've played out of turn. People thought he was playing games, but you can't play out of turn in match play; once he's away he has control. So he had to call an official to find out what to do, and it was simply a matter of replacing my ball, which I did. I think he wanted the coin to stay there so he could aim at it, which is totally legitimate. So I replaced the ball, and he putted and missed, and we halved. Then I won a couple of holes and won the match.

PETER JACOBSEN: In my singles match against Howard Clark, Howard played probably as badly as I've ever seen Howard play [Clark played for Great Britain and Ireland/Europe in six Ryder Cups]. I was playing well and hit a lot of greens, but I think he hit but six on the day. But he was just magnificent with his short game. I think he holed from off the green three or four times, including the hole-in-one on the par-3 eleventh.

I'd birdied 10 to go 1 up, and then hit a fairly good tee shot on 11, a 6-iron to twenty, twenty-one feet. Howard hit his tee shot, and the minute he hit it he turned away disgusted because he'd pulled it. The wind was blowing from left to right, and the ball got up into the wind and the wind brought it back. It landed on the slope of the green near a bunker on the left side and kicked dead to the right and, boom, went in the hole. Being a fan of golf, I thought, Oh man, that's cool, a hole-in-one. But then I thought, Oh, man, now I'm back to even.

Well, I gave him a high-five and we were laughing about it. It's the spirit of the game. If somebody makes a hole-in-one in your group, what are you going to do? Pull a Ben Hogan on him and ask him the time of day? But it was a great match. Howard won 1 up on the last green.

BRAD FAXON: The day started out okay, but in the middle of the day we started losing some matches, and other matches were getting tight. David Gilford and I were having a tight match. Gilford had been playing beautiful golf. But I knew he was a good player, and had played way better than Seve had in our four-ball match. I just didn't know what he'd be like under the gun.

At 15, I was 1 down. Gilford missed the green, and I hit it right in the middle of the green, but it ended up way back on the right. I was going to have a hard birdie but pretty much a lock two-putt. And Gilford ended up making about a twelve- to fifteen-footer for par and tied the hole. On 16 he got it up and down from a bunker for a half after I was in the middle of the green in two. At 17 he hit a pop-up, toed drive, a horrible second shot, and pitched it to about eight feet and made that for par. So on any one of those, the match could have been even. I felt comfortable, I was driving it well, and I'd hit a lot of good shots.

An amazing thing happened after we'd played 17. We were walking to the eighteenth tee when Davis Love ran out on the green. He ran up to me and said, really loud and enthusiastically, "Hey, Fax!!" Which is not typical or normal for Davis. But he just said, "Hey, Fax!!" And he looked at me, and I thought he was going to say something like "Hit a good shot!" or "Win this hole!" But that's all he said. He couldn't talk. I looked at him, and it made me kind of laugh. I just walked away thinking, What was *that* all about?

I drove it perfectly on 18. Gilford drove it short, popped it up, then hit a long straight shot, over the green, which was dead. Absolutely dead. And he couldn't even get it on the green from there; he left it on the back fringe. I'd hit my second shot into a front-left greenside bunker, but I didn't have the hardest shot. But

I hit my bunker shot just a little too hard. We were both lying three, but I was about seven, eight feet from the hole, and he was still off the green. He chipped his fourth shot fifteen feet past the hole, so he was still away. But he made that for a five. That was *huge*.

I now had a putt to win the hole and half the match to get half a point—and at the time it was a crucial half point. Because by now everything was big. The putt looked like it was going to break right-to-left, the line just outside the hole. I want to think I hit it right where I was trying to hit it, but it missed on the right edge; it hit part of the hole. And I remember being in kind of disbelief that it didn't turn and was distraught because I knew it was a big point. Frank Harmon, the golf professional at Oak Hill, told me later that he was wishing he could have come out onto the green and told me that the putt just doesn't break like it looks. Not that that made me feel any better.

JIMMY ROBERTS: Afterward, Brad Faxon was in the parking lot trying to compose himself, and he was just sobbing. And I thought, This is what this thing means.

BEN CRENSHAW: I thought that, if there was one day I could beat Colin Montgomerie, that was it. He might have been tired and made a mistake. And I think if you asked Colin he'd say he didn't play as well as he could. But I ended up making four or five mistakes, and you just can't do that. He put me away at the end, 3 and 1.

The controversial selection of Curtis Strange as one of Wadkins's captain's picks came to a head with his dramatic match against Nick Faldo—a match that some feel settled this Ryder Cup.

JIMMY ROBERTS: Lanny was on the defensive that week, first of all with his selection of Curtis, and I would imagine about some of the pairings that he made that didn't work out. There was an edge to him which I didn't really understand, probably because I didn't have much experience covering the Ryder Cup. Obviously it meant an awful lot.

CURTIS STRANGE: Lanny had tossed my name out for a year and

a half prior to the end of the qualifying period, pointing out that I'd won the U.S. Open at Oak Hill in 1989. "We'll see how Curtis is doing," he'd say. But then I got to where I was somewhere on the radar screen as far as qualifying points were concerned, and then I played a really good PGA Championship [Strange finished tied for seventeenth, with 68s in each of his last three rounds] and Lanny picked me. To set the record straight, Lanny and I never had dinner together, and there wasn't a good-old-boy connection.

I was flattered, but I also realized in a big hurry how much pressure there is on your picks, especially when you draw from down the line a little bit. If you pick eleven and twelve, then nobody can ever really question anything, but you don't pick the eleventh; you go with who you think is going to be best for the team. Lee Janzen was in the picture, and people pointed out that he'd won three tournaments before the Ryder Cup and they always include The International in the three. But what gets lost in the argument is that, although he was playing well, he won The International the week *after* Lanny made his picks. Anyway, I went to work on my golf game for the next month.

PETER JACOBSEN: I thought Curtis was a good choice at the time, and I still do. Curtis and Lanny are very much the same mold of player. They both have dogged determination, they're both very aggressive and there's no let-up in either of those guys. Lanny was looking for that type of player with his type of personality. Curtis was a fabulous leader on that team, so the fact that he had a tough finish against Faldo doesn't diminish the fact that I think he was a good choice. You know, in those situations when you make two choices from probably twelve or fourteen guys, you can't really go wrong with any of them.

CURTIS STRANGE: I told Lanny going in that my game made me better off in the foursomes, and he appreciated that. I played with Jay Haas on the second day, but I played poorly. I let Jay down [they lost 4 and 2 to Nick Faldo and Colin Montgomerie]. At this point, I was feeling some pressure. Everybody and everybody's brother was questioning my being there. But if you're rooting for the American team, why do that?

Nick and I had a hell of a singles match. We didn't say much to each other, because we knew we were in it for the long haul. He was grinding his butt off and so was I.

But then I got to 16, 1 up, and hit the worst shot of my career. He had just put it in no-man's land, and was going to make bogey, so I had to put a 6-iron on the green and make par to go 2 up with two to play. And I missed it to the right; I don't know what happened. We both made bogey, but I was still 1 up; I was okay. At 17, we both drove it well, but I fanned a 3-iron to the right on my second shot, and he hit a poor second shot, too. I chipped just okay, and he chipped just okay, but he made his putt from about eight feet. Now we were even.

I still had a hole to go, so I was okay. Faldo drove poorly. I drove well. No panic, just hang in, because all I needed was a half. He had to lay up on the hole, and I hit a poor second shot, coming up a little bit short, and I chipped poorly. He pitched from a hundred yards to about five feet or so. I missed my par putt, he made his and won the match, and it just kind of snowballed at that point.

When I was standing on the eighteenth green, I knew what was going to happen to me: They were going to hang me out to dry. And the only thing I said on television was, "You can say I played badly—but just leave it at that." It hurt me enough to know I let my teammates down. It hurt me enough that Lanny put his trust in me and I let him down.

Nobody played well that day, but I got the brunt of the criticism. Crenshaw never won a point all week either. And seven of our guys lost that day. I wasn't the only one to lose. You get over it, but it hurt for a long time because it was such a big deal.

JIMMY ROBERTS: I remember Curtis coming out of the clubhouse after that colossal meltdown, with that taciturn visage of his, and he folded his arms and stood there and held court. He talked about it. I thought to myself, My God, I could *never* do this. This guy had just failed so horribly, and this was just one of the classiest things I'd ever seen. He was a controversial selection to begin with, and I guess Lanny chose him, you know, horses for courses, and I'm sure he felt an awful lot of pressure that he had to play well.

CURTIS STRANGE: But if I can't face it, who can? People want to know what happened. And I don't help the situation if I don't talk. It was the same when I threw away The Masters in 1985 [he had a three-stroke lead over Bernhard Langer with six holes to play but finished in second place, two strokes behind him]. People want to know. The media's going to write it anyway, so I always figured, at least if they get the facts right it'll be a better story. And so I faced the music. I always have said that if you think you're good enough to be good, you'd better take the bad with it. You don't think the sun's going to come up the next day, but it does. So we talked, and it was fine.

SAM TORRANCE: I did something in my singles match with Loren Roberts that I'd never done before. On the fifteenth, the par-3, the pin was tight by the water beside the green. I was 1 up so I wasn't going for the pin. But I put such a bad swing on it that I blocked it, and it went straight at the pin. I thought I'd hit it in the water. But it was perfect, ran up to about eight, ten feet, and everybody thought it was a great shot. I was about to go 2 up, but left the birdie putt short, right on the edge. Still 1 up. Up 16, good drive in the fairway. Loren was in the fairway, too. He was away and I was just standing there. My wife, Suzanne, was over to the side, and I just wandered over to her and said, "Watch this." I was so ready, and I don't know where it came from. I hit a classic shot, to eight feet on a real tight pin placement, then dropped it in for a birdie to go 2 up with two to play. They talk about being in the zone. That's the only time in my career, really, that I was absolutely in the zone. I could have done *anything*.

On 17 I didn't even hesitate to hit 3-wood, to hit the fairway. That's a good, long par-4, and I'm not a great long iron player. With a good drive I could probably hit an 8- or a 9-iron into the green, and part of me said, "Do that, take the chance and make your second shot easier." But I didn't. I knew I was going to have to have a 4- or 5-iron into the green, but didn't care because I was in control. I hit the 3-wood perfectly and hit the 5-iron perfectly, and I was about forty feet behind the pin. So now I had two putts to win or else I was going to have to par the 18th, and nobody wants that. I had a perfect lag putt and thanks very much. Then Nick won his match against Curtis, and I thought that was it because we needed 1 more point and Philip was 3 up.

That would be Philip Walton, in the final match against Jay Haas.

SAM TORRANCE: Philip Walton—what that poor boy went through! He was 3 up with three to play. On 16, Haas was in the right bunker and had to hole the bunker shot or the match was over. Haas *bladed* it out of the bunker, but the ball hit the pin and went straight in! Like the worst blow you could ever get.

Philip then missed a par putt for a half to win the match on 17. As he was coming off the green, I went straight up to him. I said, "Come on, don't worry; you're still 1 up. Come on!" For his third shot he had a little chip from rough, and he just had to get on the green. Haas had hit a bad drive and had a chip for his fourth but knocked it past. So Philip had two putts to halve the hole and win the match. Haas conceded the second putt. Bernard [Gallacher] went up to Philip and told him, "You've just won the Ryder Cup for us."

TOM LEHMAN: I was standing with Lanny as the last match, Haas against Philip Walton, was on 18. Haas had been 3 down with three to play, and if he could win the last three holes and get half a point, the U.S. would keep the Ryder Cup. But when it became apparent that Jay was not going to win 18, and that we'd lose, Lanny turned to me and said, "Things are going to get really ugly." Meaning that it was going to be a big celebration on the 18th green, which there was, champagne popping and flowing and partying and celebrating.

Afterward, we were in shock—and it was not fun watching the Euros celebrate on the 18th. But that's all part of the Ryder Cup. It's like the Stanley Cup when people pile on the ice after it's over. The thing about sports that makes it great, I believe, is the emotion that's involved.

BRAD FAXON: Afterward in the locker room, Lanny was great. Of course he was upset; he was sad. But I think he was proud of his moment as captain, and Lanny was a great captain. He did everything that you can expect any human to do and more. Everybody was pumped; everybody loved playing for him.

BERNARD GALLACHER: When I was out there watching them play in the singles, the one player I felt the Americans lacked to turn around the match when things weren't going their way was a Lanny Wadkins–type figure—and I think that's what Lanny felt himself.

JIMMY ROBERTS: When Lanny had to go up there and make his concession speech during the closing ceremonies he put these bifocals on and started to try and praise his own team and commend his opponents. And it was obviously very difficult for him. His voice started to break and crack, and just when it looked as if he was going to be in some impossible spot, Bernard Gallacher got up.

BERNARD GALLACHER: I could see Lanny was struggling because he was so upset that they had lost, and being a losing captain is very difficult. I've *been* there. I was quite friendly with Lanny so I just stood up—it was so spontaneous—and said, "Let me help you, Lanny, I've been there before" or something like that.

JIMMY ROBERTS: That was a wonderful thing that Bernard did and another thing that just made you kind of realize that the Ryder Cup was a little bit of a different deal. It was a spontaneous display of spirit, of goodwill. As hard-boiled as the competition seemed and as bare as all the emotion had been—I mean, everybody's emotions were just *raw* that week—you just wanted to stand and cheer. You just thought, This is good. This is really, really good.

W*ith the changing of the British team to a European team in* *1979 having finally—or eventually—turned the Ryder Cup into a* *contest among equals, it was only natural that a continental Euro-* *pean venue would eventually play host. Certainly there were quali-* *ty golf courses throughout the continent. Falsterb, in Sweden; Mor-* *fontaine, in France; Penina, in Portugal. But with Spain having* *contributed more players to the Ryder Cup than any other conti-* *nental country since Seve Ballesteros and Antonio Garrido donned* *the uniform in '79, there was little doubt where it would go first. The* *question was, Which course?*

JIMMY PATINO [once a billionaire industrialist, now the owner of Valderrama, on Spain's Costa del Sol]: Around 1982 or '83, I retired from the mining business and didn't have much to do. In about 1984, '85, I bought a course at Sotogrande and had Robert Trent Jones redesign it.

The Ryder Cup came into the picture in 1989, when Seve Ballesteros and the Spanish Golf Federation put a bid in to host the 1993 Cup. There were seven people on the Ryder Cup committee, three from the European Tour, three from the British PGA, and Lord Derby sat as chairman and had the casting vote. The three people from the European Tour said give it to Spain, while the three from the British PGA wanted to go to Ireland. Lord Derby voted against Spain because the course was not up to standard, and said the Ryder Cup would go to Ireland over his dead body, because the IRA had killed his uncle, Lord Mountbatten, there. [In 1979 Lord Louis Mountbatten, also the uncle of Prince Philip, the Duke of Edinburgh, was aboard a boat bombed by the IRA.] So we went back to Belfry in '89 because no one knew where to go.

In 1991, I went to the Ryder Cup on Kiawah Island and saw how they had built a golf course and only half a clubhouse. They had one hotel. Fans were brought in from Charleston by bus to a car park, and then taken by bus twenty-five minutes to the course. I thought, if they can organize it like this, then I can organize it, too. On Easter Monday of 1992, I presented my bid to the Spanish Golf Federation. I called a press conference in London on Tuesday. The European Tour said, "We haven't decided to go to Spain yet." I replied, "Last time you turned down Spain because it didn't have a good course. Now Valderrama is ready. So you can't turn it down because of the course."

They told me that it was nice to have Valderrama in reserve, but if they were going to Spain it would be to a new course Seve was building in Madrid. I said, "I'll believe it when I see his course."

For fourteen months I was the only one with a bid for the Ryder Cup. All that time I campaigned. I spoke with players, went to the U.S. and talked to the PGA of America. I lined up as many people on my side as I could. In May 1993 they announced that the Ryder Cup would go to Spain in 1997 and that they would decide in a year on the course. Needless to say, overnight I had a lot of competitors.

They narrowed it down to six courses, then had a vote among the top players on the European Tour. About half said we should stay in the U.K., and the other half said Valderrama. But the players who said stay in Britain also said that, if we did have to go to Europe, then it should be Valderrama. One vote went to a place called Nova Sancti Petri. That was Seve's course, and he alone voted for it.

When the committee decided, I'm told, we got all six votes. In May they announced Valderrama had the Ryder Cup. Three years had gone by.

COLIN SNAPE: Political expediency came into it. There wasn't a decent venue in the whole of Spain, to be frank. Valderrama was never a good venue for access and so on, but the Madrid venues weren't much better. If you had to go to Spain, there would never have been a venue that had all the facilities that were required. But again, with Seve being captain and Seve winning and the King of Spain there, it's easy to forget shortcomings, isn't it?

BRAD FAXON: I went over on the team plane, the chartered Concorde, which was very neat. On the Sunday night before we left, we met President Clinton at the Waldorf Astoria Hotel in New York. He came to a dinner to talk to the team. I was very impressed. Physically he was good-looking; he was tall, he had a beautiful suit on, he was great at eye-to-eye contact. He knew exactly who every player was. He was very personable.

JIMMY PATINO: The opening ceremonies were fantastic. The weather was beautiful. The King and Queen of Spain were there. Prince Andrew was there. George and Barbara Bush were there—they're friends of mine and stayed at my house. Prince Andrew also stayed at my house. I moved out and went to bunk up at the golf course.

BRAD FAXON: It was just great to be over there. Valderrama is a beautiful place, but there are some strange holes. It was a course that certainly took a little bit of getting used to, things like trees in the middle of the fairways.

The course was as well-conditioned a course as we could play, but I thought the seventeenth and eighteenth holes were very tricked up. The seventeenth was similar to the par-5 fifteenth at Augusta National, in that anything hit short and landing on the front of the green would spin off and hit the water. Then they had redesigned the back of the green so it had, like, a ditch where, if you hit it over, your pitch back was very hard. The rough crossed the fairway where it made the long hitters have to hit 3-wood off the tee. So you couldn't go at the green as easily if you hit a good drive.

JIMMY PATINO: Seve designed the seventeenth hole. Trent Jones rebuilt the course with me, but we never did the seventeenth hole. He would come every two months and stay with me, and he and I would work on the course. In 1991 he said, "Jimmy, I can't come to Europe anymore because of my health." He said, "Here's a sketch. Do that." I asked, "Who do I give this to?" I thought he was going to say one of his sons, Rees or Trent Jones Jr. He said, "Give it to Seve."

So I went to Seve at the British Open at Muirfield in 1992 and asked Seve if he would design the seventeenth hole, and I gave him a copy of the sketch. He said, "I can't do this course. This is Trent Jones's course." But when I told him that Trent Jones had told me to ask him, Seve said, "Okay, I'll do it."

It wasn't until I got the Ryder Cup in 1994 that he decided to come to Valderrama. He saw the existing hole and said he wanted to change it. "The Americans can drive it too far," he said. He put the rough across the middle of the fairway.

Trent Jones came to the 1999 Ryder Cup in a wheelchair. One day he told me, "Jimmy, we have to go out to 17 and change it." I got him in a vehicle and we went down to 17. He told me move the tee a little bit, change the placing of the bunkers, change the slope around the back of the green. A few things that have made the hole a lot better. Trent Jones had a wonderful eye.

TOM LEHMAN: The Americans lost partly because of a lack of course knowledge. When it came to the golf course I felt like we were behind the eight-ball. Valderrama is a real "local knowledge" kind of course, and the European Tour played there every year for the Volvo Masters. There's a huge advantage, but the home team should have the advantage. It's like any other sport. If you're playing on my court or on my ballfield, I should have the advantage.

A lot of us really didn't read the greens very well. The course has mountains on one side and the ocean on the other. As much as it may not look like it, everything seems to break toward the ocean. I'm not sure we adjusted very well to that.

And it was a smart move by Seve to switch the format [he managed to have the four-balls in the morning and the foursomes in the afternoon when traditionally they're the other way round]. The Europeans have generally been stronger in best-ball than in alternate-shot. So you want to get off to a good start.

JIMMY PATINO: Valderrama was nearly washed away with all the rain that we had; but the Ryder Cup would never have been completed if it had been played on any course other than Valderrama.

It never rains in Spain in September, but it rained four inches in two hours on both Friday morning and Saturday morning. But the course drains beautifully, and we had a hundred people working on the golf course. We never had to play lift, clean, and replace. We never had to get the squeegees out, although we were just about to use them when it rained throughout Sunday afternoon and the course was getting saturated. I was afraid that we wouldn't be able to finish on Sunday, but we did, which was just as well because it rained even more on Monday.

BRAD FAXON: It was a tough time personally for me. In July I found out that I was getting divorced. Colin Montgomerie brought that up [at Valderrama]. I think Colin would admit that sometimes he says some stuff without thinking. He made some comments about some of the players on the team, like "Jeff Maggert—what's he ever won?" and "Faxon can't drive it in the freeway, plus he's going through a divorce, so how can he play?" Well, I read it in the paper, and I just took it with a grain of salt. That's Colin; that's the press. I wasn't too upset about it.

JIMMY ROBERTS: Monty made some comments about how maybe the divorce was why Brad was playing so poorly. But you don't have to be his best friend to understand that Brad's a good guy. And it wasn't like Brad was being unfaithful; Brad's wife left him for somebody else. All of us just felt for Brad so much. Put that together with the fact that Monty had never been the type of guy who had been very generous with the press, and I think it made him an unpopular character. I remember at the time thinking, That's not a good idea for him to say that, *not* a good idea. A lot of the American players were really pissed off about it.

I actually had a major disagreement with Monty's father over him. I was waiting for Monty near the clubhouse. As he was going in I said something like, "Colin, Jimmy Roberts from ESPN. Do you have a moment to answer a question?" And he said, "Not now. Talk to you later, talk to you later," then went into the clubhouse. His father was trailing along and said something about how "He doesn't want to have anything to do with your sort." I went right back after him. I don't remember specifically what I said to him, but I wasn't taking any of his guff. I told him that his son was at times a miserable human being and he could do with being a little bit more honest and a little bit less contemptuous of people that he didn't know. We went back and forth for quite some time.

BRAD FAXON: But [the pending divorce] *had* affected my play. Starting in mid-August at the PGA, I hadn't played well for a while. Tom Kite, our captain, was great about it. We'd been good friends for a long time, and he tried to cheer me up and just keep me positive.

In the morning four-balls, Tom Lehman played with Jim Furyk against Jesper Parnevik and Per-Ulrik Johansson, an exciting encounter marred only by the fact that Seve Ballesteros told Johansson that he wouldn't be playing in the afternoon—and informed him during play.

TOM LEHMAN: That was a good match, Jim's first match, and he was nervous. He didn't play very well at the beginning but played much better on the back nine. The two Euro guys really ham-and-egged it. Johansson would go birdie, birdie, double, double, but Jesper would go double, double, birdie, birdie. It was a great team. When you play well and you lose, especially when it comes down to 18, you can feel good about it even though you lose. Those guys did a little better.

Faxon, meanwhile, was paired with Fred Couples against the formidable pairing of a young, strong Lee Westwood and the veteran Nick Faldo.

BRAD FAXON: The last hole was big. We were 1 up. Freddie kind of drove it out of play to the left, so he didn't really have a shot at the green. Faldo and I drove it close to each other. I hit first, into a bunker left of the green. The pin was left. Faldo hit a beautiful iron shot to about seven feet, pin high right. I hit a pretty good shot out of the bunker, ending up right next to his coin, probably so close that I had to move my coin away. Westwood made par, so

Faldo's putt for birdie was to win the hole and half a point. If he missed and I made mine, we'd halve the hole and win the match.

Faldo had Fanny [Sunesson] caddying for him at the time, and she was standing behind his putt to see if he was aiming properly. I was trying to stand as close as I could without imposing on him, just to watch the line, see what the putt did. And I had pretty much read it as straight. Well, as he was getting ready to putt, she said, "You still aim to the left. You still aim to the left." And he stood away from the putt. He looked like his rhythm was thrown off. So he went back through the whole deal. She said, "That's good," and he pushed it wide. Now I had a lot of things going through my mind because I hadn't played particularly well that day. I'd made a couple of great par-saving putts, but I don't think I'd made any birdies. And I thought about 1995 at Oak Hill, the eighteenth hole, where I'd missed a big putt to halve a match. I thought, I can do something here to redeem myself.

I knew it was going in before I hit it, and it was a great feeling when I did hit it because I hit it dead square, right in the middle. When it went in, Fred gave me a big Freddie hug, and, to tell you the truth, I was in tears.

On the second day, Lehman paired in the morning four-balls with Phil Mickelson against Ignacio Garrido—the nephew of Antonio Garrido, who played for Europe in 1979—and Olazábal.

TOM LEHMAN: We were all-square going into seventeen Phil drove it in the right rough off the tee, then hit a 2-iron out of the rough over water to the front-right pin, which is the toughest on the green. He nearly hit it in the hole!

In My Greatest Shot *(by Ron Cherney and Michael Arkush, HarperResource, 2004), Mickelson cited this approach. "I had 247 to the front of the green, 249 to the hole," he wrote. "That's a green that slopes severely from back to front. Hit the approach long and you're in a back bunker with almost no way to stop a shot in front of the green. Short, and you're down the bank and into water. Even if you lay up, it can be hard to hold the green with a sand wedge*

*and it was getting late in this key match. I had an uphill lie in the
first cut of rough and hit a 2-iron straight up in the air. As luck
would have it, it was right at the hole, carried 248 and ended up
seven feet above the hole for eagle."*

TOM LEHMAN: It looked like it was advantage us, especially after
José Maria hit it in the water. Obviously Garrido's not going near
the water, so he knocked it into a bunker, ten yards over the green.

Now he had a bunker shot which had to land on the fringe,
barely trickle over a plateau, and roll down to the hole—*and* stay
out of the water. Guys had been chipping it and putting it into the
water all day long, because it's a virtually impossible shot. Garrido's shot landed just on the fringe, just trickled onto the green, just
barely got over the plateau to the slope, rolled past the hole, broke
to the right and somehow stopped on the fringe before it went in
the water, about fifteen feet away. Then he made it for birdie! It was
the most incredible up-and-down I have ever seen. *Ever*. Then Phil
had an eight-footer for an eagle to win the hole, but he missed it.
So we tied the hole.

On 18, they both drove it way left. Phil and I were in the left
rough. Phil missed the green. I hit a pretty good shot about thirty
to forty feet from the hole. They both were on in three, but no better than thirty feet. Phil chipped up and would make a five. I putted
up about four feet short. Garrido missed, and José Maria made his
putt for par. Now I had to make a four-footer just to halve—which
I made but it looked like we were going to win both the last two
holes, and we ended up halving. It really was a great match.

PETER OOSTERHUIS: I covered Valderrama on Friday for USA Net-
work in America and then Saturday and Sunday for [satellite network]
Sky Sports. The match I remember most was Nick Faldo and Lee
Westwood against Scott Hoch and Jeff Maggert in the foursomes on
Saturday afternoon. On the seventh green, the balls were much the
same distance apart. The referee had kind of gone up and casually
just said, "It's European ball." Hoch marched up, had a look for himself, and said, "I don't think that's correct. I'd like you to remeasure."

So he got a few jeers for that. Then the referee was pacing off the putts and the crowd was counting, "One . . . two . . . three!" as the guy was walking. And the American ball *was* away. Hoch had been right. But now the tone of the match had changed. It seemed Scott Hoch was just needling everybody. Anyway, it was rained out, and they finished the next morning. Hoch and Maggert won [2 and 1].

BRAD FAXON: One day I almost didn't make it to the course. I was picked up at our hotel by a driver who was to take me to the course. They'd built these back roads for us to drive on because they didn't want us on the main roads for traffic reasons. My driver was Spanish, and couldn't speak much English, and I couldn't speak any Spanish. And he got lost. I'm like, "This is a set-up." And it didn't take us that long, but it took us twenty-five minutes to get there instead of ten. I remember driving through these dirt roads, thinking, "I may never get to the Ryder Cup."

Whether it was course knowledge or the conditions or simply superior play, Europe opened up a five-point lead by the end of the four-balls and foursomes. Not even Tiger Woods, making his Ryder Cup debut, could make things happen. Of the four matches he played before the singles, he won one and halved another. And worse was to come.

JIMMY PATINO: On Saturday evening I was hosting a dinner for about two hundred people in the clubhouse. Everyone was there: the PGA European Tour, the PGA Tour, the United States Golf Association, the Royal & Ancient Golf Club; and George Bush was the guest of honor. I was waiting to welcome him when Tom Kite came over and asked, "Jimmy, I'd like George Bush to speak to our players. Would you mind if I ask him when he comes in?"

George came up the steps right on time. I said, "Tom Kite would like to have a quick word with you." Kite asked him if he would nip over and say a few words. George said to me, "Jimmy do you mind?" I said, "Of course not. People are drinking. They can drink for another fifteen minutes."

BRAD FAXON: Kite opened the door and there was President

Bush. You thought, Oh, there's President Bush. I don't know if he'd come over specifically for the Ryder Cup. But he came in and gave a little "Win one for the Gipper" sort of speech.

That was followed by a videotape made by Dallas-based film producer Mickey Holden.

MICKEY HOLDEN: In 1995 I did a videotape for the PGA of America in which all of the living Ryder Cup captains were interviewed. We turned that into a fifteen-minute tape that was shown at Oak Hill in 1995, and the players loved it because it helped drive home the history and the tradition of what it was that made this event special. Tom was planning to show that tape again to the players on Saturday night at Valderrama and I thought, Okay, what else can we do? And we came up with the idea of doing a highlight tape on his team, the best shots and the best moments that each guy had had in his career as a way, again, to remind his team how good they were.

The title of the tape was from a Tina Turner song, "Simply the Best." And it almost ties in, too, with Ben Hogan's famous introduction of his team when he was captain at Champions in 1967: "Ladies and gentlemen, the best golfers in the world." I think that was part of Tom's thinking.

It was very important to Tom that players be shuffled throughout the tape. It's not like he would start at A and go to W. Or that you would go best player down to number twelve. He just wanted to drive home the idea of a team, so he'd have a shot of Tiger followed by a shot of Phil followed by a shot of Freddie Couples and, again, remind his players of how good they were. Tom wanted to put his own stamp on things, improve what had been done before and advance it.

TOM LEHMAN: We were five points back going into the singles, and had to win nearly every match. One of the things that worked against us in the overall course of the matches was the delay caused by the big rainstorm on the first day. After that it was non-stop golf. You played, you kept on playing, it got dark and then you kept on playing, kept on playing. There was never a chance to regroup, perhaps in the middle of the day between the foursomes and the four-balls. For the team that had the momentum it was easy to keep it going, but for the team that didn't, it was hard to turn it around. Not having a chance to regroup really hurt us. It's like in a basketball game when you have one team dominating. At half-time the other team gets a break, comes back out, and they just roar back to life and turn it around. Well, we never had that half-time.

RENTON LAIDLAW: But there were some great games. Costantino Rocca beating Tiger Woods was a terrific scalp for Rocca [Rocca won 4 and 2 and later said it was the best he'd ever played]. And Fred Couples just annihilated Ian Woosnam [8 and 7].

PETER OOSTERHUIS: I had fun the final day following Rocca and Woods. Tiger obviously wasn't firing on all cylinders, and Rocca was playing solidly and making the putts he needed. But the course didn't suit Tiger because it took away his advantage of power. He had to lay up on a lot of holes and on the holes where he could hit it a long way you had to be particularly straight. He just wasn't in tune.

They finished on the sixteenth green, so I just cut from there a hundred yards over to the 11th fairway and joined up with Colin Montgomerie and Scott Hoch. Montgomerie kind of glanced over at me and gave me a raise of the eyebrow. He was taking deep breaths like he knew his match was becoming more and more significant. And then he just ground it out.

BRAD FAXON: I was 3 down to Bernhard Langer after eight, and when I looked at the scoreboard all I thought was, Oh my gosh. And then I had a stretch where I won three out of four holes and pulled the match to even going to 13. The thirteenth hole is a quirky, downhill, dogleg-right, with trees encroaching to the point that, if you hit it just a little in the rough, you could really be blocked out. I was so pumped up off the tee I hit a 3-wood. I'd hit it in the other two rounds perfectly, but I hit this one so hard it went through the fairway and I was blocked out and ended up making a bogey. I went back to 1 down, which is tough after having won three holes in a row.

I don't know if Bernhard birdied another hole, but I was 2 down going to sixteenth when Tiger showed up to cheer me on. I thought it was cool that Tiger had come out. I had to lay up on 17 and so did Langer. He was in the right rough and I thought I had a big advantage. I thought that from the right rough he'd have a tough time getting it on the green. But he drew a good line, hit a good shot. I hit a pretty good third shot, just inside him. He putted first and missed. I had this twelve-footer to keep the match alive. And I remember missing it, just on the left side. And it turned out to be the clinching point for the tie. That was the match that did it. [Europe won by a single point, 14½–13½.]

TOM LEHMAN: I played Garrido and won 7 and 6. I think I was last man out and first to finish, or close to it. I played about as well as I could play, and Ignacio didn't play his best.

JIMMY PATINO: Seve was driving about the golf course like a madman. Like a madman!. He was everywhere. He was telling his players how to play, and they didn't like it. In a practice round he took a club out of Thomas Björn's hand—this was Björn's first Ryder Cup—and gave him a different club!

JIMMY ROBERTS: Kite took way too much heat for losing at Valderrama. All you heard about was Seve dashing here and dashing there in his cart. You know what? Seve didn't make any birdies. I'm sure he did a lot to encourage people. For example, in Olazábal's singles match, he'd driven it left on 18, and Seve pulled up and cheered him on, but way too much was made of that. Seve got too much credit. Too many people desperately wanted some kind of resonant story. I thought it was nonsense.

RENTON LAIDLAW: Seve was not the ideal captain, because he wanted to do everything himself. He went over to one player and said, "'I want to suggest so–and–so," and the player said, "Listen, do you mind just going away? I'm fully aware of the situation. I know what I have to do. I'm trying to win the point. Let me win it."

PETER OOSTERHUIS: In the four-balls on the second day, Darren Clarke was with Colin Montgomerie. Darren was in the rough and Colin was in a perfect position on the fairway. Seve was rushing around trying to tell them the sequence of shots they should hit. Darren was away, but he wanted Monty to hit first, and then Darren could take a chance on his recovery shot. But both of them were like, "Get out of the way; we can handle it." So, as people said at the time, you didn't know whether Europe won because of Seve or in spite of Seve.

RENTON LAIDLAW: But Seve wanted to be everywhere. He was described by one journalist as "the frantic conductor of the orchestra." You know how you see some of these conductors standing the podium going absolutely crazy? And, of course, he wasn't going to be content with a draw. He didn't want to draw the match and keep the Cup. He wanted to win the match and *keep* the Cup.

JIMMY PATINO: Seve not only wanted to win; he *had* to win.

JIMMY ROBERTS: When it was all over, I had an odd meeting with former President Bush. Two years earlier, I was preparing a story about the history of presidential golf for our coverage of the 1997 U.S. Open, which was to be at Congressional Country Club, just outside Washingon, D.C., and I wanted to interview the former president. The guy who was my kind of mentor in the industry, a guy by the name of Dorrance Smith, had worked in the Gerald Ford White House, was friendly with the Bush family, and eventually worked for President Bush. I wrote the president a letter that was channeled through Dorrance, asking if we could come interview him. He invited me to come to Kennebunkport, in Maine, and play golf with him.

We flew up, stayed overnight at a bed-and-breakfast, and the next day the president, myself, the club professional there, Ken Raynor, and Mark Plummer [an amateur of note from Maine who lost to Tiger Woods in the semifinals of the 1995 U.S. Amateur] played a course called Cape Arundel. We had a great, great day.

Now it was Sunday at Valderrama, and the matches were over.

The clubhouse at Valderrama sits at the top of a hill, and I'd left all my gear in an area way down below, far away from the clubhouse, so I didn't have my rain suit or an umbrella or anything with me. When I was up at the clubhouse it started pouring, and if I'd gone to get my umbrella I would have been absolutely soaked through by the time I reached it. Instead I found a big plastic garbage bag and poked a hole in the top for my head and two more for my arms. I was walking around looking like a vagrant.

Then I saw the president, surrounded not only by other dignitaries but a covey of security as well. I wanted to go over and say hello. He wasn't the sitting president, so the security arrangements were a little different, and I was able to get close to him. It was really pouring hard and he passed by without noticing me, so I shouted out, "Mr. President!" and he turned around. I stuck my hand out and said, "Mr. President—Hi! How are you? Jimmy Roberts from ESPN. We played golf together up in Kennebunkport." Now, my head was soaked from all the rain, so my hair was all matted down, and I was absolutely soaking wet, I'd just introduced myself to the former president of the United States while wearing a large garbage bag. I would have been a prime candidate to be hustled away, but he looked at me just for a second and then he completely remembered our game, who we played with. Everything. But I did catch a glimpse of one of the security guys with the oddest look on his face. He was like, "Are you *kidding* me?"

NO, *THIS* WAS THE COMEBACK

*G*ood lord, what a way to end the century. Never in the entire history of the Ryder Cup had the U.S. been underdogs. Even though it took losing to Europe to finally put the contest on even terms, to make the Ryder Cup into a must-see, the U.S. always came into the Cup as the stronger, deeper team. Even when Europe won impressively in 1985, that was the first U.S. loss in almost thirty years. Even when it lost at Valderrama in 1997, it came in with Tiger Woods making his debut—and how could you bet against that? But on a Saturday evening in 1999, at The Country Club in Brookline, Massachusetts, a suburb of Boston, the U.S. players' fortunes had never sunk lower. They were down and out, 10–6 down with twelve singles remaining, the Europeans playing with a bubbling intensity that seemed invincible. The U.S. was as dead as the Ryder Cup itself had been twenty years earlier. But rather than capitulate, the U.S. responded with one of the craziest, most controversial and exhilarating days in the annals of the game, if not all sport.

And to think that it all began quite innocently. . . .

BEN CRENSHAW [U.S. captain in 1999]: Jim Awtrey, the PGA of America president, was in Texas on other business and asked me meet him. I thought I was one of four or so people he would talk to before making any decision on the captaincy, but at the end of our meeting he told me the PGA wanted me to captain the Ryder Cup team in 1999. I was surprised. One of the first people I called was Curtis Strange, because The Country Club means so much to him—he won the U.S. Open there in 1988—and he had to have been in the picture. I told him they'd offered me the job because I was older and he was very gracious. He said, "Well, they can't have two captains."

The Country Club meant a lot to me. I'd gone there to play the U.S. Junior in 1968. I also knew about it because I learned from the first golf book my dad bought me about how the young American Francis Ouimet had beaten [British greats] Harry Vardon and Ted Ray there in the U.S. Open in 1913. It also was my first exposure to eastern golf courses, which were very, very different from what I'd been playing in Texas. I loved the place. I also played quite well there in the 1988 U.S. Open, I think finishing twelfth.

Crenshaw then chose as his support team Bruce Lietzke, Bill Rogers, and the late Bruce Edwards—best known as Tom Watson's caddie when he won the 1982 U.S. Open he died of Lou Gehrig's disease in April 2004—and Crenshaw's own caddie, Linn Strickler.

BEN CRENSHAW: We're all close friends. Bruce had caddied for Tom Watson and Greg Norman, and I'd known him for a long time. He was awfully good at reading players, seeing who was on or who was not, and spotting many different things. If any of the players hadn't seen Bill play, they at least had seen his name—on The Open Championship trophy [which he won at Royal St. George's in 1981]. But they enjoyed being around him an awful lot.

BRUCE LIETZKE: The day after Ben was asked to be captain, he called and asked me if I'd like to be an assistant. He called Bill Rogers right after me. I waited a day to accept, because it was truly going to be at least a one-week responsibility, and I wanted to check with my family first. Golf had gone down on my priority list since 1983, when my first child was born and my family became my top priority.

I also wanted to find out what my duties would be. My only stipulation was that I would not have to be involved in all the nightly social dinners. That was the captain's job. I just wanted to help Ben, mainly as an extra set of eyes, tell him who's winning a match, who's playing well. I told Ben, "As long as I can finish my day on the golf course and quietly go back to my hotel and prepare for the next day, I'll accept." He said, "That's the way it is planned. You won't be part of the official party." I said, "Okay, sign me up."

Ben and I go back a long way. The first time we played against each other was in junior high. He lived in Austin, Texas, and I lived in Beaumont. We played lots of state high school and junior tournaments against each other. Then he went to the University of Texas, and I went to the University of Houston. We played match after match. He even was in my wedding party.

BEN CRENSHAW: Before the Cup, Bruce, Bill, and I got together and went bass fishing. We just sat all day talking about things like which pairs would work together. How about this? How about that?

BRUCE LIETZKE: Bill lives in San Antonio, Ben's in Austin, I'm in Dallas, so we met at least three times in San Antonio, which is kind of central. Bill had a member at his club who had a hundred-acre lake about an hour southwest of San Antonio, so we'd get together on a boat and would fish and talk strategy.

Ben knew by heart who the top ten point guys were as he was starting to formulate some ideas about captain's choices. Eventually the picks became Steve Pate and Tom Lehman.

TOM LEHMAN: I had been out for three or four months of the previous year with a separated shoulder [suffered while showing his children how to do a handstand!]. I had surgery and missed the first few months of 1999, but once I came back I played well and got up to eleventh on the points list, so he selected me.

BRUCE LIETZKE: Tom and Steve's ages had a lot to do with it, as we already had a pretty young team. Lengthwise, with Tiger and [David] Duval and Mickelson we had a lot of strength. We had two very experienced players in Mark O'Meara and Payne Stewart, but it had been a while since Payne had been on a team [1991]. So I think Ben wanted more of the leadership, the guidance, that a very tough player like Lehman would bring. And Steve Pate is a tremendously popular player. He proved to be the one guy that Tiger Woods was comfortable with and won a point with. We threw Tiger and David Duval together, the number one and two players in the world, and they lost. So they were looking for chemistry, and Steve kind of provided it, while playing a lot of good golf on his own.

One time when we were on the lake, Crenshaw's cell phone went off. He talked for about twenty, thirty minutes, hung up, and said, "Bruce, I have some disappointing news for you." He said that the European captain Mark James had insisted that his assistant captains Ken Brown and Sam Torrance be part of the official party. They would be invited to every function, they would have the full wardrobe, pants, golf bag, and the whole deal, and the PGA had agreed. So now I was going to every party with the team. It made the days extraordinarily long, but my wife loved it, and really it became an honor to do it.

Payne Stewart brought something to the team that no other player could have. A few months before the Ryder Cup, Crenshaw and I were at Firestone Country Club in Akron [during a World Golf Championships event] and were greeting some of the other players, when Payne walked up to our table.

BEN CRENSHAW: Payne told me he had thought of something that could really help us, and I said, "Okay, what is it?" and he said, "A Ping-Pong table."

BRUCE LIETZKE: He looked Ben straight in the eye and said, "I don't know anything about this suite where the players will have food and stuff like that, but at the end of the day, a Ping-Pong table will be a great way for guys to relax and enjoy themselves or blow off some steam." And Ben made a mental note.

BEN CRENSHAW: Payne was right. It was a great idea. One of the hardest things to do in the Ryder Cup is play your own game. There is just so much else going on that it's difficult even to *find* your own game, so the ability to relax and have some fun really helped us.

BRUCE LIETZKE: There are emotions that have to be vented, because the Ryder Cup has become such a huge event. A Ping-Pong table or something like that seemed to make sense.

I also remember that every night Payne wore a pair of pajama pants that had hot chili peppers on them. He didn't wear them to any of the formal functions, but there were nights when I would put a nice shirt on for dinner in our suite, and Payne always had his chili pepper pants on. Even though he was very intense on the golf course, he was very, very relaxed. And he was the one player in that group that could make fun of a guy. Maybe somebody had lost both his points that day—Payne still might have a little jab for them. Nobody else could get away with those kind of things.

All was not rosey, however. The issue of payments for players, previously unheard of, blew up into a controversy, with such players as Mark O'Meara maintaining that the players deserved a piece of the income. In the end the PGA of America agreed to donate to charities chosen by each player, but the players were hammered in the media as spoiled rich kids just getting greedier.

DAVID FEHERTY: They were made to feel like they weren't worthy of being there and that they were greedy and money-grabbing. And it was such a crock of shit. You know, the PGA of America runs its entire operation on the profits that it makes because of the generosity of those players providing their services for free. And when they ask for—what, 5 percent—the proper answer to that question should be, "Certainly. Where would you like me to send the check?" There is *no* argument. They just want to have some power over a little portion of that money to direct toward causes that they feel are worthwhile. It should never, never have been an argument.

BEN CRENSHAW: I knew the subject of payments had been discussed and was there. But no, I did not think players should be paid for playing in the Ryder Cup.

LARRY NELSON: I think the players should be paid *a lot*. Yeah, it is an honor but sometimes that honor is not the way it used to be. You have guys making $7 million, $8 million a year. The Ryder Cup they play for free and then are made to sound greedy when they ask for some sort of compensation. It used to cost us to play in the Ryder Cup. But times change. It was not as commercialized as it is now. So yeah, I think guys should be compensated.

BILLY CASPER: When I played we got a very small fee, $2,000 or $3,000 to cover expenses. It was never an issue because there was never any money made on the Ryder Cup. But you know, they had that pro shop at Brookline, and I don't know how many thousand people went through the first part of the week. Jeepers creepers! The money that they make off the Ryder Cup is unbelievable now. When you have sixty-odd or seventy corporate tents out there, they're making a lot of money. And I really feel that they should have made some kind of arrangement before it ever started. This shouldn't have gotten blown way out of proportion as it did. It should have been handled in-house, taken care of between the players and the PGA.

One supporter of payment for play was Duval, who also likened the Ryder Cup to an "exhibition."

DAVID FEHERTY: David Duval asked over and over and over again why there's such an obsession with what's basically an exhibition match. And I was thinking, After he's played in one he will understand.

Then I saw him in his first match. He holed a putt and punched the air and I thought, There you go. *Now* you understand. When was the last time you punched the air after a seven—and before the tournament was even over?

But that's what the Ryder Cup is about. It makes you feel the best you've ever felt on the golf course, and it makes you feel the worst.

BEN CRENSHAW: We [Crenshaw and his wife Julie] received an invitation to go to former President Bush's place in Kennebunkport before the Ryder Cup and went up there for a couple of days. John Major, who'd been prime minister of Britain, was there. President Bush just sort of said, "Ben, I'd like you to meet John Major, the ex–prime minister of Great Britain." Jimmy Patino also was there.

Although the organization of the U.S. effort had been delegated to Crenshaw, much of the actual on-site organization of the event went to a young man from Connecticut named Dan Baker.

DAN BAKER [tournament director at the Country Club]: I ran the Walker Cup at Quaker Ridge [in Westchester County, outside New York City] in 1997, and a guy called Mike Gilligan was the tournament director for the PGA Championship, which was played at Winged Foot the following week. Winged Foot was literally across the road, so we would talk all the time about vendors and such and we became friends. About six weeks before the Walker Cup we were playing golf together when he asked, "What are you doing after the Walker Cup?" I said, "I don't know, I need to get some other gigs." And he said, "I might have something for you. We're going to need a tournament director in Boston for the Ryder Cup."

I'd never been to a Ryder Cup, but I wasn't nervous as I've been running events for years. When I was ten, I started caddying at a little club in Connecticut—Freddie Couples's caddie Joe LaCava caddied with me—and by the time I was fourteen I was running the bag room. By the time I was seventeen I was managing the golf shop and when I'd go to various golf events, I'd always find myself thinking, Hmm, that sign should be over there, or this should go there.

In some ways the Walker Cup is similar to the Ryder Cup. It's a three-day event, and the Ryder Cup is a three-day event. It's on a much smaller scale than the Ryder Cup, but you still have to create a transportation system, you have to feed people, you have to provide them services, whether it be bleachers or bathrooms or whatever. You have to have security; you have to have marshals.

When I got there the hospitality tents were pretty much sold. Our main concerns, being an event six miles from downtown Boston, were transportation, parking, and shuttles, and not sales or marketing—the Ryder Cup kind of sells itself. We spent a lot of time with the town of Brookline, the city of Boston, and neighborhood associations.

When the week began, I'd get to the Country Club at four-thirty each morning and get home at midnight. On the Wednesday night I was waiting at the club for [Eagles guitarist] Glenn Frey, who was going to do a one-hour show before the opening ceremonies on Thursday. He was late, so he didn't get there until about nine-thirty. We still had to do a sound-check, and so we didn't get that done until ten-thirty, and I realized I hadn't had any dinner. Now, we had this massive catering compound, but it was all shut down. Trucks were unloading bread, lettuce, ice, you name it, everything for the next day, and I thought this was kind of funny: Here I was, tournament director of the Ryder Cup, there's all this food right here, and I'm *starving*—and I can't even get a turkey sandwich!

There was this little pub right across the street from the house I'd been staying in, so I called and confirmed that they did takeout, then ordered a hamburger and some chicken wings. At eleven-thirty at night I walked into this pub and ran into some friends. They're like, "What are you *doing* here? Aren't you in the middle of running the biggest golf tournament on earth?" And I said, "I just came to get something to eat!" Like this was business as usual.

BRUCE LIETZKE: Going in, the mood of the squad was wonderful. The team had a great mixture of veterans and younger players and was a mesh of wonderful personalities. And only one or two guys appeared to be struggling with their games.

There were huge, huge crowds, even during the practice rounds, twenty thousand people sitting around the practice tee. The fans were very vocal, and the players really struggled with their focus during practice rounds. But nobody knew the golf course, and Ben thought it was important to get those practice rounds in.

CHI CHI RODRIGUEZ: I watched a practice round at The Country Club. The Europeans were so nice when they came out, relaxed and signing autographs for the kids. Our guys looked like zombies, like robots. Guys that had given their brains to a psychologist. The only friendly one was Mark O'Meara. To me a golfer or any athlete that turns down a kid for an autograph, I don't care for them.

SAM TORRANCE [assistant to Europe's captain Mark James]: We did so much work that week on the gallery, as we always do. You're there for four days before the matches begin, so the galleries see a lot of you. The players would go over into the crowd, get their pictures taken, smile, laugh, get them on our side. And at The Country Club, it was unbelievable. They really were on our side. And then on Sunday the whole thing changed.

BRUCE LIETZKE: Once play began, usually I stayed with the first match out or sometimes the first two, and then Bill Rogers would come behind me. I had a walkie-talkie to keep Ben informed. Most of the time he stayed near the clubhouse, as he had deadlines to meet, doing interviews, filling out lineup cards. When it got closer to the pairing deadline, he was very interested in who was playing well.

TOM LEHMAN [who paired with Tiger Woods against Jesper Parnevik and Sergio Garcia]: I hit the first drive, Tiger missed the green, and I chipped in. And that was the highlight of the day. After that it was drive in the fairway, hit it on the green thirty feet from the hole and two-putt. Sergio and Jesper played decently, but it was one of those matches where I don't feel like we put our best foot forward. Rather than them beating us, we kind of beat ourselves. We lost 2 and 1.

BRUCE LIETZKE: At the end of the first day, we were not discouraged but just truly perplexed that we were behind [6–2, having lost the foursomes 2½–1½ and the four-balls 3½–½]. I had seen some great golf, from Colin Montgomerie as well as Hal Sutton, who was probably the best player we had. I think Colin Montgomerie was the best player on the golf course between both teams. He truly was magical in a really tough situation.

Having dispatched Lehman and Woods in the morning, the odd couple of Parnevik and Garcia took care of Phil Mickelson and Jim Furyk in the afternoon. This was the star pairing for Europe, although their tendency to leap and jump around animatedly when they won a hole began to work up the galleries.

BRUCE LIETZKE: We fully expected to make up a lot of ground on Saturday. We were very disappointed to be behind on Friday, so we changed a lot of the pairings, and we played some good golf. Hal Sutton and Jeff Maggert came through in their matches, and we just kept sending Hal back out. He was truly worn out by the end—he played all five matches.

I watched Payne play with Justin Leonard on Saturday morning. They were losing and Payne was not playing well, and eventually Crenshaw called on the radio and asked, "How are your two guys playing?" I told him that Payne was not having a good day and that, unless Ben had a hunch, he probably should leave Payne out in the afternoon. They ended up losing on the fifteenth or sixteenth hole [3 and 2 loss to Parnevik-Garcia], and Payne walked over to me—I was going to give him a ride back to the clubhouse—and put his face right next to mine. He had tears in his eyes and said, "I don't deserve to play this afternoon." And it had to have just torn his heart out because he had been so motivated to make that team. He had won the U.S. Open that year, but he had said early in the year that his motivation had been that he had not played on a Ryder Cup team in years. I'll never forget looking at his teary eyes as he said something he did not want to have to say. But he knew it was best for the team.

MIKE HICKS: I don't think Ben Crenshaw did a whole lot of homework, because Payne was like 150th in total driving [a combination of driving distance and driving accuracy statistical rankings] going into Brookline, but he was third or fourth in birdies per round. The way I looked at it, he wouldn't be a good foursomes player, because he's going to hit some foul balls, but he would have been a great fourball player, playing his own ball. Now, earlier in his career, in the late '80s and early '90s, Payne was as good as anybody. When he was driving with a wooden club, he could shape the shot right to left, left to right. But a metal driver is designed to go straight, and he had problems with that.

So we played both foursomes matches—which was not good. With Davis Love against Miguel Angel Jiménez and Padraig Harrington, we halved. With Justin Leonard against Sergio Garcia and Jesper Parnevik, we lost. I just can't believe that Ben didn't see that.

At the end of the second day, with the United States down 10–6, Crenshaw addressed the media. He looked battered and bedraggled, exactly like a captain who had watched his players first be slammed by the media as greedy and then be mugged in their own backyard by a European team that didn't even have the benefit of Ballesteros. His players couldn't have felt much better. "The mood was dejection," Bill Rogers said in a thrilling reconstruction of the final day that appeared in Golf Digest. *And on NBC, analyst Johnny Miller even suggested that the best thing Justin Leonard could do for his team on Sunday was to stay home. The air was ugly.*

BRUCE LIETZKE: Bill Rogers and I were in the locker room, which is just off of the pressroom, and were watching the press conference live on a big screen television. All the players had headed back to the hotel; only a couple of caddies were in there with us. Ben was very tired, under a tremendous amount of pressure, and he started rambling. Bill and I kind of made a comment to each other that we needed to save Ben by getting him off the stage. But really he saved himself.

We were going to walk in and start wrapping things up, because we did have a big night of things to do. Before we could work our way back to where the media was, Ben collected himself, because I think he realized he was rambling. And that's when he started wagging his finger.

BEN CRENSHAW: I looked at everyone and pointed my finger and said, "I'm going to leave you with one thought. I'm a big believer in fate. I have a good feeling about this. That's all I'm going to tell you."

BRUCE LIETZKE: If it had been anybody else in the world of golf, I would have written it off as just a pep-talk for his team. But I've known Ben for a long time, and he has a passion for golf and a sense of history of golf that I've never felt. He truly had a feeling, and I believed him. When he wagged his finger at me I felt like he was pointing it right at me, and when he said, "I have a good feeling about this," I believed him. And I don't think I would have believed anybody else.

MIKE HICKS: Typical Ben, you know. But I don't really think it inspired anybody. Realistically you know there's always a chance. But you also know that with a 10–6 deficit in the Ryder Cup, you pretty much are done. I'll be honest: I thought it was over. And so did everybody else.

That Saturday night we were all inside the locker room, determining the order in which we would go out. Obviously we [caddies] didn't voice our opinions, but we were there listening as they did it right there in kind of a bar area. It was pretty unbelievable, really. Crenshaw was sitting down, and it was like everybody else was standing around him. Ben was asking opinions from the players, where they wanted to play, who they thought should go first.

BRUCE LIETZKE: We had Lehman near the end, but Ben said, "Lehman has put in a request to be the first man out." Bill and I said, "We have no problem with that."

TOM LEHMAN: To put me out first was one of the great compliments of my golf career. Ben said to me, "You're a strong man, I know you can get the job done for us." But we all felt we had a chance. We're four points down; we can still win. We can win eight out of twelve singles matches; we can do this.

But there was some debate about how to go about the pairings, and Ben and Lietzke and Rogers had an original line-up, which had Tiger, for example, at the end. The guys got together and said, "Ben, if we're going to have any chance to win, start out as strongly as we can. With this line-up, there's a good chance that Tiger's match won't even matter. We want to make sure that our best player contributes. They had some more conversation and loaded the front end.

MIKE HICKS: We needed to win the first five or six matches or it was over, so the guys who were playing the best were to go out first. Although there was a little concern about Hal playing early because he had played every match and needed some rest, they all pretty much agreed on the first five or six guys, and Ben just kind of filled it in from there.

BRUCE LIETZKE: We wanted those first matches to be going our way because, for one thing, that gets us closer to even. But it also is great inspiration for the guys in the later tee times who are practicing and seeing the board with American numbers up there.

MIKE HICKS: Payne was out tenth. He didn't really say anything about it. He went wherever Ben put him. And I don't think he had a problem playing that late. But other than that—I mean, Payne didn't say a word. He just went where he was put. That's kind of how he was.

And he was taking everything in and making mental notes on how he would or would not do things, because he was going to be captain here, maybe after Curtis [Strange].

There then followed an extraordinary evening. Once the pairings came out—pairings that only encouraged the U.S. players—they looked at a videotape. By now this had become something of a tradition, and usually the plan was to inspire the players—footage of great shots, rousing music, the works.

MICKEY HOLDEN [who produced the videotape]: Ben and his wife, Julie, had been actively involved in putting the tapes together. Ben had an idea to for a video that would use the Queen song "We Are the Champions." It opened with a shot of the Ryder Cup, accompanied by the first few riffs of the song, then five minutes of European celebration, just to remind the team what was at stake. And it ended with a graphic that said: "Memo to Europe: The party's over."

Ben showed that one on Thursday. On Friday night he showed

a sort of general highlights video, very similar to what Tom Kite had done at Valderrama. These videos are very common in team sports, but in golf it's very unusual. Every college football team in America has this kind of stuff, but pro golfers don't. And the players I think not only enjoy watching their own shots but they enjoy watching the other guys' shots, too, because when they're out on the golf course they don't see what their peers are doing.

Saturday night's video would be very, very different.

MICKEY HOLDEN: Over the course of the preceding six months, Julie had surreptitiously contacted every guy's wife or girlfriend to find out what his favorite music was, who his sports heroes were, which people he looked up to, and we got most of the people to appear on tape and say things specifically to the players. We told them, "Look, this is a big secret, but we want you to say a few words to the Ryder Cup team, and in particular to this particular player." Like the guy who said to Jim Furyk, "Jim, I know you're a big Pittsburgh Steelers fan; I want you to go out and win this for the country."

It was a terrific program. It opened up with that famous clip from *Patton* where George C. Scott talks about what it means to fight for your country. It had John Belushi's speech from *Animal House*. Bill Murray in *Caddyshack*. And while he's telling the Cinderella story, we cut to highlights of Mark O'Meara winning the Masters. We had the Dallas Cowboy cheerleaders singing a song to Justin Leonard. We had lots of cheerleaders actually. We had the Centenary College cheerleaders for Hal Sutton. For Steve Pate, we had the UCLA song girls do a dance and a cheer. Payne Stewart had the SMU cheerleaders. Phil Mickelson, Arizona State; David Duval, Georgia Tech. Tom Lehman had his pastor, and the guy was hilariously funny. You never would have guessed he was a pastor.

TOM LEHMAN: In addition to being a pastor, he's a professional musician and my best friend. He did a little song and dance thing, then a spoof of *Deliverance* where he was out there in the swamp, and he's like, "Come on, boys, I want you to go kick some Euro tail. If you don't kick some Euro tail, I'm going to do that *Deliverance* thing." [Lehman mimics banjo music.]

MICKEY HOLDEN: For Davis Love, we had Mike Mills from the band REM and Huey Lewis. We had several music ones, in fact. Can't remember what Mark O'Meara's bit was. Tiger's hero was his dad, so he was on there. And the musician Keith Sweat.

Who else was on there . . . the actor Matthew McConaughey. The older President Bush. Coach Mack Brown, football coach at the University of Texas. Dan Marino. Randy Johnson of the Arizona Diamondbacks. Cordell Stewart of the Pittsburgh Steelers. Jay Leno. Pamela Anderson Lee. She said, "Just go get 'em." Nothing terribly memorable. We didn't even know if she liked golf, but it was the reaction of the guys we wanted because it was so out of left field.

Not only was it inspirational to have all these major figures in American life reminding these guys that the people were behind them and the country cared, but there was a lot of humor mixed into it. And when the Cowboys cheerleaders were singing, "We love you, Justin," to Conrad Birdie's "We Love You, Birdie," it was just great fun.

A video is the kind of vehicle that can break down barriers, allow the guys to get to know each other better. Did they know Jim Furyk was a big Steelers fan? They all knew Tom Lehman was very religious, but did they know his pastor was a total cut-up? When the Centenary cheerleaders were saying, "Hal, Hal, he's our man, if he can't do it, nobody can," Ashley Sutton [his wife] was saying, "Hal? Who *are* those girls? Do you *know* those girls?" A video like that gives them something to chuckle over and a way to see each other in a new light.

Another nice touch: The team had played pretty well on Saturday and got nothing for it, so I went over to the NBC truck and cut in highlights from that day into the movie. We were a little late getting it there because of it, but I think that that made a big difference as well to remind these guys that, despite what was showing up on the scoreboard, the team was playing very, very well.

BRUCE LIETZKE: Then we had a dinner planned. The players had already eaten, but this was when the players and wives would sit and just talk about what was on their minds. But before that happened, Governor George W. Bush [soon to be U.S. president] came into the room.

According to an article in T&L Golf by Harry Hurt, Crenshaw had approached Bush a few weeks earlier to ask him to speak. "What speech do you want me to deliver?" Bush had replied. "My economics speech or my foreign policy speech?"

"What about reading the letter Colonel William Barret Travis wrote from the Alamo?" Crenshaw had replied. "We could be in a tight spot."

That speech in full:

> *Fellow citizens & compatriots, I am besieged, by a thousand or more of the Mexicans under Santa Anna. I have sustained a continual bombardment & cannonade for 24 hours & have not lost a man. The enemy has demanded a surrender at discretion, otherwise, the garrison are to be put to the sword, if the fort is taken. I have answered the demand with a cannon shot, & our flag still waves proudly from the walls. I shall never surrender or retreat. Then, I call on you in the name of Liberty, of patriotism & every thing dear to the American character, to come to our aid, with all dispatch. The enemy is receiving reinforcements daily & will no doubt increase to three or four thousand in four or five days. If this call is neglected, I am determined to sustain myself as long as possible & die like a soldier who never forgets what is due to his own honor & that of his country.*
>
> *VICTORY OR DEATH.*

BRUCE LIETZKE: Not that the Ryder Cup has a place in world history alongside the Alamo, but the speech had some chilling words in it. And you just couldn't help but feel like we felt fairly surrounded even in our home country and that the European team seemed fresher than we were. It was a great speech, and just as quickly as he came in, he wished us luck and walked out. I was terribly impressed with it and I know all the players were. Of course, American players are pretty famously Republican, so Bush was in friendly surroundings anyway. But the players were very impressed.

Then the players and their wives each had something to say. Players were trying to relieve themselves of pressure. The message was, "I am playing as hard as I can. I believe in you; I want you to believe in me." There was nothing like, "I was really trying to make that putt on 16 today, I don't want you all to think . . ." It was players really pouring their hearts out. Almost to a man they talked about what Ben Crenshaw meant as their captain—and that meant an awful lot to me. In the 1981 Ryder Cup at Walton Heath, I had really wanted to win for our captain Dave Marr; I had truly grown to love him. And on Sunday afternoon, once the champagne was flowing, the players said, "We did this for Ben Crenshaw." That was great.

And the wives had great things to say. Robin Love had words from [legendary golf instructor] Harvey Penick. She said, "Davis and Ben and Tom Kite all had one great teacher, and he lived by three words. These are words that you guys can live by tomorrow: 'Take dead aim.'" That was very emotional. It was just players and wives truly speaking from the heart.

Tiger was a very quiet member of the team. He spoke when he wanted to, but he left it to the veteran players and to the captain to make choices. Actually, it probably would have shocked me to see Tiger get up and give a big rah-rah speech. And I think in the long run that helped the team because we certainly didn't want to think—we didn't want the weight of the team to be on Tiger's hands even though he's the number one player in the world.

Instead he let guys like Payne carry the leadership. Tom Lehman also had that, and by the end of the week, Hal Sutton carried the torch. Early in the week I don't know that I would have put Hal as kind of a spiritual leader. Payne for sure. Lehman for sure. By Sunday, Hal Sutton was a spiritual leader.

MICKEY HOLDEN: Hal Sutton later said, "I really opened up and became friends with these guys. I've never allowed them to get that close to me before. And I really regret that." But that's really what happens that week: These phenomenally deep friendships are formed.

When the pairings came up, European captain Mark James had done an extraordinary thing. After starting with two of his horses, Lee Westwood and Darren Clarke, he followed with Jarmo Sandelin, Jean Van de Velde, and Andrew Coltart, and none of this trio had hit a shot in an actual match. Which meant if the U.S. could handle the first two matches—and Westwood and Clarke are Clydesdales, not show ponies, which could suffer in the heat and the pace of the third hectic day—the U.S. could forseeably win the first five singles.

BRUCE LIETZKE: Mark played into our hands just a little bit by putting Van de Velde, Sandelin, and Coltart back to back after they'd been left completely out of the foursomes and four-balls Friday and Saturday. That was a critical mistake. We expected him to kind of hide them or put one out early, one in the middle, one in the back. As it turned out, Coltart had not played a shot, and he was playing Tiger Woods! On Saturday night, we saw pairings of Tiger Woods and Andrew Coltart, and said, "That's a point." We saw Davis Love against Van de Velde. "That's another." Phil Mickelson against Sandelin, I believe. "That's a point." All of a sudden, on Saturday night, we were even.

TOM LEHMAN: Then when we saw the pairings we all felt that it absolutely could not have gone any better for us. Hal [who was out second] and I both felt that if our team had any chance to win at all, we had to win our matches, *period*. Because the next three players hadn't played. I don't mean any disrespect. They're all very, very good players, but they hadn't played. Then we would be ahead on points, and follow that up with David Duval playing Jesper. We felt that if things went just a little bit right, we could win the first six points.

BRUCE LIETZKE: And as it turned out, we won the first seven!

The U.S. might have won none at all had this been a best-dressed contest. Although the vast amount of golfers are not known for their sartorial splendor—can someone say Aureus, mid- 1980s?—the Crenshaw-designed shirts for the final day quickly became legendary: black-and-white photographs of previous U.S. Ryder Cup teams (winning teams) on a burgundy background.

BEN CRENSHAW: The idea for the shirts began back in 1995, when I won the Masters wearing a shirt that bore a lot of images of Bobby Jones. Julie and I thought we could come up with something similar. We got some photographs together of some previous winning U.S. Ryder Cup teams and asked a shirt company if it was possible to put them on shirts. They said, "Sure." When we showed them to the players, there were some raised eyebrows. But most of them just said, "Yup, that'll work." But, of course, they weren't meant to be a fashion statement. They were a symbol.

BRUCE LIETZKE: The shirts really weren't an issue, because there were so many more important things. We saw them, and there were a few chuckles, and I'm sure Payne had something to say about it.

TOM LEHMAN: I know the shirts weren't real popular, but the psychology behind them was really good.

BRUCE LIETZKE: On Sunday morning, there were twelve groups going off now so I, Bill Rogers, Bruce Edwards, and Linn Strickler hopped in carts. I was off with the first three pairs. We were carrying towels, rain gear, umbrellas, and things like that, but the main thing was that we had to have walkies-talkies out there. Ben wanted to know how these matches stood even before the scoreboards were showing them. He wanted to know almost shot-for-shot how things were going.

I was right there when Darren Clarke chipped in on the first hole against Hal Sutton. Hal walked right past me and said, "I lost the first hole yesterday to a chip-in and won. Doesn't bother me a bit." He was truly incredible.

In the early groups I was with, the crowds were very vocal, especially when the Americans starting to make a move on the leaderboard.

TOM LEHMAN: You had to have seen the scoreboard. It was all red. And not just red but *big* red. It was 1 up, 2 up, 3 up, 4 up in every match. All red. Duval was 4 up, 5 up, 6 up. Davis was 5 up, 6 up. It was a whuppin'.

MIKE HICKS: When Payne and I got on the range, we could see that every U.S. player was leading, and now you're going, well, there is a chance after all. The first two days had taken so much out of Darren Clarke and Lee Westwood. Same with Garcia and Parnevik. The only chance Mark James had was to play those guys every match, hope he could get a big lead, and hope they hung on. Sunday showed how exhausted those guys really were. But they had played phenomenal golf for two days.

BRUCE LIETZKE: On the golf course you could tell American roars, you could tell European roars, just by the sound, the decibels. It was incredible. And once we had our first four or five groups winning and more groups were starting to tee off, it started becoming really loud.

DAN BAKER: I don't know exactly how many spectators there were, but it was probably thirty thousand. At the 1988 Open here, they had thirty thousand, maybe slightly over. The problem—or the difference—is that, in the Ryder Cup, they follow four groups at a time, twelve on Sunday, while in an Open people are teeing off all day long. So it was more of a challenge for the spectators, and that's why we came up with seven JumboTron TV screens positioned around the course. We had one on the practice range with four thousand bleacher seats so people could watch the teams warm up and a couple of thousand people just would sit there from time to time and just watch the matches on the JumboTron. And you could get headsets that had a BBC radio broadcast that was specific to the JumboTron television broadcast, or you could switch to a channel that had the NBC television broadcasters on. You could listen to what [announcers] Dick Enberg and Johnny Miller and those guys were saying. I wasn't out spectating much, but it seemed like a pretty good atmosphere, and every day we got positive feedback about crowd control and all that. The first I heard of any problems was Sunday.

Bruce Lietzke: The crowds didn't start getting really boisterous until the afternoon guys started teeing off—and, of course, the beer had been flowing since mid-morning. And then around one or two o'clock in the afternoon, it got pretty bad.

Mike Hicks: It was a tough day for Monty. He played wonderfully, but the crowds were just relentless on him. I mean, *relentless*. Payne did everything in his power to keep the crowd under control, but there was verbal abuse, profanity, things an avid golf fan would never think about saying. Monty really admired Payne for speaking up. The old Payne Stewart, back in, say, 1989, '90, '91, would have felt like that was an advantage to him, and wouldn't have said a word. That's how much he had changed over the years. But he didn't want an edge. If he beat Monty, he wanted it to be with his golf.

Dan Baker: I saw what happened to Colin Montgomerie on television. Somebody said something about him, and Payne Stewart had pointed the heckler out to the security. The incident wasn't anything that I needed to worry about because we had people that worked with that. He [the heckler] definitely was removed from the area and probably would have been then removed from the golf course if he continued. But I don't know where he ended up. To my knowledge, there were no arrests made.

But the crowds were pretty good. We didn't really have any complaints. You get a couple of people who were maybe a little intoxicated or a little rowdy, but you get that at every event, and you're talking about a handful of people. At a golf tournament, where almost every spectator is very reverential and respectful of the players, four or five loud and obnoxious people in a gallery of ten thousand would stand out like a sore thumb. I mean, if some guy in the fifty-second row at Giants Stadium [at an NFL game] is yelling, you can't even hear him, but at a golf event, it's dead quiet, so everybody can hear them. The thing is, there's a difference between being loud and being disrespectful, and I think the people that crossed the line were disrespectful.

MIKE HICKS: The behavior at Brookline was out of hand. There was too much alcohol, and too many people there to begin with. When the Ryder Cup is played in Europe, there the fans pull just as hard. In '93 at the Belfry I really started to hear the cheering when you missed a putt or you hit one in the water. That's really when I started to realize that this was serious stuff—and not necessarily good. But over here it seems more of an us-against-them type of atmosphere. More of a football mentality, which I don't think is good at all.

At the Country Club, you had football people who really didn't know about golf. They'd just heard about the Ryder Cup, thinking, "Man, I want to go to that." And they were all liquored up.

DAVID FEHERTY: Everyone in Boston is fuckin' pissed off. They're digging a hole in the middle of that city that looks like every Irishman ever came here is trying to dig his way home. Takes you forty-five minutes to go anywhere. And the people in Boston are a little forward at times, you know? So they're a little forward, we've got twenty thousand too many of them, and half of them are drunk. What do you expect?

JIMMY PATINO: But the Europeans started it. Mark James should have put a stop to it on the first day. Parnevik was playing with Sergio Garcia, who is a very enthusiastic little boy. Parnevik sank a putt, and Garcia ran across the green and jumped in his arms. I said, "For God's sake, what is this? This is not a bullfight." I was appalled. Mark James should have told Sergio immediately, "Congratulate your partner, pat him on the back, but don't jump in his arms and don't run around the greens. This is a game of golf." For two days the European players were jumping around because they were winning, and thirty thousand American fans had to keep their mouths shut and look on in dismay.

DAN BAKER: A private security firm handled security but, in terms of the galleries, it was really the marshals, and they came from different clubs. Each hole was marshaled by a different club in the area.

RENTON LAIDLAW: The stewards [marshals] have to look after the crowds, but while fans were shouting at the top of Colin Montgomerie's backswing, the stewards were doing nothing about it. Instead of watching the crowds, they were watching the golf. And encouraging the Americans as well.

SAM TORRANCE: Jarmo Sandelin was walking on the second green in his match against Phil Mickelson when he put his hand in his pocket to get his ball mark and found he had a hole in his pocket and all his markers were gone. He really didn't have a marker. Of course, the crowd all believe that he's hanging about, waiting for Mickelson to give him a putt, and they started booing him. He had to go and borrow a coin from someone, and he got so much shit from the crowd for this.

As the day went on, it seemed that the early optimism would not be enough. While the U.S. won seven of the first eight matches, Europe needed only three points to retain the Cup and both Paul Lawrie and José Maria Olazábal were in good shape—Lawrie 4 up through nine holes against Jeff Maggert, and Olazábal 4 up through eleven against Justin Leonard.

BRUCE LIETZKE: When Lehman finished his match [he beat Westwood 3 and 2] he fell back and watched the others—none of the players wanted to go back to the clubhouse. And when Davis won his match, on the thirteenth hole, he looked at the board and saw Justin was down at the time. He got on my radio and called Ben Crenshaw and said, "Ben, let me go out and be with Justin. I can help him." I gave Davis a ride back out to 10 tee box, Justin had just had lost 9 and was in the process of losing 10 to go 4 down. As soon as Davis got out of the cart, he walked up to him and said something like, "If you want me to leave I will, or else I'll stay with you." Justin looked very teary-eyed himself, very distraught. And he said, "Stay with me." And he ended up winning us the Cup. That was pretty emotional.

Meanwhile, when Mickelson was finished [he beat Sandelin 4 and 3], he went to watch Pater [Steve Pate] play. And Tiger [who beat Coltart 3 and 2] went to watch O'Meara play. And that's the spirit. That's what the Ryder Cup is all about. Guys had won their individual matches and could have been patting themselves on the back, but they were concerned about the other players.

When Woods caught up with O'Meara, he was witness to the stalling tactics of the European team.

JIMMY ROBERTS: On Sunday afternoon I was with a group of American players on the fifteenth hole, a par-4. Several matches were over, and the players had come back to pick up the Mark O'Meara–Padraig Harrington match. I think it was all square at the time.

Both players had hit safely from the tee. Harrington was away. But after getting to his ball and checking his yardages, he walked slowly all the way up the green to check the green and the pin position or whatever, then walked slowly all the way back. I had never seen anything like it before. We've come to understand how deliberate a player Harrington is, and I do believe he wanted to inspect the condition of something on the green to see how it would affect his play. I won't name any names, but many of the American players who were following the match were quietly but visibly apopleptic. I think they questioned Harrington's motives. They were amazed that anybody would do this. They believed it was gamesmanship and inappropriate.

Two matches back of that came Leonard versus Olazábal. But no one was prepared for what happened next.

Tom Lehman: Ben had been saying all week that the history of the Country Club showed that the seventeenth hole always was good to American players; it was always a big hole. The seventeenth hole is where it always seemed to turn.

Ben Crenshaw: The seventeenth was the hole Francis Ouimet birdied to get into a playoff with Harry Vardon and Ted Ray for the 1913 U.S. Open, then birdied again in the playoff. And Ouimet lived not far from the seventeenth green.

Bruce Lietzke: At that time O'Meara was on 17 playing Padraig Harrington, and it appeared that this match could be the winning point, so that was kind of where the group started assembling, wives and caddies and players and everything.

O'Meara made a great putt on 17, but just for a par to tie. If he'd won seventeenth, his point would have been the winning point. But he tied, so all he had to do was tie 18. Most of us went to watch O'Meara play the last hole. But he lost the last hole, so everybody on 18 dropped right back to 17, and that's when Justin was in the middle of the fairway.

José María hit first, kind of a heavy shot that ended up on the front part of the green. Justin hit a really good shot that flew up to the top of the green, near the pin, then spun even farther back than José's putt. That was pretty discouraging.

We were looking at the board, and Crenshaw had done the math. We needed half a point from either O'Meara, Leonard, or Payne Stewart. O'Meara lost his match, so then it came down to Justin and Payne Stewart, who was in the group behind Justin with Colin Montgomerie.

Neither Justin nor Olazábal had a makeable putt, so I was already formulating, "If they both two-putt, they will go to 18, tied. But if Justin wins 17, which we didn't really think about, that would put him 1 up and the worst he could do was a tie and that half point was going to be all we needed." So we're thinking, Well, Justin's just going to have to tie.

Crenshaw had said he knew about Francis Ouimet having

holed a big putt on 17 to win the 1913 U.S. Open, but he's the only one that knows about all this weird history. None of us realistically thought this putt was going to go in. And that's why, you know, it caught everybody off guard as Justin came running toward the back of the green when the putt went in.

MIKE HICKS: Payne and I were standing in the left rough back down the seventeenth, when Justin made the putt. I said, "It's over." Payne said, "What do you mean, Jack, it's over?" I said, "He's guaranteed half a point. That gives us the Cup." Payne looks up. He says, "Yeah, that's right, isn't it?" I'm thinking to myself, "Praise the Lord, man, because I'm glad it ain't coming down on me."

DAN BAKER: When the putt went in, I was preparing for them to finish and get the Closing Ceremonies ready. So I was actually looking at the eighteenth hole, not the seventeenth, and the amazing thing was, the putt went in and you heard the roar from the crowd on seventeenth, but there was a tape delay on the video broadcast on the JumboTron on the eighteenth, maybe two or three seconds. I heard the actual roar, then a roar of people telling their friends what happened, then a roar from the people wearing the radio headsets, then another roar when we saw it on the JumboTron. You heard three or four different roars. It was like this multiple wave.

TOM LEHMAN: We were thinking, you know, he makes this putt, we get that last half point, we win. Obviously, our thinking was misguided, because José Maria still had a putt to tie. But because the way the last four or five holes had gone, with Justin winning so many and José Maria losing, we felt that, if Justin made it, there was no way José Maria was going to make that putt to tie. So when Justin's putt went in, we went dancing across the green, and the rest is, unfortunately, history.

BRUCE LIETZKE: It was just kind of a natural reaction from some of the players. Some of the players and a couple of caddies got up and slapped high-fives. I stood there and clapped, and then I started to go toward Justin, but then I looked over and I saw José Maria and he was getting ready to put his ball down. I thought, He hasn't putted yet. I was truly lost in the moment, too. It just caught everybody off guard.

The "dancing across the green" also turned out to be the most controversial incident in Ryder Cup history.

HALE IRWIN: Spontaneity is one thing, but professionalism is another. Our players had been pushed to the limit of their patience with the slow pace of play by the Europeans. The Ryder Cup should be a competitive experience among professionals, and you certainly have pride in what you're doing, but let's not let behavior get in the way of etiquette.

TOM LEHMAN: If it was an intentional breach of etiquette, gamesmanship, that's one thing. If I accidentally step in your line, is it a breach of etiquette? Well, yeah, it is, but it wasn't intentional, and the motivation wasn't to hurt you or to cause you a problem. It was an accident, and accidents sometimes happen. It was in the heat of the moment, it was something that I and a lot of guys felt bad about. I sent José Maria a letter and apologized. You know, if we could do everything over, I would hope that we could have stayed put. But if you have ever played team sports, you would understand what happened there.

DOW FINSTERWALD: I certainly understand how it happened. I just wish it hadn't. With all the emotion and being so far behind, and for them to come back so marvelously, I understand how their emotions could take over and in that short period of time, but even as short as it was, I still wish it hadn't happened.

DAN BAKER: NBC played some tapes for me later, all the different angles, and I didn't see anybody run in José Maria's line. But I talked to him about it. I saw him at Pebble Beach the next year. It seemed to me like he had long forgotten about it. Put it out of his mind.

TONY JACKLIN: Nobody would have been running on the green if Mark James had done his singles pairings properly. I looked at the pairings with Peter Oosterhuis and I said, "Shit, if these first two guys get beaten, they've given all of the game away." Of course, it happened exactly like that. If James had gone in there with Mont-gomerie and Parnevik and the strength from the off, they'd have blasted them out of the water.

PETER OOSTERHUIS: I was in the studio, and, to be honest, I thought the match had been decided. It was an easy mistake to make, but it wasn't quite over. The reaction was over the top, but bearing in mind everything else that had gone on, maybe it was excusable.

JIMMY PATINO: It was terrible. Terrible! Ben Crenshaw should have said, "Give Olazábal the putt for a half. Go to the next hole." They probably would have lynched Gentle Ben if he had done that, but you can't expect Olazábal to putt in an atmosphere like that.

PETER JACOBSEN: It's not in the spirit of the game. I was embar-rassed and dumbfounded as to why a teammate or a wife or a caddy or an official would feel they needed to run out there and hug Justin. It wasn't over. But I really give Olazábal a lot of credit. He just stood there and looked at them and waited for them to fin-ish. If it had been Seve, he would have been over there swinging and biting somebody's ear off. We would have seen Mike Tyson before Mike Tyson.

DAVID FEHERTY: When you step back and look with hindsight at what happened, it was an understandable reaction. This was a group of players that had been lambasted in the press. They had been villified.

MICKEY HOLDEN: They'd been beaten up so badly, for the loss at Oak Hill, the loss at Valderrama. Then they got beat up coming into the Country Club for the pay-for-play issue. They got beat up as wussy prima donnas for falling behind 6–2. And then they were gutless cowards for being behind 10–6. And they knew they were getting hammered. They knew Johnny Miller was saying, "I've got a hunch Justin should watch this on TV." I mean they *knew* it. And they really had a feeling of "us against the world"—but we'll show 'em. And a lot of that came out in a spontaneous celebration at the seventeenth.

DAVID FEHERTY: This was an "Up yours!" to all those people that had given them such a hard time, that said they didn't like each other, that they weren't a team. Well, that sure as hell looked like a team to me.

BRUCE LIETZKE: If Justin's putt had not gone in, and even if Justin had lost his match on 18, I'm convinced that Payne Stewart would have done the job. Remember that he conceded his match to Colin Montgomerie because it didn't mean anything. But he would have won his match. He would have done whatever it had taken. Colin was the best player on the ground for that week, but I'm convinced now that Payne would have either won 17 or 18.

I actually left my cart out on 17. I called the club pro later that night and I said, "You know, I forgot, I left my cart out there." And he said, "We found it, and your rain jacket—I had some personal items in there—we got everything." But there were so many people there that the golf cart just couldn't go anyplace.

MIKE HICKS: We were the last match coming in, and it was a three-ring circus on 18. People everywhere. At that point it really didn't matter. I'm not going to say it was one of my fondest memories of the Ryder Cup, but it was quite a scene. It was fun.

TOM LEHMAN: People were sprinting down the 18th fairway toward the green. There's no way you're going to get through the crowd once they got there, so we all ran with them so we could make sure we could be ready to celebrate when the match was over.

MIKE HICKS: On the final putt, Payne looked at me and said, "I'm going to give it to him." I said, "Yeah, give it to him; it's over. What does it matter?" And so he walked over and picked up Monty's coin and said, "That's it." Which I thought was a great gesture.

DAVID FEHERTY: That was just Payne. He has a long history of doing the right thing at the Ryder Cup.

PETER JACOBSEN: I loved when Payne gave Colin Montgomerie his putt on the last hole. He was done. And that just showed you the kind of person that Payne was. If Payne had been thinking about his own personal Ryder Cup record, he would have made him putt it. But he gave it to him, and I think that gave Colin the match [it did, 1 up]. There were ugly things, like what happened on the seventeenth hole, but many good things come out as well.

RENTON LAIDLAW: What happened at Brookline has drawn attention away from the wonderful golf that was played by the Americans in the final day. They came out with all guns firing, and it's just a pity that the crowds, the stewards, some of the players got carried away.

Strangely enough it's the kind of thing that happens in Boston. Way back in 1913 when Francis Ouimet, Ted Ray, and Harry Vardon played off for the U.S. Open and the young boy Ouimet beat the two stars of the day, the crowd scenes were so bad in terms of shouting and hysteria that the *New York Times* wrote something along the lines that unless something's done about crowd behavior, golf will be ruined!

TOM LEHMAN: But it was the most emotionally charged experience I've ever been a part of. I grew up playing team sports, and the only comparison I can think of is when your team is down at half time by 30 in basketball and you make a comeback, and make a buzzer-beater to win. The crowd pours onto the court and you tear down the nets. That's the feeling.

DAVID FEHERTY: Our judgment is clouded, naturally enough, by the fact that we Europeans lost, but that was one of the most remarkable afternoons in sport that I have ever seen. That tension built up and up and it looked like it might happen, looked like it might happen, but, you know, it could *never* happen. But it did. It was incredible.

BRUCE LIETZKE: Afterward, the team didn't quite make it to the clubhouse; they were on a balcony above the locker room spraying champagne over everyone. Tom Lehman took his shirt off and threw it to the crowd. It was on eBay the next day.

TOM LEHMAN: I was standing below this balcony, and said to the head pro, Brendan Walsh, "Brendan, how do we get up there?" He said, "Follow me!" So we all just followed him upstairs, to where they stored all their goods for the pro shop, all the extra shirts and extra golf balls, and we started pushing our way through boxes and all kinds of stuff to get to the window. And suddenly there we were, out on this balcony. It was the perfect place to celebrate.

DAN BAKER: At that time I was making sure the trophy was ready for the closing ceremonies, and then suddenly the U.S. players were up on the balcony above the locker room celebrating. And they were spraying champagne and all that. I got on the radio with the club's operations manager and asked him, "Can that porch hold their weight?" Because they climbed out of this window and there were, like, eight or nine people on this tiny little porch. Tiger was up there and I think Lehman and maybe Duval and a couple of caddies. We were worried because nobody had ever really stepped out on that porch in probably twenty years. And I thought, Oh, gosh, if that thing collapses . . . So I really couldn't enjoy the celebration, thinking, That thing could fall down. But it was fine.

I remember I sat down on the steps that led to the U.S. locker room. Norman Fletcher, the assistant executive director of the British PGA sat down next to me. I guess I looked a bit dejected because he said, "Why do you look so sad? You just won the Ryder Cup." Now, people would always ask me if I rooted for the U.S. and I'd always say, "I just want it to be close. I want it to be exciting for the fans and all of the volunteers and people who put so much time and effort into it. I want it to come down to the final putt and whoever wins, so be it, but I want it to be close and exciting. And that's what it was. But as I told Sandy as we were sitting there, I'd just realized that two years of my life were over—and I didn't know what to do next.

But I had really fond memories. On the Saturday three of us were in my office, watching on television. We were all a little exhausted and were taking a breather. The fourteenth green was right behind our office, and I remember thinking, We're sitting here in the office and the biggest golf tournament in the world's going on right outside the door. Let's go enjoy it for an hour. So we went out and stood up on this hill and watched the people go through. And then we walked up to 15 and just listened to people. Everybody was talking about what a great time they were having. Everybody was so positive and happy and having a good time. But, as I said, it was a weird feeling when it was over. I was sitting there thinking, I don't know what to do next. [Baker soon became tournament director of the PGA Tour's Greater Hartford Open.]

Then I had to sort of regroup and get the closing ceremonies set up. I got through this and then saw that Ben Crenshaw was leaving. He'd lost his dad shortly before the Ryder Cup, maybe that year sometime, and I think that had a big impact on him. I think my dad's the greatest person on earth, so as we both prepared for the Ryder Cup we talked about our dads a lot. He gave me a big hug and told me I should be really proud of what a great job I did. And I said to him, "You know, the proudest guys are our dads."

Then he and the U.S. team left, and I decided to walk down to the club's front gate, where we had all these crews picking up all the fencing and bike racks that were out in the streets. I wanted to make sure they knew what they were loading it all into. On my way down, I saw this guy who looked like he was stealing a television from the media center. I went up to him and asked, "Where are you going?" He said, "Oh, it's all right, I work here." I said, "You don't work here." And with that he started running across the fifteenth hole!

Behind me were two supervisors from our security company. I called to them. "Hey, can you tell the gate to stop this guy?" One of them said, "Sure" and the other hopped in a golf cart, and said, "Let's get him." So we took off.

Now, it was dark out, and the other security guys started yelling at us, but we didn't hear them because we were in a noisy, gas-powered cart. Next thing I knew I was waking up in our security compound at the front gate, and all these people were around me. I also was sitting in the passenger seat of the cart and I thought, I was driving; how did I get here? I looked around me and somebody was holding my head and our security director, who was a good friend, was looking at me, saying, "Dan, everything's all right; the ambulance is on its way." I looked down and saw that my white shirt was red with blood. I looked back at him and he said, "It's okay, head wounds bleed a lot. You're fine." I still wasn't sure what had happened.

It turned out we'd hit the gallery rope on the fifteenth hole with the front of the cart, pulled the rope taut, and a gallery stake, which now was behind us, came out of the ground and hit me right in the back of the head, splitting my head open. It could have killed me. In fact, our vice chairman of operations at the club called later and said, "I'm so glad to hear you're all right. Two years ago at a charity event here in Boston a guy got hit like you did, but the stake went right through his head and killed him." That shook me up a little bit.

Anyway, the ambulance came and they started working on me as they took me to hospital. I think they let me go at about three or four in the morning. So that was my Ryder Cup victory celebration.

BRUCE LIETZKE: After the closing ceremonies, we went into the locker room, and there was a lot of celebrating and hugging and drinking going on. Then Crenshaw sent the team back because they were ready to do some serious partying and the golf course wasn't the place to do it. But they all did interviews first.

We had a huge party that night. I got back to my room at about eleven-thirty P.M. and cleaned up a little. I hadn't eaten, so I went into the suite with the players—but they were already through eating and had obviously started drinking long before we got there. They were partying and dancing and Payne Stewart had his chili pepper pants on already! I ate a bite of food and hung around for about half an hour, just kind of walked around to the individual players and told everybody how proud we were of them.

They were passing tequila around. The last time I saw David Duval that night, he had several jiggers of tequila sitting in front of him and about four empties that he had already turned over. I had to get up early the next morning, and so did Bill, so we didn't participate much. I drank a little tequila, had a little wine, and left the room about twelve-thirty A.M. The party was still going strong.

The only player I saw the next morning was Payne. He was eating breakfast and trying to recuperate, but he clearly was in pain. And he still had his chili pepper pants on!

And that's the last time I ever saw Payne Stewart, so that's how I'll always remember him. In his chili pepper pants.

$$\boxed{\textbf{EVEN YEARS}}$$

The 1999 Ryder Cup changed everything. If the 1991 Ryder Cup had seen partisanship taken to extremes, the 1999 version had gone warp speed beyond that. Not for the first time had players bared their emotions at the moment of victory, but for the first time the players had acted like fans and, whether or not you condoned the behavior of the U.S. players when Leonard holed that winning putt, it was clear that this was conduct courting disaster. Maintaining the spirit of the competition in 2001, while at the same time enouraging support and controlling the atmosphere, would be top of the agenda for captains Curtis Strange and Sam Torrance.

CURTIS STRANGE: But the day the announcement was made that I was the 2001 U.S. Ryder Cup captain was probably the toughest day I've ever had as a professional, because that was the day Payne Stewart died [a private jet in which Stewart was riding lost cabin pressure, and eventually ran out of fuel and crashed in South Dakota]. The captaincy announcement was held in the morning in PGA headquarters in Palm Beach Gardens, and afterward PGA president Jim Awtrey said, "We might have a problem here." I'm thinking, What have I done already? But then he told us what had happened. We stayed another day for meetings, but it was tough to focus. Everybody knew Payne was going to be Ryder Cup captain one day.

MIKE HICKS: It hadn't been confirmed that Payne would be made captain after Curtis, but it was pretty much a done deal. His vice captains were going to be Sutton and Azinger. He would have been a wonderful captain, because he was a team kind of guy, and that would have rubbed off on the guys who aren't used to team matches or team concepts. Ben was a great captain just because he's a wonderful person. But he didn't have authority. He doesn't have that personality. He was always asking for other people's opinions.

CURTIS STRANGE: You can take on as much as you want or you can let the PGA do as much as you want them to do. My wife, Sarah, and I decided that we wanted to enjoy this two-year stint— at the time it was going to be two years—to the max. But I wasn't going to let it run my life like it seemed to take over Crenshaw's.

I talked to just about every previous captain, and most said the same thing: Go with your instincts. You've been there. Enjoy it. One person I spoke to had statistics and percentages, like your chance of losing in the singles if you play three matches or four matches, all this stuff. He said, "I still have it if you want me to fax it to you." I said, "Don't waste my fax paper." He was making my head scramble.

I had a list of specific things that I wanted to get done. From day one I started writing down anything that popped into my head. One was to reinstate the Sunday night cocktail party after the matches. Sam [Torrance] agreed completely. When I played, it was a stuffy, sit-down, coat-and-tie dinner. I actually enjoyed it, but the losers don't want to be there forever. Nor do the winners. They want to relax and have a couple of beers in their team room. So this would be very short, very sweet. Come for thirty minutes, have a beer, that kind of thing.

And when we eventually did it, everybody showed and thoroughly enjoyed it. Some stayed for thirty minutes, some for two hours. Jesper Parnevik also invited us up to their team room Sunday night. He'd hired some Swedish comedians—and they were *sick.* [Parnevik's father, Bo, was Sweden's most famous comedian, based partly on his wicked imitations of Ronald Reagan and Lieutenant Columbo!] I went with my two boys, Tom and David. Hal Sutton went; David Duval went. But when you get down to it, that's what the Ryder Cup is. Win, lose, or draw, I always had a great week.

For the second time in history the Ryder Cup was postponed (remember the hiatus during World War II). The reason? It was scheduled for September 28–30, 2001, and the terrorist atrocities in New York, Washington, D.C., and rural Pennsylvania earlier that month changed more than just the golf world completely.

CURTIS STRANGE: I was in Colorado Springs, Colorado, doing an outing at the Broadmoor for Hewlett-Packard, and was supposed to fly that evening to St. Louis to work the World Golf Championships for ABC. I was walking to the golf shop when I got a call on my cell phone from Julius Mason [director of public relations for the PGA of America]. "Get in front of a TV right now," he said. There was a TV in the pro shop. I watched it there.

SAM TORRANCE: I was at Sunningdale Golf Club [just outside London]. I'd just got out of my car and one of my friends said, "Have you seen what's happened?"

CURTIS STRANGE: At first it never occurred to me that this would have any repercussions on the Ryder Cup. In fact, we were all stuck there, people from out of town, so we went ahead and played golf. I hate to even admit that, but what else were we to do?

Anyway, I did a clinic and during it somebody asked how this would affect the Ryder Cup. I said, "I don't know." The next day I started driving to St. Louis. I was halfway there when the St. Louis tournament was canceled, so I just continued driving home to Virginia. It took about twenty-seven hours and during that time I talked to every player numerous times, to Tim Finchem [PGA Tour commissioner], and to the PGA of America, to feel the pulse, and I think putting off the Ryder Cup was without question the right decision. There were some short-sighted people out there that thought we should have gone ahead and played, but that would have been wrong.

At that point, [Strange's wife] Sarah and I had had everything in place. We were supposed to be leaving town [for England] in twelve days. Some people from the PGA of America had been planning to leave in two days. So we just laid low. Everything was put on hold for six months, then we started the preparations all over again.

A small controversy arose when both sides decided the teams would remain the same, even if one or more players suffered a consequent loss of form, or other players did exactly the opposite. It was true that this could result in one or both teams not being represented by the best performers going into the Ryder Cup, but the overall sentiment was that anyone who had played well enough to qualify should play, no matter the year.

CURTIS STRANGE: When it came to captain's picks, I was in an enviable position because I had five or six guys not on the team who were playing really well. Paul Azinger, Frank Lickliter, Scott Verplank. I just love the way Scott Verplank plays. He's aways in play, so he was picked for the alternate shot, and that's all he played. And you know what? He probably appreciated being picked as much as anybody ever has. Some people thought I was going out on a limb picking a rookie—he's the first rookie ever to be a captain's pick—and my response to that is, "This guy's no rookie." Look what he's gone through in life. He's come back from such a serious slump. He's had injuries his whole life. He's diabetic. "Rookie" is the last thing you should call him. In fact, both my picks came back from such illness and adversity, Azinger from cancer. He ended up like twenty-second on the points list, but he was playing well; he's a competitor and he brings a lot to the locker room. Azinger is the whole deal.

Over in Europe, Philip Price, a thirty-five-year-old Welshman with no Ryder Cup experience, had indeeed slumped since the post-ponement. Going into the Belfry, he lay forty-fifth on the European money list. The UK media called for his head.

SAM TORRANCE: Philip Price step down? What a lot of bullshit. The boy made the team. Christ, how could you take that away from him? Obviously you work on a iittle bit on confidence, but if you start going too heavy on that, then you have an adverse effect. "Why the hell is he telling me this?" The whole team was at the Belfry a month prior to the matches, apart from Garcia and Parnevik, and we had a competition. I put Fulke and Price together and they had the best score of all the teams. Killed everyone, won all the money. So they were okay.

But Mark James was asked to step down as assistant captain. It had to do with Faldo's good-luck telegram [in his book *Into the Bearpit,* about the 1999 Ryder Cup, James claimed he threw a good-luck note from Nick Faldo, who didn't make the 1999 team, into the garbage]. But it was flippant, and it was meant as fun. Faldo took umbrage to it, created a huge furor with the press, and it just got too big. But when Mark was asked to step down, I had no doubt in my mind that he would still be coming and doing exactly the same job. He just had to lose the title. Woosie [Ian Woosnam] ended up being my vice captain but Woosie, Mark James, and Joakim Haeggman [Swedish golfer who played in the 1993 Ryder Cup] were all doing the same job.

When the teams did arrive a year later—the President's Cup also moved up a year to accommodate it—the horror of September 11 was supplanted by the bizarre. An earthquake measuring 4.8 on the Richter scale rocked the Belfry (its epicenter was only a few miles away). Few players had arrived, but one was Jesper Parnevik, who, purely by coincidence, had been in New York City on September 11.

CURTIS STRANGE: We were still in Ireland at the World Golf Championship event when the earthquake hit the Belfry Sunday night. Now we're saying, "Shoot, what else can go wrong?"

Not a lot, because the mood of this edition of the Ryder Cup was much different. First there was the conscious effort by Strange and Torrance to return civility and sportsmanship to the event in the wake of the Country Club. Then there was the awareness of why the matches were being played a year later. Oh, the players played hard, and the fans were as into it as ever, but if ever there was a Ryder Cup in which it didn't matter who won or lost that much, this was it.

Much of the early media coverage focused, as expected, on the tenth hole. But not on its risk and reward—on the fact that Sam Torrance had moved the tee back, effectivily taking the "go for it" out of play. Now it was a lay-up hole.

CURTIS STRANGE: Sam did what he had to do. He took our length, which was our strength, away from us. He pinched in all the fairways. My guys started complaining the first day. Scott Hoch's pissing and moaning, they're all pissing and moaning, but I said, "Guys, I don't want to hear it one more time because there's not a goddamn thing you can do about it. You're better iron players, you're better putters, you're better drivers. Okay, you're not going to hit many drivers, but you can still beat them with your irons. You're better players. Get over it." And it all pretty much stopped. I knew the game was on though.

And Sam really took our strength away by making 10 our lay-up hole all week long. The tenth is one of the great match-play holes of all time, if you can put it on the green. But you couldn't do it. Maybe one or two guys went for it. But that was it.

SAM TORRANCE: I need to get this about the tenth hole cleared up, because all the criticism was bullshit. When we played the Ryder Cup at the Belfry in '85 and '89, the tenth hole was like a good 3-wood. At the Benson & Hedges European Tour tournament the year prior to the Ryder Cup, in 2001, they were hitting 3-irons onto the green. To me that wasn't right. I wanted it set up so if you had to go for it, it was a driver, or down-breeze it was 3-wood. So I went back to where we'd always played it. And that was it. It was a tough, demanding shot to put it on the green, and that's what I wanted. It wasn't really done to take away any advantage. I did it to restore the quality of the hole and the way the hole should be played.

DAVID FEHERTY: I was worried about Sam Torrance. I was just hoping his team didn't paint half their arses blue at the opening ceremony. "You can take our cup, but you'll never take our frrrrrreedom! Play ball!"

CURTIS STRANGE: During the matches I just watched if you talk to the players who played at Valderrama in 1997, they'll tell you they hated every bit of Seve's driving around and telling them what to do. My deal was to be there if they needed me for anything, but not to go to them. I would be where they could see me. And if anything else needed to be done, I had two assistants, my two sons, Tom and David, over there with me. The boys had radios, and were out on the course relaying messages about what was going on. I also had [PGA Tour pro] Mike Hulbert helping out. Mike is one of the most likable people on Tour; he's everybody's best friend. He was surprised to be involved, but I didn't pick him for experience; I was going to make those decisions. I had twelve of the best players in the world to run things off of, if I wanted to. I didn't need another guy. Mike is the type of person that no chore is too little for him to do. And there are a lot of little things that have to be done that somebody else might say, "Screw you, you go do it, I don't want to do that." Know what I'm saying? Mike loved doing everything that was asked of him. Everything. He was great.

I had some pairings that had been done for a year. I thought David Toms's and Phil Mickelson's personalities meshed well. I always liked Tiger and Calc and Tiger and Zinger, because I thought Calc was a wonderful best-ball player and Azinger was a great alternate-shot player. But I switched that at the last minute. We were all in a little meeting one night and I said, "Okay, Calc, playing with Tiger Woods, best ball or alternate shot?" He said, "Alternate shot." Both Calc and Zinger said they were comfortable in the opposite of how I'd paired them. Tiger said it didn't matter to him. Tiger and Calc lost in the afternoon foursomes [2 and 1, to Sergio Garcia and Lee Westwood]. In the morning, Azinger and Tiger played really well in the four-balls and lost. Their match against Darren Clarke and Thomas Björn had nineteen birdies. We were 1 down on the last hole, and Azinger stuck a 4-iron in there to three feet. The Europeans both hit it to twenty or twenty-five feet, and Björn made it. All you can do is applaud. But if I could take something back, I wouldn't have switched Calc and Zinger.

SAM TORRANCE: Darren Clarke got off to a roaring start, but it wasn't just that one match. There were four matches, and we won three of them. [Sergio Garcia and Lee Westwood beat David Duval and Davis Love 4 and 3, while Colin Montgomerie and Bernhard Langer beat Scott Hoch and Jim Furyk by the same score.] It was just a great start. We also were up in three of the afternoon four-balls, but ended up losing two of them and halving one. So we ended the day just one point ahead.

CURTIS STRANGE: Everybody on our team was guaranteed one match before the singles. I don't believe in hiding anybody. You make the team, you play. I thought it was important that everybody got in the first day, and then it would be easier to sit someone out the second day. And you're so fired up at the Opening Ceremony to get started—then you have to wait a day? Get in the matches!

I put Davis Love with Tiger on the second day because I wanted to get Tiger on the scoreboard. One, it was important for Tiger to get a win, to get the press and everybody else off his ass. Two, it was important for the team to have Tiger win.

And win he did, the pair playing flawlessly in beating Clarke and Björn 4 and 3. With the teams splitting the morning scores and the United States taking a 2½–1½ edge in the afternoon, the scores were tied at 8–8 going into the singles.

CURTIS STRANGE: On Saturday evening we held what's sort of a ritual where people get up and say thanks to the captain and his wife and to all the other players. A lot of the theme that night was, "We're even on points, we're in good shape, but we still have to play tomorrow." Sarah and I spoke last, then Sarah punched me and said, "Tom wants to speak." Think about that: my nineteen-year-old son getting up in front of twelve of the best golfers in the world—and he was so nervous he was quivering. He told everyone how great it all had been for him and his brother David—he spoke for his brother, too—and thanked everyone for making them feel welcome. His last comment was, "I'll never forget what my dad said at the opening ceremony—that we're all one team now." Then Tom said, "Guys, that shit ain't gonna fly tomorrow." And the whole place came down! I was proud of him being able to do that.

But Sunday is tough because you're so spread out and you feel like you're missing somebody all the time. Eventually things settled down to where everything was coming to the end, so I went back to try to get Davis in. Davis didn't birdie 17, the par-5, so now we were doomed [he was all square with Pierre Fulke]. Mickelson was still 3 down. He was 3 down after eight holes. I'd ridden up to him and said,"You all right?" He said, "I'm okay. I'm okay." I said, "Well, I hope so." But what are you going to say? I mean, they're big boys.

SAM TORRANCE: Philip Price played magnificently against Mickelson. Some of the shots he hit on that last day were some of the best shots hit by anyone all week. On the sixth hole, Mickelson had hit a great second to about two feet. Philip has one foot in a hazard, the ball about two feet above him, and hit an incredible shot to three feet. He holed it, and Mickelson missed. A huge swing around there. [Price eventually won 3 and 2.]

CURTIS STRANGE: Tell you who I did say something to, and it was half-comical. Zinger was getting beat a couple down through 7. All week long he'd been the one talking about how "You gotta strap 'em on, boys. You gotta strap on this pair of balls and go get 'em." Always telling them, "You got to strap 'em on." That became the theme for the week.

So I went up to him when he was going to the eighth green, when he was 2 down to Niclas Fasth, and I said, "Hey, come here a minute. What have you been talking about all week? You've been telling them to strap 'em on, haven't you?" He said, "Yeah." I said, "Well, you better fuckin' strap 'em on right now, because we need you."

I was dead serious, and he knew it. But I could say that with Zinger's personality. And we kind of both got a little chuckle over it. And he did it, too. He *really* did it. He got a half back for us.

SAM TORRANCE: At one point we had a lead in seven of the first eight matches, but I made a stupid mistake. I thought we'd won it on the eighteenth when Niclas Fasth was about twenty-five feet away, lying two and putting, and Azinger was in the bunker. We needed only a half on the hole for a point and that would win us the Cup. And we all know what happened.

CURTIS STRANGE: I was on the seventeenth fairway trying to get Davis through, and I heard this enormous roar. But there was something strange about it—it wasn't one of their roars. It wasn't a prolonged roar. And then over the radio came this screaming, and it was Mike Hulbert trying to tell me that Zinger had holed a bunker shot on 18 for a half with Niclas Fasth. But he was screaming. It was funny, but I had to tell them all, *"Settle down."*

JIMMY ROBERTS: A lot of these players can hole bunker shots, but you think of the circumstances, and you just shake your head and think, Oh, man, Azinger . . . A lot of players love playing in the Ryder Cup, but Zinger *really* loves it. I do really think some people are born to do certain things. Azinger was born to play in the Ryder Cup. It's in his DNA.

And look at the putt [Irishman] Paul McGinley made to win the Cup [he halved with Jim Furyk]. This was not a tap-in. It was maybe fifteen feet, and you have to understand that when it comes down to it, there is no air at the eighteenth green during the Ryder Cup. And he made it. That will be the highlight of his life, maybe not up there with the birth of his children or his wedding day, but definitely his golf highlight.

SAM TORRANCE: Paul McGinley hit a wonderful putt on 17 and an even better one on 18. On 17, Furyk was just outside him, and missed first, which was big, because he was 1 up. Paul suddenly sees light at the end of the tunnel—and there was no train coming the other way. And he knocked in a great putt and then again on 18 for a tie, and we claimed the Cup.

There was one moment of, shall we say, questionable behavior. With the Cup clinched, and Love and Fulke on 18, Sergio Garcia went sprinting out onto the eighteenth fairway to hug the Swede before falling on the ground in mock exhaustion. Embarrassed, Fulke offered to concede the match to Love—they were all square at the time—but they instead agreed on half a point each and picked up their balls.

CURTIS STRANGE: Sergio should grow up. Sergio's world revolves around Sergio. What he did in the Ryder Cup didn't affect the outcome, but it does show the world that you have to think sometimes. I just think the game has taught him better than that. He was crying after losing the first day, and then he's doing this "prince has come home to visit" thing on the back of a cart, waving to the crowd. Come on, get some kind of even keel going here.

Afterward Strange was roundly criticized for his Sunday lineup, specifically that by putting Tiger Woods out last and losing by 15½–12½, the Cup was in Europe's hands before Woods's match could matter. Torrance, on the other hand, front-loaded his lineup with his best players, the after-effect, of course, of his having been an assistant at the Country Club in 1999, when the U.S. comeback was fueled by front-loading.

CURTIS STRANGE: I figured there were three possibilities on Sunday. One, that we would win going away, which was not a big possibility because we weren't playing that well and they weren't playing well either. Two, that we would lose in a close match. And three, that we would win in a close match. I never gave it a thought that they would win going away. I thought it was going to be a really close match and everybody else in the world thought it was going to be a close match, so I have to have some meat at the end. Tiger Woods is the best player in the world and, as long as I'm captain, he is going to play last, or maybe second from last. That's my philosophy. Some of the criticism said that Tiger's point didn't count. Well, all the points count, okay?

But Tiger was always even in his match with Jesper, and that never sent a positive message to the rest of the team. He and I have talked about this. Worse was Mickelson going 3 down so early to Philip Price in the second-to-last match. On Saturday night, after we saw the pairings, I said, "Guys, it looks like there might be a lot of blue [for Europe] on the board tomorrow, but if you stay patient and if you do your job, the red will come back around. It's a long day. Don't panic. Don't worry about other people; worry about your own match." I don't think we did that.

And what if I had Tiger in seventh or eighth, and we went to the final match with Joe Shmuck? What now?

JIMMY ROBERTS: Just as Seve didn't win the Ryder Cup at Valderrama, Curtis didn't lose it at the Belfry. I certainly didn't see him scoring any bogeys. Really, Phil Mickelson should have beaten Philip Price. Had he done that, then Tiger would have had to have beaten Jesper Parnevik, and Tiger seldom loses when he has to win. So if they both had won, then the matches would have been tied and the U.S. would have retained the Ryder Cup. Curtis took way too much heat.

CURTIS STRANGE: When the matches were over, I first I sought out Sam [Torrance] on the eighteenth green. Then I tried to see every one of their players, and then every one of mine. I felt that, win, lose, or draw, it was going to be such an emotional release, and it really was.

But what do you do? You just kind of get on with your business. Do some press; try to keep it together for that. It started quickly, though. When I was walking across the putting green with Sarah and a lot of my guys, people were applauding. But Rich Lerner from the Golf Channel asked me all the second-guessing questions already. Doesn't take you long, does it? Jesus, it was brutal.

But you know what? I was and am happy for Sam Torrance and

his family. You could lose to somebody you don't care for much, but Sam is well loved by everyone. People understood that Sam and I were trying to get out this message of "Let's be civil and respectful and get back to the etiquette of the game." And we did that. The last thing I did before we went into the pressroom on Sunday night, after we'd lost, was get the guys together and tell them, "Don't fuck up now. This has been a great week, other than that we lost, so watch what you say in this pressroom. We're not going to talk about Sergio, we're not going to talk about whatever else might have happened out there."

The closing ceremonies were extremely emotional. I couldn't speak much about my team because I'd have lost it. The opening ceremonies are stuffy and rigid, and you have to do proper things. But at the closing ceremonies, it's over with. You thank the people that put it on.

Then you come home, and there's the initial shock of some of the stuff written in the press. People criticized Tiger because he didn't wear the exact team uniform on Sunday. But he just had a different configuration [warmer clothes] because he had the flu. And you know what? I didn't care what he wore. Tiger had the flu on Saturday night, and he still stayed in the team room until eleven o'clock, until the last person spoke, and that speaks volumes. You know, some people think that's the only thing a captain does is pick out the clothes for the Ryder Cup team. But the least of your list of priorities is the clothes. The players talked to me about shoes. I told Scott Hoch, "I don't give a damn what kind of shoes you wear as long as your feet are comfortable."

But I did have to remind the team about the delay of a year. I said, "Guys, let me tell you something, if you put on weight or lose weight, the clothes are your responsibility." They knew I was dead serious, because I didn't want to mess with it. A couple of players had to get their clothes altered. Tiger went over and found that one pair of his pants didn't fit. I said, "Let me ask you this, how long have you had your slacks? Oh, one year and a half?

Have you tried them on? No? Then screw you. It's your fault, not mine."

But you really do make friends at the Ryder Cup. People tend to forget about all that. Not only with the players, which the whole thing is about, but with the people behind the scenes, the people that come over and cater dinner for you, and you just want to have them sit down and eat with you. And the people at the Belfry could not have been any nicer. Geez, they were nice. In our team room, we had four or five people in charge of us, and I honestly think they were rooting for us. Sarah and all of them were crying when we were getting on the bus to leave the Belfry on Monday morning.

So you certainly want to win, and you want your players to enjoy success. But if my twelve guys and their wives or girlfriends had the best week of their lives, then my week was a success. Believe me, that was the greatest week of my life. Honestly, it really does become more than just winning or losing.

They got the guy at the Country Club who stole the TV.

APPENDIX
THE WHOLE NINE YARDS

Note: Although the British team was known only as "Great Britain" until 1973, when "& Ireland" was incorporated into the team name, Irish players actually had been playing on the "British" side since 1953, when Harry Bradshaw, born in County Wicklow, was selected. Accordingly, all teams until the change to "Europe" are listed here as "GB&I."

1927
WORCESTER COUNTRY CLUB, WORCESTER, MASSACHUSETTS
Captains: Walter Hagen (USA), Ted Ray (GB&I)
GB&I 2½ USA 9½

GB&I		USA	
FOURSOMES			
Ted Ray & Fred Robson	0	Walter Hagen & Johnny Golden (2 & 1)	1
George Duncan & Archie Compston	0	Johnny Farrell & Joe Turnesa (8 & 6)	1
Arthur Havers & Herbert Jolly	0	Gene Sarazen & Al Watrous (3 & 2)	1
Aubrey Boomer & Charles Whitcombe (7 & 5)	1	Leo Diegel & Bill Mehlhorn	0

SINGLES

Archie Compston	0	Bill Mehlhorn (1 up)	1
Aubrey Boomer	0	Johnny Farrell (5 & 4)	1
Herbert Jolly	0	Johnny Golden (8 & 7)	1
Ted Ray	0	Leo Diegel (7 & 5)	1
Charles Whitcombe	½	Gene Sarazen	½
Arthur Havers	0	Walter Hagen (2 & 1)	1
Fred Robson	0	Al Watrous (3 & 2)	1
George Duncan (1 up)	1	Joe Turnesa	0

1929

MOORTOWN GOLF CLUB, LEEDS, ENGLAND
Captains: Walter Hagen (USA), George Duncan (GB&I)
USA 5 GB&I 7

USA		GB&I	
FOURSOMES			
Johnny Farrell & Joe Turnesa	½	Charles Whitcombe & Archie Compston	½
Leo Diegel & Al Espinosa (7 & 5)	1	Aubrey Boomer & George Duncan	0
Gene Sarazen & Ed Dudley	0	Abe Mitchell & Fred Robson (2 & 1)	1
Johnny Golden & Walter Hagen (2 up)	1	Ernest Whitcombe & Henry Cotton	0
SINGLES			
Johnny Farrell	0	Charles Whitcombe (8 & 6)	1
Walter Hagen	0	George Duncan (10 & 8)	1
Leo Diegel (8 & 6)	1	Abe Mitchell	0
Gene Sarazen	0	Archie Compston (6 & 4)	1
Joe Turnesa	0	Aubrey Boomer (4 & 3)	1
Horton Smith (4 & 2)	1	Fred Robson	0
Al Watrous	0	Henry Cotton (4 & 3)	1
Al Espinosa	½	Ernest Whitcombe	½

1931

SCIOTO COUNTRY CLUB, COLUMBUS, OHIO
Captains: Walter Hagen (USA), Charles Whitcombe (GB&I)
GB&I 3 USA 9

GB&I		USA	
FOURSOMES			
Archie Compston & William Davies	0	Gene Sarazen & Johnny Farrell (8 & 7)	1
George Duncan & Arthur Havers	0	Walter Hagen & Denny Shute (10 & 9)	1
Abe Mitchell & Fred Robson (3 & 1)	1	Leo Diegel & Al Espinosa	0
Syd Easterbrook & Ernest Whitcombe	0	Billy Burke & Wiffy Cox (3 & 2)	1
SINGLES			
Archie Compston	0	Billy Burke (7 & 6)	1
Fred Robson	0	Gene Sarazen (7 & 6)	1
William Davies (4 & 3)	1	Johnny Farrell	0
Abe Mitchell	0	Wiffy Cox (3 & 1)	1
Charles Whitcombe	0	Walter Hagen (4 & 3)	1
Bert Hodson	0	Denny Shute (8 & 6)	1
Ernest Whitcombe	0	Al Espinosa (2 & 1)	1
Arthur Havers (4 & 3)	1	Craig Wood	0

1933

SOUTHPORT & AINSDALE GOLF CLUB, SOUTHPORT, ENGLAND
Captains: Walter Hagen (USA), J. H. Taylor (GB&I)
USA 5½ GB&I 6½

USA		GB&I	
FOURSOMES			
Gene Sarazen & Walter Hagen	½	Percy Alliss & Charles Whitcombe	½
Olin Dutra & Denny Shute	0	Abe Mitchell & Arthur Havers (3 & 2)	1

| Craig Wood & Paul Runyan | 0 | William Davies & Syd Easterbrook (1 up) | 1 |
| Ed Dudley & Billy Burke (1 up) | 1 | Alf Padgham & Alf Perry | 0 |

SINGLES

Gene Sarazen (6 & 4)	1	Alf Padgham	0
Olin Dutra	0	Abe Mitchell (9 & 8)	1
Walter Hagen (2 & 1)	1	Arthur Lacey	0
Craig Wood (4 & 3)	1	William Davies	0
Paul Runyan	0	Percy Alliss (2 & 1)	1
Leo Diegel	0	Arthur Havers (4 & 3)	1
Denny Shute	0	Syd Easterbrook (1 up)	1
Horton Smith (2 & 1)	1	Charles Whitcombe	0

1935

RIDGEWOOD COUNTRY CLUB, RIDGEWOOD, NEW JERSEY
Captains: Walter Hagen (USA), Charles Whitcombe (GB&I)
GB&I 3 USA 9

GB&I		USA	

FOURSOMES

Alf Perry & Jack Busson	0	Gene Sarazen & Walter Hagen (7 & 6)	1
Alf Padgham & Percy Alliss	0	Henry Picard & Johnny Revolta (6 & 5)	1
Wiffy Cox & Ted Jarman	0	Paul Runyan & Horton Smith (9 & 8)	1
Charles Whitcombe & Ernest Whitcombe (1 up)	1	Olin Dutra & Ky Laffoon	0

SINGLES

Jack Busson	0	Gene Sarazen (3 & 2)	1
Dick Burton	0	Paul Runyan (5 & 3)	1
Reg Whitcombe	0	Johnny Revolta (2 & 1)	1
Alf Padgham	0	Olin Dutra (4 & 2)	1
Percy Alliss (1 up)	1	Craig Wood	0
Wiffy Cox	½	Horton Smith	½

| Ernest Whitcombe | 0 | Henry Picard (3 & 2) | 1 |
| Alf Perry | ½ | Sam Parks | ½ |

1937

SOUTHPORT & AINSDALE COUNTRY CLUB, SOUTHPORT, ENGLAND

Captains: Ben Hogan (USA), Henry Cotton (GB&I)

USA 8 GB&I 4

USA		GB&I	
FOURSOMES			
Ed Dudley & Byron Nelson	1	Alf Padgham & Henry Cotton (4 & 2)	0
Ralph Guldahl & Tony Manero (2 & 1)	1	Arthur Lacey & Wiffy Cox	0
Gene Sarazen & Denny Shute	½	Charles Whitcombe & Dai Rees	½
Henry Picard & Johnny Revolta	0	Percy Alliss & Dick Burton (2 & 1)	1
SINGLES			
Ralph Guldahl (8 & 7)	1	Alf Padgham	0
Denny Shute	½	Sam King	½
Byron Nelson	0	Dai Rees (3 & 1)	1
Tony Manero	0	Henry Cotton (5 & 3)	1
Gene Sarazen (1 up)	1	Percy Alliss	0
Sam Snead (5 & 4)	1	Dick Burton	0
Ed Dudley (2 & 1)	1	Alf Perry	0
Henry Picard (2 & 1)	1	Arthur Lacey	0

1947

PORTLAND GOLF CLUB, PORTLAND, OREGON
Captains: Ben Hogan (USA), Henry Cotton (GB&I)
GB&I 1 USA 11

GB&I		USA	
FOURSOMES			
Henry Cotton & Arthur Lees	0	Ed "Porky" Oliver & Lew Worsham (10 & 8)	1
Fred Daly & Charlie Ward	0	Sam Snead & Lloyd Mangrum (6 & 5)	1
Jimmy Adams & Max Faulkner	0	Ben Hogan & Jimmy Demaret (2 up)	1
Dai Rees & Sam King	0	Byron Nelson & Herman Barron (2 & 1)	1
SINGLES			
Fred Daly	0	Dutch Harrison (5 & 4)	1
Jimmy Adams	0	Lew Worsham (3 & 2)	1
Max Faulkner	0	Lloyd Mangrum (6 & 5)	1
Charlie Ward	0	Ed "Porky" Oliver (4 & 3)	1
Arthur Lees	0	Byron Nelson (2 & 1)	1
Henry Cotton	0	Sam Snead (5 & 4)	1
Dai Rees	0	Jimmy Demaret (3 & 2)	1
Sam King (4 & 3)	1	Herman Keiser	0

1949

GANTON GOLF CLUB, SCARBOROUGH, ENGLAND
Captains: Ben Hogan (USA), Charles Whitcombe (GB&I)
USA 7 GB&I 5

USA		GB&I	
FOURSOMES			
Dutch Harrison & Johnny Palmer	0	Max Faulkner & Jimmy Adams (2 & 1)	1
Bob Hamilton & Skip Alexander	0	Fred Daly & Ken Bousfield (4 & 2)	1

Jimmy Demaret & Clayton Heafner (4 & 3)	1	Charlie Ward & Sam King	0
Sam Snead & Lloyd Mangrum	0	Dick Burton & Arthur Lees (1 up)	1

SINGLES

Dutch Harrison (8 & 7)	1	Max Faulkner	0
Johnny Palmer	0	Jimmy Adams (2 & 1)	1
Sam Snead	1	Charlie Ward (6 & 5)	0
Bob Hamilton	0	Dai Rees (6 & 4)	1
Clayton Heafner (3 & 2)	1	Dick Burton	0
Chick Harbert (4 & 3)	1	Sam King	0
Jimmy Demaret (7 & 6)	1	Arthur Lees	0
Lloyd Mangrum (4 & 3)	1	Fred Daly	0

1951

PINEHURST COUNTRY CLUB, PINEHURST, NORTH CAROLINA
Captains: Sam Snead (USA), Arthur Lacey (GB&I)
GB&I 2½ USA 9½

GB&I		USA	
FOURSOMES			
Max Faulkner & Dai Rees	0	Clayton Heafner & Jack Burke Jr. (5 & 3)	1
Charlie Ward & Arthur Lees (2 & 1)	1	Ed "Porky" Oliver & Henry Ransom	0
Jimmy Adams & John Panton	0	Sam Snead & Lloyd Mangrum (5 & 4)	1
Fred Daly & Ken Bousfield	0	Ben Hogan & Jimmy Demaret (5 & 4)	1
SINGLES			
Jimmy Adams	0	Jack Burke Jr. (4 & 3)	1
Dai Rees	0	Jimmy Demaret (2 up)	1
Fred Daly	½	Clayton Heafner	½
Harry Weetman	0	Lloyd Mangrum (6 & 5)	1
Arthur Lees (2 & 1)	1	Ed "Porky" Oliver	0
Charlie Ward	0	Ben Hogan (3 & 2)	1

| John Panton | 0 | Skip Alexander (8 & 7) | 1 |
| Max Faulkner | 0 | Sam Snead (4 & 3) | 1 |

1953

WENTWORTH GOLF CLUB, WENTWORTH, ENGLAND
Captains: Lloyd Mangrum (USA), Henry Cotton (GB&I)
USA 6½ GB&I 5½

USA		GB&I	
FOURSOMES			
Dave Douglas & Ed "Porky" Oliver (2 & 1)	1	Harry Weetman & Peter Alliss	0
Lloyd Mangrum & Sam Snead (8 & 7)	1	Eric Brown & John Panton	0
Ted Kroll & Jack Burke Jr. (7 & 5)	1	Jimmy Adams & Bernard Hunt	0
Walter Burkemo & Cary Middlecoff	0	Fred Daly & Harry Bradshaw (1 up)	1
SINGLES			
Jack Burke Jr. (2 & 1)	1	Dai Rees	0
Ted Kroll	0	Fred Daly (9 & 7)	1
Lloyd Mangrum	0	Eric Brown (2 up)	1
Sam Snead	0	Harry Weetman (1 up)	1
Cary Middlecoff (3 & 1)	1	Max Faulkner	0
Jim Turnesa (1 up)	1	Peter Alliss	0
Dave Douglas	½	Bernard Hunt	½
Fred Haas	0	Harry Bradshaw (3 & 2)	1

1955

Thunderbird Golf & Country Club, Palm Springs, California
Captains: Chick Harbert (USA), Dai Rees (GB&I)
GB&I 4 USA 8

GB&I		USA	
FOURSOMES			
John Fallon & John Jacobs (1 up)	1	Chandler Harper & Jerry Barber	0
Eric Brown & Syd Scott	0	Doug Ford & Ted Kroll (5 & 4)	1
Arthur Lees & Harry Weetman	0	Jack Burke Jr. & Tommy Bolt (1 up)	1
Harry Bradshaw & Dai Rees	0	Sam Snead & Cary Middlecoff (3 & 2)	1
SINGLES			
Christy O'Connor Sr.	0	Tommy Bolt (4 & 2)	1
Syd Scott	0	Chick Harbert (3 & 2)	1
John Jacobs (1 up)	1	Cary Middlecoff	0
Dai Rees	0	Sam Snead (3 & 1)	1
Arthur Lees (3 & 2)	1	Marty Furgol	0
Eric Brown (3 & 2)	1	Jerry Barber	0
Harry Bradshaw	0	Jack Burke Jr. (3 & 2)	1
Harry Weetman	0	Doug Ford (3 & 2)	1

1957

LINDRICK CLUB, YORKSHIRE, ENGLAND
Captains: Jack Burke (USA), Dai Rees (GB&I)
USA 4½ GB&I 7½

USA		GB&I	
FOURSOMES			
Doug Ford & D. Finsterwald (2 & 1)	1	Peter Alliss & Bernard Hunt	0
Art Wall & Fred Hawkins	0	Ken Bousfield & Dai Rees (3 & 2)	1
Ted Kroll & Jack Burke Jr. (4 & 3)	1	Max Faulkner & Harry Weetman	0

Dick Mayer & Tommy Bolt (7 & 5)	1	Christy O'Connor Sr. & Eric Brown	0

SINGLES

Tommy Bolt	0	Eric Brown (4 & 3)	1
Jack Burke Jr.	0	Peter Mills (5 & 3)	1
Fred Hawkins (2 & 1)	1	Peter Alliss	0
Lionel Herbert	0	Ken Bousfield (4 & 3)	1
Marty Furgol	0	Dai Rees (7 & 6)	1
Doug Ford	0	Bernard Hunt (6 & 5)	1
Dow Finsterwald	0	Christy O'Connor Sr. (7 & 6)	1
Dick Mayer	½	Harry Bradshaw	½

1959

ELDORADO COUNTRY CLUB, PALM DESERT, CALIFORNIA
Captains: Sam Snead (USA), Dai Rees (GB&I)
GB&I 3½ USA 8½

GB&I		USA	

FOURSOMES

Bernard Hunt & Eric Brown	0	Bob Rosburg & Mike Souchak (5 & 4)	1
Dai Rees & Ken Bousfield	0	Julius Boros & Dow Finsterwald (2 up)	1
Christy O'Connor Sr. & Peter Alliss (3 & 2)	1	Art Wall & Doug Ford	0
Harry Weetman & Dave Thomas	½	Sam Snead & Cary Middlecoff	½

SINGLES

Norman Drew	½	Doug Ford	½
Ken Bousfield	0	Mike Souchak (3 & 2)	1
Harry Weetman	0	Bob Rosburg (6 & 5)	1
Dave Thomas	0	Sam Snead (6 & 5)	1
Christy O'Connor Sr.	0	Art Wall (7 & 6)	1
Dai Rees	0	Dow Finsterwald (1 up)	1
Peter Alliss	½	Jay Herbert	½
Eric Brown (4 & 3)	1	Cary Middlecoff	0

1961

ROYAL LYTHAM & ST. ANNE'S, ST. ANNE'S, ENGLAND
Captains: Jerry Barber (USA), Dai Rees (GB&I)
USA 14½ GB&I 9½

USA		GB&I	
FOURSOMES: MORNING			
Doug Ford & Gene Littler	0	Christy O'Connor Sr. & Peter Alliss (4 & 3)	1
Art Wall & Jay Herbert (4 & 3)	1	John Panton & Bernard Hunt	0
Billy Casper & Arnold Palmer (2 & 1)	1	Dai Rees & Ken Bousfield	0
Bill Collins & Mike Souchak (1 up)	1	Tom Haliburton & Neil Coles	0
FOURSOMES: AFTERNOON			
Art Wall & Jay Herbert (1 up)	1	Christy O'Connor Sr. & Peter Alliss	0
Billy Casper & Arnold Palmer (5 & 4)	1	John Panton & Bernard Hunt	0
Bill Collins & Mike Souchak	0	Dai Rees & Ken Bousfield (2 & 1)	1
Jerry Barber & Dow Finsterwald (1 up)	1	Tom Haliburton & Neil Coles	0
SINGLES: MORNING			
Doug Ford (1 up)	1	Harry Weetman	0
Mike Souchak (5 & 4)	1	Ralph Moffitt	0
Arnold Palmer	½	Peter Alliss	½
Billy Casper (5 & 3)	1	Ken Bousfield	0
Jay Herbert	0	Dai Rees (2 & 1)	1
Gene Littler	½	Neil Coles	½
Jerry Barber	0	Bernard Hunt (5 & 4)	1
Dow Finsterwald (2 & 1)	1	Christy O'Connor Sr.	0
SINGLES: AFTERNOON			
Art Wall (1 up)	1	Harry Weetman	0
Bill Collins	0	Peter Alliss (3 & 2)	1

Mike Souchak (2 & 1)	1	Bernard Hunt	0
Arnold Palmer (2 & 1)	1	Tom Haliburton	0
Doug Ford	0	Dai Rees (4 & 3)	1
Jerry Barber	0	Ken Bousfield (1 up)	1
Dow Finsterwald	0	Neil Coles (1 up)	1
Gene Littler	½	Christy O'Connor Sr.	½

1963

EAST LAKE COUNTRY CLUB, ATLANTA, GEORGIA
Captains: Arnold Palmer (USA), John Fallon (GB&I)
GB&I 9 USA 23

GB&I		USA	
FOURSOMES: MORNING			
Brian Huggett & George Will (3 & 2)	1	Arnold Palmer & Johnny Pott	0
Peter Alliss & Christy O'Connor Sr.	0	Billy Casper & Dave Ragan (1 up)	1
Neil Coles & Bernard Hunt	½	Julius Boros & Tony Lema	½
Dave Thomas & Harry Weetman	½	Gene Littler & Dow Finsterwald	½
FOURSOMES: AFTERNOON			
Dave Thomas & Harry Weetman	0	Billy Maxwell & Bob Goalby (4 & 3)	1
Brian Huggett & George Will	0	Arnold Palmer & Billy Casper (5 & 4)	1
Neil Coles & Geoff Hunt (2 & 1)	1	Gene Littler & Dow Finsterwald	0
Tom Haliburton & Bernard Hunt	0	Julius Boros & Tony Lema (1 up)	1
FOUR-BALLS: MORNING			
Brian Huggett & Dave Thomas	0	Arnold Palmer & Dow Finsterwald (5 & 4)	1
Peter Alliss & Bernard Hunt	½	Gene Littler & Julius Boros	½

| Harry Weetman & George Will | 0 | Billy Casper & Billy Maxwell (3 & 2) | 1 |
| Neil Coles & Christy O'Connor Sr. | 0 | Bob Goalby & Dave Ragan (1 up) | 1 |

FOUR-BALLS: AFTERNOON

Neil Coles & Christy O'Connor Sr.	0	Arnold Palmer & Dow Finsterwald (3 & 2)	1
Peter Alliss & Bernard Hunt	0	Tony Lema & Johnny Pott (1 hole)	1
Tom Haliburton & Geoff Hunt	0	Billy Casper & Billy Maxwell (2 & 1)	1
Brian Huggett & Dave Thomas	½	Bob Goalby & Dave Ragan	½

SINGLES: MORNING

Geoff Hunt	0	Tony Lema (5 & 3)	1
Brian Huggett (3 & 1)	1	Johnny Pott	0
Peter Alliss (1 up)	1	Arnold Palmer	0
Neil Coles	½	Billy Casper	½
Dave Thomas	0	Bob Goalby (3 & 2)	1
Christy O'Connor Sr.	0	Gene Littler (1 up)	1
Harry Weetman (1 up)	1	Julius Boros	0
Bernard Hunt (2 up)	1	Dow Finsterwald	0

SINGLES: AFTERNOON

George Will	0	Arnold Palmer (3 & 2)	1
Neil Coles	0	Dave Ragan (2 & 1)	1
Peter Alliss	½	Tony Lema	½
Tom Haliburton	0	Gene Littler (6 & 5)	1
Harry Weetman	0	Julius Boros (2 & 1)	1
Christy O'Connor Sr.	0	Billy Maxwell (2 & 1)	1
Dave Thomas	0	Dow Finsterwald (4 & 3)	1
Bernard Hunt	0	Bob Goalby (2 & 1)	1

1965

ROYAL BIRKDALE GOLF CLUB, SOUTHPORT, ENGLAND
Captains: Byron Nelson (USA), Harry Weetman (GB&I)
USA 19½ GB&I 12½

USA		GB&I	
FOURSOMES: MORNING			
Julius Boros & Tony Lema (1 up)	1	Lionel Platts & Peter Butler	0
Arnold Palmer & Dave Marr	0	Dave Thomas & George Will (6 & 5)	1
Billy Casper & Gene Littler (2 & 1)	1	Bernard Hunt & Neil Coles	0
Ken Venturi & Don January	0	Peter Alliss & Christy O'Connor Sr. (5 & 4)	1
FOURSOMES: AFTERNOON			
Arnold Palmer & Dave Marr (6 & 5)	1	Dave Thomas & George Will	0
Billy Casper & Gene Littler	0	Peter Alliss & Christy O'Connor Sr. (2 & 1)	1
Julius Boros & Tony Lema (5 & 4)	1	Jimmy Martin & Jimmy Hitchcock	0
Ken Venturi & Don January	0	Bernard Hunt & Neil Coles (3 & 2)	1
FOUR-BALLS: MORNING			
Don January & Tommy Jacobs (1 up)	1	Dave Thomas & George Will	0
Billy Casper & Gene Littler	½	Lionel Platts & Peter Butler	½
Arnold Palmer & Dave Marr (6 & 4)	1	Peter Alliss & Christy O'Connor Sr.	0
Julius Boros & Tony Lema	0	Bernard Hunt & Neil Coles (1 up)	1
FOUR-BALLS: AFTERNOON			
Arnold Palmer & Dave Marr	0	Peter Alliss & Christy O'Connor Sr. (2 up)	1

Don January & Tommy Jacobs (1 up)	1	Dave Thomas & George Will	0
Billy Casper & Gene Littler	½	Lionel Platts & Peter Butler	½
Ken Venturi & Tony Lema (1 up)	1	Bernard Hunt & Neil Coles	0

SINGLES: MORNING

Arnold Palmer (3 & 2)	1	Jimmy Hitchcock	0
Julius Boros (4 & 2)	1	Lionel Platts	0
Tony Lema (1 up)	1	Peter Butler	0
Dave Marr (2 up)	1	Neil Coles	0
Gene Littler	0	Bernard Hunt (2 up)	1
Tommy Jacobs (2 & 1)	1	Dave Thomas	0
Billy Casper	0	Peter Alliss (1 up)	1
Don January	½	George Will	½

SINGLES: AFTERNOON

Tony Lema (6 & 4)	1	Christy O'Connor Sr.	0
Julius Boros (2 & 1)	1	Jimmy Hitchcock	0
Arnold Palmer (2 up)	1	Peter Butler	0
Ken Venturi	0	Peter Alliss (3 & 1)	1
Billy Casper	0	Neil Coles (3 & 2)	1
Gene Littler (2 & 1)	1	George Will	0
Dave Marr (1 up)	1	Bernard Hunt	0
Tommy Jacobs	0	Lionel Platts (1 up)	1

1967

CHAMPIONS GOLF CLUB, HOUSTON, TEXAS
Captains: Ben Hogan (USA), Dai Rees (GB&I)
GB&I 8½ USA 23½

GB&I		USA	

FOURSOMES: MORNING

Brian Huggett & George Will	½	Billy Casper & Julius Boros	½
Peter Alliss & Christy O'Connor Sr.	0	Arnold Palmer & Gardner Dickinson (2 & 1)	1

Tony Jacklin & Dave Thomas (4 & 3)	1	Doug Sanders & Gay Brewer	0
Bernard Hunt & Neil Coles	0	Bobby Nichols & Johnny Pott (6 & 5)	1

FOURSOMES: AFTERNOON

Brian Huggett & George Will	0	Billy Casper & Julius Boros (1 up)	1
Malcolm Gregson & Hugh Boyle	0	Gardner Dickinson & Arnold Palmer (5 & 4)	1
Tony Jacklin & Dave Thomas (3 & 2)	1	Gene Littler & Al Geiberger	0
Peter Alliss & Christy O'Connor Sr.	0	Bobby Nichols & Johnny Pott (2 & 1)	1

FOUR-BALLS: MORNING

Peter Alliss & Christy O'Connor Sr.	0	Billy Casper & Gay Brewer (3 & 2)	1
Bernard Hunt & Neil Coles	0	Bobby Nichols & Johnny Pott (1 up)	1
Tony Jacklin & Dave Thomas	0	Gene Littler & Al Geiberger (1 up)	1
Brian Huggett & George Will	0	Gardner Dickinson & Doug Sanders (3 & 2)	1z

FOUR-BALLS: AFTERNOON

Bernard Hunt & Neil Coles	0	Billy Casper & Gay Brewer (5 & 3)	1
Peter Alliss & Malcolm Gregson	0	Gardner Dickinson & Doug Sanders (3 & 2)	1
George Will & Hugh Boyle	0	Arnold Palmer & Julius Boros (1 up)	1
Tony Jacklin & Dave Thomas	½	Gene Littler & Al Geiberger	½

SINGLES: MORNING

Hugh Boyle	0	Gay Brewer (4 & 3)	1
Peter Alliss	0	Billy Casper (2 & 1)	1
Tony Jacklin	0	Arnold Palmer (3 & 2)	1
Brian Huggett (1 up)	1	Julius Boros	0

Neil Coles (2 & 1)	1	Doug Sanders	0
Malcolm Gregson	0	Al Geiberger (4 & 2)	1
Dave Thomas	½	Gene Littler	½
Bernard Hunt	½	Bobby Nichols	½

SINGLES: AFTERNOON

Brian Huggett	0	Arnold Palmer (5 & 3)	1
Peter Alliss (2 & 1)	1	Gay Brewer	0
Tony Jacklin	0	Gardner Dickinson (3 & 2)	1
Christy O'Connor Sr.	0	Bobby Nichols (3 & 2)	1
George Will	0	Johnny Pott (3 & 1)	1
Malcolm Gregson	0	Al Geiberger (2 & 1)	1
Bernard Hunt	½	Julius Boros	½
Neil Coles (2 & 1)	1	Doug Sanders	0

1969

ROYAL BIRKDALE GOLF CLUB, SOUTHPORT, ENGLAND
Captains: Sam Snead (USA), Eric Brown (GB&I)
USA 16 GB&I 16

USA		GB&I	
FOURSOMES: MORNING			
Miller Barber & Raymond Floyd	0	Neil Coles & Brian Huggett (3 & 2)	1
Lee Trevino & Ken Still	0	Bernard Gallacher & Maurice Bembridge (2 & 1)	1
Dave Hill & Tommy Aaron	0	Tony Jacklin & Peter Townsend (3 & 1)	1
Billy Casper & Frank Beard	½	Christy O'Connor Sr. & Peter Alliss	½
FOURSOMES: AFTERNOON			
Dave Hill & Tommy Aaron (1 up)	1	Neil Coles & Brian Huggett	0
Lee Trevino & Gene Littler (1 up)	1	Bernard Gallacher & Maurice Bembridge	0
Billy Casper & Frank Beard	0	Tony Jacklin & Peter Townsend (1 up)	1

Jack Nicklaus & Dan Sikes (1 up)	1	Peter Butler & Bernard Hunt	0

FOUR-BALLS: MORNING

Dave Hill & Dale Douglass	0	Christy O'Connor Sr. & Peter Townsend (1 up)	1
Raymond Floyd & Miller Barber	½	Brian Huggett & Alex Caygill	½
Lee Trevino & Gene Littler (1 up)	1	Brian Barnes & Peter Alliss	0
Jack Nicklaus & Dan Sikes	0	Tony Jacklin & Neil Coles (1 up)	1

FOUR-BALLS: AFTERNOON

Billy Casper & Frank Beard (2 up)	1	Peter Butler & Peter Townsend	0
Dave Hill & Ken Still (2 & 1)	1	Brian Huggett & Bernard Gallacher	0
Tommy Aaron & Raymond Floyd	½	Maurice Bembridge & Bernard Hunt	½
Lee Trevino & Miller Barber	½	Tony Jacklin & Neil Coles	½

SINGLES: MORNING

Lee Trevino (2 & 1)	1	Peter Alliss	0
Dave Hill (5 & 4)	1	Peter Townsend	0
Tommy Aaron	0	Neil Coles (1 up)	1
Billy Casper	1	Brian Barnes (1 up)	0
Frank Beard	0	Christy O'Connor Sr. (5 & 4)	1
Ken Still	0	Maurice Bembridge (1 up)	1
Raymond Floyd	0	Peter Butler (1 up)	1
Jack Nicklaus	0	Tony Jacklin (4 & 3)	1

SINGLES: AFTERNOON

Dave Hill (4 & 2)	1	Brian Barnes	0
Lee Trevino	0	Bernard Gallacher (4 & 3)	1
Miller Barber (7 & 6)	1	Maurice Bembridge	0
Dale Douglass	0	Peter Butler (3 & 2)	1

Dan Sikes (4 & 3)	1	Neil Coles	0
Gene Littler (2 & 1)	1	Christy O'Connor Sr.	0
Billy Casper	½	Brian Huggett	½
Jack Nicklaus	½	Tony Jacklin	½

1971

OLD WARSON COUNTRY CLUB, ST. LOUIS, MISSOURI
Captains: Jay Hebert (USA), Eric Brown (GB&I)
GB&I 13½ USA 18½

GB&I		USA	

FOURSOMES: MORNING

Neil Coles & Christy O'Connor Sr. (2 & 1)	1	Billy Casper & Miller Barber	0
Peter Townsend & Peter Oosterhuis	0	Arnold Palmer & Gardner Dickinson (1 up)	1
Brian Huggett & Tony Jacklin (3 & 2)	1	Jack Nicklaus & Dave Stockton	0
Maurice Bembridge & Peter Butler (1 up)	1	Charles Coody & Frank Beard	0

FOURSOMES: AFTERNOON

Harry Bannerman & Bernard Gallacher (2 & 1)	1	Billy Casper & Miller Barber	0
Peter Townsend & Peter Oosterhuis	0	Arnold Palmer & Gardner Dickinson (1 up)	1
Brian Huggett & Tony Jacklin	½	Lee Trevino & Mason Rudolph	½
Maurice Bembridge & Peter Butler	0	Jack Nicklaus & J. C. Snead (5 & 3)	1

FOUR-BALLS: MORNING

Christy O'Connor Sr. & Brian Barnes	0	Lee Trevino & Mason Rudolph (2 & 1)	1
Neil Coles & John Garner	0	Frank Beard & J. C. Snead (2 & 1)	1
Peter Oosterhuis & Bernard Gallacher	0	Arnold Palmer & Gardner Dickinson (5 & 4)	1
Peter Townsend & Harry Bannerman	0	Jack Nicklaus & Gene Littler (2 & 1)	1

FOUR-BALLS: AFTERNOON

Bernard Gallacher &		Lee Trevino &	
Peter Oosterhuis (1 up	1	Billy Casper	0
Tony Jacklin & Brian Huggett	0	Gene Littler & J. C. Snead (2 & 1)	1
Peter Townsend &		Arnold Palmer &	
Harry Bannerman	0	Jack Nicklaus (1 up)	1
Neil Coles &		Charles Coody &	
Christy O'Connor Sr.	½	Frank Beard	½

SINGLES: MORNING

Tony Jacklin	0	Lee Trevino (1 up)	1
Bernard Gallacher	½	Dave Stockton	½
Brian Barnes (1 up)	1	Mason Rudolph	0
Peter Oosterhuis (4 & 3)	1	Gene Littler	0
Peter Townsend	0	Jack Nicklaus (3 & 2)	1
Christy O'Connor Sr.	0	Gardner Dickinson (5 & 4)	1
Harry Bannerman	½	Arnold Palmer	½
Neil Coles	½	Frank Beard	½

SINGLES: AFTERNOON

Brian Huggett	0	Lee Trevino (7 & 6)	1
Tony Jacklin	0	J. C. Snead (1 up)	1
Brian Barnes (2 & 1)	1	Miller Barber	0
Peter Townsend	0	Dave Stockton (1 up)	1
Bernard Gallacher (2 & 1)	1	Charles Coody	0
Neil Coles	0	Jack Nicklaus (5 & 3)	1
Peter Oosterhuis (3 & 2)	1	Arnold Palmer	0
Harry Bannerman (2 & 1)	1	Gardner Dickinson	0

1973

MURFIELD GOLF CUB, MURFIELD, SCOTLAND
Captains: Jack Burke (USA), Bernard Hunt (GB&I)
USA 19 GB&I 13

USA		GB&I	
FOURSOMES: MORNING			
Lee Trevino & Billy Casper	0	Brian Barnes & Bernard Gallacher (1 up)	1
Tom Weiskopf & J.C. Snead	0	Christy O'Connor Sr. & Neil Coles (3 & 2)	1
Chi Chi Rodriguez & Lou Graham	½	Tony Jacklin & Peter Oosterhuis	½
Jack Nicklaus & Arnold Palmer (6 & 5)	1	Maurice Bembridge & Eddie Polland	0
FOUR-BALLS: AFTERNOON			
Tommy Aaron & Gay Brewer	0	Brian Barnes & Bernard Gallacher (5 & 4)	1
Arnold Palmer & Jack Nicklaus	0	Maurice Bembridge & Brian Huggett (3 & 1)	1
Tom Weiskopf & Billy Casper	0	Tony Jacklin & Peter Oosterhuis (3 & 1)	1
Lee Trevino & Homero Blancas (2 & 1)	1	Christy O'Connor Sr. & Neil Coles	0
FOURSOMES: MORNING			
Jack Nicklaus & Tom Weiskopf (1 up)	1	Brian Barnes & Peter Butler	0
Arnold Palmer & Dave Hill	0	Peter Oosterhuis & Tony Jacklin (2 up)	1
Chi Chi Rodriguez & Lou Graham	0	Maurice Bembridge & Brian Huggett (5 & 4)	1
Lee Trevino & Billy Casper (2 & 1)	1	Neil Coles & Christy O'Connor Sr.	0
FOUR-BALLS: AFTERNOON			
J. C. Snead & Arnold Palmer (2 up)	1	Brian Barnes & Peter Butler	0

Gay Brewer & Billy Casper (3 & 2)	1	Tony Jacklin & Peter Oosterhuis	0
Jack Nicklaus & Tom Weiskopf (3 & 2)	1	Clive Clark & Eddie Polland	0
Lee Trevino & Homero Blancas	½	Maurice Bembridge & Brian Huggett	½

SINGLES: MORNING

Billy Casper (2 & 1)	1	Brian Barnes	0
Tom Weiskopf (3 & 1)	1	Bernard Gallacher	0
Homero Blancas (5 & 4)	1	Peter Butler	0
Tommy Aaron	0	Tony Jacklin (3 & 1)	1
Gay Brewer	½	Neil Coles	½
J. C. Snead (1 up)	1	Christy O'Connor Sr.	0
Jack Nicklaus	½	Maurice Bembridge	½
Lee Trevino	½	Peter Oosterhuis	½

SINGLES: AFTERNOON

Homero Blancas	0	Brian Huggett (4 & 2)	1
J. C. Snead (3 & 1)	1	Brian Barnes	0
Gay Brewer	1	Bernard Gallacher	0
Billy Casper (2 & 1)	1	Tony Jacklin	0
Lee Trevino	1	Neil Coles (6 & 5)	0
Tom Weiskopf	½	Christy O'Connor Sr.	½
Jack Nicklaus (2 up)	1	Maurice Bembridge	0
Arnold Palmer	0	Peter Oosterhuis (4 & 2)	1

1975

LAUREL VALLEY GOLF CLUB, LIGONIER, PENNSYLVANIA
Captains: Arnold Palmer (USA), Bernard Hunt (GB&I)
GB&I 11 USA 21

GB&I		USA	

FOURSOMES: MORNING

Brian Barnes & Bernard Gallacher	0	Jack Nicklaus & Tom Weiskopf (5 & 4)	1
Norman Wood & Maurice Bembridge	0	Gene Littler & Hale Irwin (4 & 3)	1

Tony Jacklin & Peter Oosterhuis	0	Al Geiberger & Johnny Miller (3 & 1)	1
Tommy Horton & John O'Leary	0	Lee Trevino & J. C. Snead (2 & 1)	1

FOUR-BALLS: AFTERNOON

Peter Oosterhuis & Tony Jacklin (2 & 1)	1	Billy Casper & Raymond Floyd	0
Eamonn Darcy & Christy O'Connor Jr.	0	Tom Weiskopf & Lou Graham (3 & 2)	1
Brian Barnes & Bernard Gallacher	½	Jack Nicklaus & Bob Murphy	½
Tommy Horton & John O'Leary	0	Lee Trevino & Hale Irwin (2 & 1)	1

FOUR-BALLS: MORNING

Peter Oosterhuis & Tony Jacklin	½	Billy Casper & Johnny Miller	½
Tommy Horton & Norman Wood	0	Jack Nicklaus & J. C. Snead (4 & 2)	1
Brian Barnes & Bernard Gallacher	0	Gene Littler & Lou Graham (5 & 3)	1
Eamonn Darcy & Guy Hunt	½	Al Geiberger & Raymond Floyd	½

FOURSOMES: AFTERNOON

Tony Jacklin & Brian Barnes (3 & 2)	1	Lee Trevino & Bob Murphy	0
Christy O'Connor Jr. & John O'Leary	0	Tom Weiskopf & Johnny Miller (5 & 3)	1
Peter Oosterhuis & Maurice Bembridge	0	Hale Irwin & Billy Casper (3 & 2)	1
Eamonn Darcy & Guy Hunt	0	Al Geiberger & Lou Graham (3 & 2)	1

SINGLES: MORNING

Tony Jacklin	0	Bob Murphy (2 & 1)	1
Peter Oosterhuis (2 up)	1	Johnny Miller	0
Bernard Gallacher	½	Lee Trevino	½

Tommy Horton	½	Hale Irwin	½
Brian Huggett	0	Gene Littler (4 & 2)	1
Eamonn Darcy	0	Billy Casper (3 & 2)	1
Guy Hunt	0	Tom Weiskopf (5 & 3)	1
Brian Barnes (4 & 2)	1	Jack Nicklaus	0

SINGLES: AFTERNOON

Tony Jacklin	0	Raymond Floyd (1 up)	1
Peter Oosterhuis (3 & 2)	1	J. C. Snead	0
Bernard Gallacher	½	Al Geiberger	½
Tommy Horton (2 & 1)	1	Lou Graham	0
John O'Leary	0	Hale Irwin (2 & 1)	1
Maurice Bembridge	0	Bob Murphy (2 & 1)	1
Norman Wood (2 & 1)	1	Lee Trevino	0
Brian Barnes (2 & 1)	1	Jack Nicklaus	0

1977

ROYAL LYTHAM & ST. ANNE'S, ST. ANNE'S, ENGLAND
Captains: Dow Finsterwald (USA), Brian Huggett (GB&I)
USA 12½ GB&I 7½

USA		GB&I	
FOURSOMES			
Lanny Wadkins & Hale Irwin (3 & 1)	1	Bernard Gallacher & Brian Barnes	0
Dave Stockton & Jerry McGee (1 up)	1	Neil Coles & Peter Dawson	0
Raymond Floyd & Lou Graham	0	Nick Faldo & Peter Oosterhuis (2 & 1)	1
Ed Sneed & Don January	½	Eamonn Darcy & Tony Jacklin	½
Jack Nicklaus & Tom Watson (5 & 4)	1	Tommy Horton & Mark James	0
FOUR-BALLS			
Tom Watson & Hubert Green (5 & 4)	1	Brian Barnes & Tommy Horton	0

Ed Sneed & Lanny Wadkins (5 & 3)	1	Neil Coles & Peter Dawson	0
Jack Nicklaus & Raymond Floyd	0	Nick Faldo & Peter Oosterhuis (3 & 1)	1
Dave Hill & Dave Stockton (5 & 3)	1	Tony Jacklin & Eamonn Darcy	0
Hale Irwin & Lou Graham (1 up)	1	Mark James & Ken Brown	0

SINGLES

Lanny Wadkins (4 & 3)	1	Howard Clark	0
Lou Graham (5 & 3)	1	Neil Coles	0
Don January	0	Peter Dawson (5 & 4)	1
Hale Irwin	0	Brian Barnes (1 up)	1
Dave Hill (5 & 4)	1	Tommy Horton	0
Jack Nicklaus	0	Bernard Gallacher (1 up)	1
Hubert Green (1 up)	1	Eamonn Darcy	0
Raymond Floyd (2 & 1)	1	Mark James	0
Tom Watson	0	Nick Faldo (1 up)	1
Jerry McGee	0	Peter Oosterhuis (2 up)	1

1979

THE GREENBRIER, WHITE SULPHUR SPRINGS, WEST VIRGINIA
Captains: Billy Casper (USA), John Jacobs (Europe)
EUROPE 11 USA 17

Europe		USA	

FOUR-BALLS: MORNING

Antonio Garrido & Seve Ballesteros	0	Lanny Wadkins & Larry Nelson (2 & 1)	1
Ken Brown & Mark James	0	Lee Trevino & Fuzzy Zoeller (3 & 2)	1
Peter Oosterhuis & Nick Faldo	0	Andy Bean & Lee Elder (2 & 1)	1
Bernard Gallacher & Brian Barnes (2 & 1)	1	Hale Irwin & John Mahaffey	0

FOURSOMES: AFTERNOON

Ken Brown & Des Smyth	0	Hale Irwin & Tom Kite (7 & 6)	1
Seve Ballesteros & Antonio Garrido (3 & 2)	1	Fuzzy Zoeller & Hubert Green	0
Sandy Lyle & Tony Jacklin	½	Lee Trevino & Gil Morgan	½
Bernard Gallacher & Brian Barnes	0	Lanny Wadkins & Larry Nelson (4 & 3)	1

FOURSOMES: MORNING

Tony Jacklin & Sandy Lyle (5 & 4)	1	Lee Elder & John Mahaffey	0
Nick Faldo & Peter Oosterhuis (6 & 5)	1	Andy Bean & Tom Kite	0
Bernard Gallacher & Brian Barnes (2 & 1)	1	Fuzzy Zoeller & Mark Hayes	0
Seve Ballesteros & Antonio Garrido	0	Lanny Wadkins & Larry Nelson (3 & 2)	1

FOUR-BALLS: AFTERNOON

Seve Ballesteros & Antonio Garrido	0	Lanny Wadkins & Larry Nelson (5 & 4)	1
Tony Jacklin & Sandy Lyle	0	Hale Irwin & Tom Kite (1 up)	1
Bernard Gallacher & Brian Barnes (3 & 2)	1	Lee Trevino & Fuzzy Zoeller	0
Nick Faldo & Peter Oosterhuis (1 up)	1	Lee Elder & Mark Hayes	0

SINGLES

Bernard Gallacher (3 & 2)	1	Lanny Wadkins	0
Seve Ballesteros	0	Larry Nelson (3 & 2)	1
Tony Jacklin	0	Tom Kite (1 up)	1
Antonio Garrido	0	Mark Hayes (1 up)	1
Michael King	0	Andy Bean (4 & 3)	1
Brian Barnes	0	John Mahaffey (1 up)	1
Nick Faldo (3 & 2)	1	Lee Elder	0
Des Smyth	0	Hale Irwin (5 & 3)	1
Peter Oosterhuis	0	Hubert Green (2 up)	1

Ken Brown (1 up)	1	Fuzzy Zoeller	0
Sandy Lyle	0	Lee Trevino (2 & 1)	1
Mark James (injured, halved)	½	Gil Morgan (halved, match not played)	½

1981

WALTON HEATH GOLF CLUB, SURREY, ENGLAND
Captains: Dave Marr (USA), John Jacobs (Europe)
USA 18½ EUROPE 9½

USA		Europe	
FOURSOMES: MORNING			
Lee Trevino & Larry Nelson (1 up)	1	Bernhard Langer & Manuel Piñero	0
Bill Rogers & Bruce Lietzke	0	Sandy Lyle & Mark James (2 & 1)	1
Hale Irwin & Raymond Floyd	0	Bernard Gallacher & Des Smyth (3 and 2)	1
Tom Watson & Jack Nicklaus (4 & 3)	1	Peter Oosterhuis & Nick Faldo	0
FOUR-BALLS: AFTERNOON			
Tom Kite & Johnny Miller	½	Sam Torrance & Howard Clark	½
Ben Crenshaw & Jerry Pate	0	Sandy Lyle & Mark James (3 & 2)	1
Bill Rogers & Bruce Lietzke	0	Des Smyth & José Maria Canizares (6 & 5)	1
Hale Irwin & Raymond Floyd (2 & 1)	1	Bernard Gallacher & Eamonn Darcy	0
FOUR-BALLS: MORNING			
Lee Trevino & Jerry Pate (7 & 5)	1	Nick Faldo & Sam Torrance	0
Larry Nelson & Tom Kite (1 up)	1	Sandy Lyle & Mark James	0
Raymond Floyd & Hale Irwin	0	Bernard Langer & Manuel Piñero (2 & 1)	1

Jack Nicklaus & Tom Watson (3 & 2)	1	José Maria Canizares & Des Smyth	0

Foursomes: Afternoon

Lee Trevino & Jerry Pate (2 & 1)	1	Peter Oosterhuis & Sam Torrance	0
Jack Nicklaus & Tom Watson (3 & 2)	1	Bernhard Langer & Manuel Pinero	0
Bill Rogers & Raymond Floyd (3 & 2)	1	Sandy Lyle & Mark James	0
Tom Kite & Larry Nelson (3 & 2)	1	Des Smyth & Bernard Gallacher	0

Singles

Lee Trevino (5 & 3)	1	Sam Torrance	0
Tom Kite (3 & 2)	1	Sandy Lyle	0
Bill Rogers	½	Bernard Gallacher	½
Larry Nelson (2 up)	1	Mark James	0
Ben Crenshaw (6 & 4)	1	Des Smyth	0
Bruce Lietzke	½	Bernhard Langer	½
Jerry Pate	0	Manuel Piñero (4 & 2)	1
Hale Irwin (1 up)	1	José Maria Canizares	0
Johnny Miller	0	Nick Faldo (2 & 1)	1
Tom Watson	0	Howard Clark (4 & 3)	1
Raymond Floyd (1 up)	1	Peter Oosterhuis	0
Jack Nicklaus (5 & 3)	1	Eamonn Darcy	0

1983

PGA National Golf Club,
Palm Beach Gardens, Florida
Captains: Jack Nicklaus (USA), Tony Jacklin (Europe)
EUROPE 13½ USA 14½

Europe		USA	

Foursomes: Morning

Bernard Gallacher & Sandy Lyle	0	Tom Watson & Ben Crenshaw (5 & 4)	1

Nick Faldo & Bernhard Langer (4 & 2)	1	Lanny Wadkins & Craig Stadler	0
José Maria Canizares & Sam Torrance (4 & 3)	1	Raymond Floyd & Bob Gilder	0
Seve Ballesteros & Paul Way	0	Tom Kite & Calvin Peete (2 & 1)	1

FOUR-BALLS: AFTERNOON

Brian Waites & Ken Brown (2 & 1)	1	Gil Morgan & Fuzzy Zoeller	0
Nick Faldo & Bernard Langer	0	Tom Watson & Jay Haas (2 & 1)	1
Seve Ballesteros & Paul Way (1 up)	1	Raymond Floyd & Curtis Strange	0
Sam Torrance & Ian Woosnam	½	Ben Crenshaw & Calvin Peete	½

FOUR-BALLS: MORNING

Brian Waites & Ken Brown	0	Lanny Wadkins & Craig Stadler (1 up)	1
Nick Faldo & Bernhard Langer (4 & 2)	1	Ben Crenshaw & Calvin Peete	0
Seve Ballesteros & Paul Way	½	Gil Morgan & Jay Haas	½
Sam Torrance & Ian Woosnam	0	Tom Watson & Bob Gilder (5 & 4)	1

FOURSOMES: AFTERNOON

Nick Faldo & Bernhard Langer (3 & 2)	1	Tom Kite & Raymond Floyd	0
Sam Torrance & José Maria Canizares	0	Gil Morgan & Lanny Wadkins (7 & 5)	1
Seve Ballesteros & Paul Way (2 & 1)	1	Tom Watson & Bob Gilder	0
Brian Waites & Ken Brown	0	Jay Haas & Curtis Strange (3 & 2)	1

SINGLES

Seve Ballesteros	½	Fuzzy Zoeller	½
Nick Faldo (2 & 1)	1	Jay Haas	0
Bernhard Langer (2 holes)	1	Gil Morgan	0
Gordon J. Brand	0	Bob Gilder (2 up)	1

Sandy Lyle	0	Ben Crenshaw (3 & 1)	1
Brian Waites	0	Calvin Peete (1 up)	1
Paul Way (2 & 1)	1	Curtis Strange	0
Sam Torrance	½	Tom Kite	½
Ian Woosnam	0	Craig Stadler (3 & 2)	1
José Maria Canizares	½	Lanny Wadkins	½
Ken Brown (4 & 3)	1	Raymond Floyd	0
Bernard Gallacher	0	Tom Watson (2 & 1)	1

1985

THE BELFRY GOLF & COUNTRY CLUB, SUTTON COLDFIELD, ENGLAND

Captains: Lee Trevino (USA), Tony Jacklin (Europe)

USA 11½ EUROPE 16

USA		Europe	
FOURSOMES: MORNING			
Curtis Strange & Mark O'Meara	0	Seve Ballesteros & Manuel Piñero (2 & 1)	1
Calvin Peete & Tom Kite (3 & 2)	1	Bernhard Langer & Nick Faldo	0
Lanny Wadkins & Raymond Floyd (4 & 3)	1	Sandy Lyle & Ken Brown	0
Craig Stadler & Hal Sutton (3 & 2)	1	Howard Clark & Sam Torrance	0
FOUR-BALLS: AFTERNOON			
Fuzzy Zoeller & Hubert Green	0	Paul Way & Ian Woosnam (1 up)	1
Andy North & Peter Jacobsen	0	Seve Ballesteros & Manuel Pinero (2 & 1)	1
Craig Stadler & Hal Sutton	½	Bernhard Langer & José Maria Canizares	½
Raymond Floyd & Lanny Wadkins (1 up)	1	Sam Torrance & Howard Clark	0

FOUR-BALLS: MORNING

Tom Kite & Andy North	0	Sam Torrance & Howard Clark (2 & 1)	1
Hubert Green & Fuzzy Zoeller	0	Paul Way & Ian Woosnam (4 & 3)	1
Mark O'Meara & Lanny Wadkins (3 & 2)	1	Seve Ballesteros & Manuel Pinero	0
Craig Stadler & Curtis Strange	½	Bernhard Langer & Sandy Lyle	½

FOURSOMES: AFTERNOON

Tom Kite & Calvin Peete	0	José Maria Canizares & José Rivero (4 & 3)	1
Craig Stadler & Hal Sutton	0	Seve Ballesteros & Manuel Piñero (5 & 4)	1
Curtis Strange & Peter Jacobsen (4 & 2)	1	Paul Way & Ian Woosnam	0
Raymond Floyd & Lanny Wadkins	0	Bernhard Langer & Ken Brown (3 & 2)	1

SINGLES

Lanny Wadkins	0	Manuel Pinero (3 & 1)	1
Craig Stadler (2 & 1)	1	Ian Woosnam	0
Raymond Floyd	0	Paul Way (2 up)	1
Tom Kite	½	Seve Ballesteros	½
Peter Jacobsen	0	Sandy Lyle (3 & 2)	1
Hal Sutton	0	Bernhard Langer (5 & 4)	1
Andy North	0	Sam Torrance (1 up)	1
Mark O'Meara	0	Howard Clark (1 up)	1
Calvin Peete (1 up)	1	José Rivero	0
Hubert Green (3 & 1)	1	Nick Faldo	0
Fuzzy Zoeller	0	José Maria Canizares (2 up)	1
Curtis Strange (4 & 2)	1	Ken Brown	0

1987

MUIRFIELD VILLAGE GOLF CLUB, DUBLIN, OHIO

Captains: Jack Nicklaus (USA), Tony Jacklin (Europe)

EUROPE 15 USA 13

Europe		USA	
FOURSOMES: MORNING			
Sam Torrance & Howard Clark	0	Curtis Strange & Tom Kite (4 & 2)	1
Ken Brown & Bernhard Langer	0	Hal Sutton & Dan Pohl (2 & 1)	1
Nick Faldo & Ian Woosnam (2 up)	1	Lanny Wadkins & Larry Mize	0
Seve Ballesteros & José Maria Olazábal (1 up)	1	Larry Nelson & Payne Stewart	0
FOUR-BALLS: AFTERNOON			
Gordon Brand Jr. & José Rivero (3 & 2)	1	Ben Crenshaw & Scott Simpson	0
Sandy Lyle & Bernhard Langer (1 up)	1	Andy Bean & Mark Calcavecchia	0
Nick Faldo & Ian Woosnam (2 & 1)	1	Hal Sutton & Dan Pohl	0
Seve Ballesteros & José Maria Olazábal (2 & 1)	1	Curtis Strange & Tom Kite	0
FOURSOMES: MORNING			
José Rivero & Gordon Brand Jr.	0	Curtis Strange & Tom Kite (3 & 1)	1
Nick Faldo & Ian Woosnam	½	Hal Sutton & Larry Mize	½
Sandy Lyle & Bernhard Langer (2 & 1)	1	Lanny Wadkins & Larry Nelson	0
Seve Ballesteros & José Maria Olazábal (1 up)	1	Ben Crenshaw & Payne Stewart	0
FOUR-BALLS: AFTERNOON			
Nick Faldo & Ian Woosnam (5 & 4)	1	Curtis Strange & Tom Kite	0

Eamonn Darcy & Gordon Brand Jr.	0	Andy Bean & Payne Stewart (3 & 2)	1
Seve Ballesteros & José Maria Olazábal	0	Hal Sutton & Larry Mize (2 & 1)	1
Sandy Lyle & Bernhard Langer (1 up)	1	Lanny Wadkins & Larry Nelson	0

SINGLES

Ian Woosnam	0	Andy Bean (1 up)	1
Howard Clark (1 up)	1	Dan Pohl	0
Sam Torrance	½	Larry Mize	½
Nick Faldo	0	Mark Calcavecchia (1 up)	1
José Maria Olazábal	0	Payne Stewart (2 up)	1
José Rivero	0	Scott Simpson (2 & 1)	1
Sandy Lyle	0	Tom Kite (3 & 2)	1
Eamonn Darcy (1 up)	1	Ben Crenshaw	0
Bernhard Langer	½	Larry Nelson	½
Seve Ballesteros (2 & 1)	1	Curtis Strange	0
Ken Brown	0	Lanny Wadkins (3 & 2)	1
Gordon Brand Jr.	½	Hal Sutton	½

1989

THE BELFRY GOLF & COUNTRY CLUB, SUTTON COLDFIELD, ENGLAND
Captains: Raymond Floyd (USA), Tony Jacklin (Europe)
USA 14 EUROPE 14

USA		Europe	
FOURSOMES: MORNING			
Tom Kite & Curtis Strange	½	Nick Faldo & Ian Woosnam	½
Lanny Wadkins & Payne Stewart (1 up)	1	Howard Clark & Mark James	0
Tom Watson & Chip Beck	½	Seve Ballesteros & José Maria Olazábal	½
Mark Calcavecchia & Ken Green (2 & 1)	1	Bernhard Langer & Ronan Rafferty	0

FOUR-BALLS: AFTERNOON

Curtis Strange & Paul Azinger	0	Sam Torrance & Gordon Brand Jr. (1 up)	1
Fred Couples & Lanny Wadkins	0	Howard Clark & Mark James (3 & 2)	1
Mark Calcavecchia & Mark McCumber	0	Nick Faldo & Ian Woosnam (2 up)	1
Tom Watson & Mark O'Meara	0	Seve Ballesteros & José Maria Olazábal (6 & 5)	1

FOURSOMES: MORNING

Lanny Wadkins & Payne Stewart	0	Ian Woosnam & Nick Faldo (3 & 2)	1
Chip Beck & Paul Azinger (4 & 3)	1	Gordon Brand Jr. & Sam Torrance	0
Mark Calcavecchia & Ken Green (3 & 2)	1	Christy O'Connor Jr. & Ronan Rafferty	0
Tom Kite & Curtis Strange	0	Seve Ballesteros & José Maria Olazábal (1 up)	1

FOUR-BALLS: AFTERNOON

Chip Beck & Paul Azinger (2 & 1)	1	Nick Faldo & Ian Woosnam	0
Tom Kite & Mark McCumber (2 & 1)	1	Bernhard Langer & José Maria Canizares	0
Payne Stewart & Curtis Strange	0	Howard Clark & Mark James (1 up)	1
Mark Calcavecchia & Ken Green	0	Seve Ballesteros & José Maria Olazábal (4 & 2)	1

SINGLES

Paul Azinger (1 up)	1	Seve Ballesteros	0
Chip Beck (3 & 2)	1	Bernhard Langer	0
Payne Stewart	0	José Maria Olazábal (1 up)	1
Mark Calcavecchia	0	Ronan Rafferty (1 up)	1
Tom Kite (8 & 7)	1	Howard Clark	0
Mark O'Meara	0	Mark James (3 & 2)	1
Fred Couples	0	Christy O'Connor Jr. (1 up)	1
Ken Green	0	José Maria Canizares (1 up)	1

Mark McCumber (1 up)	1	Gordon Brand Jr.	0
Tom Watson (3 & 1)	1	Sam Torrance	0
Lanny Wadkins (1 up)	1	Nick Faldo	0
Curtis Strange (2 up)	1	Ian Woosnam	0

1991

Ocean Course, Kiawah Island, South Carolina
Captains: Dave Stockton (USA), Bernard Gallacher (Europe)
Europe 13½ USA 14½

Europe		USA	
Foursomes: Morning			
Seve Ballesteros & José Maria Olazábal (2 & 1)	1	Paul Azinger & Chip Beck	0
Bernhard Langer & Mark James	0	Raymond Floyd & Fred Couples (2 & 1)	1
David Gilford & Colin Montgomerie	0	Lanny Wadkins & Hale Irwin (4 & 2)	1
Nick Faldo & Ian Woosnam	0	Payne Stewart & Mark Calcavecchia (1 up)	1
Four-balls: Afternoon			
Sam Torrance & David Feherty	½	Lanny Wadkins & Mark O'Meara	½
Seve Ballesteros & José Maria Olazábal (2 & 1)	1	Paul Azinger & Chip Beck	0
Steven Richardson & Mark James (5 & 4)	1	Corey Pavin & Mark Calcavecchia	0
Nick Faldo & Ian Woosnam	0	Raymond Floyd & Fred Couples (5 & 3)	1
Foursomes: Morning			
David Feherty & Sam Torrance	0	Hale Irwin & Lanny Wadkins (4 & 2)	1
Mark James & Steven Richardson	0	Mark Calcavecchia & Payne Stewart (1 hole)	1
Nick Faldo & David Gilford	0	Paul Azinger & Mark O'Meara (7 & 6)	1

Seve Ballesteros &		Fred Couples &	
José Maria Olazábal (3 & 2)	1	Raymond Floyd	0

FOUR-BALLS: AFTERNOON

Ian Woosnam &		Paul Azinger &	
Paul Broadhurst (2 & 1)	1	Hale Irwin	0
Bernhard Langer &		Corey Pavin &	
Colin Montgomerie (2 & 1)	1	Steve Pate	0
Mark James &		Lanny Wadkins &	
Steven Richardson (3 & 1)	1	Wayne Levi	0
Seve Ballesteros &		Payne Stewart &	
José Maria Olazábal	½	Fred Couples	½

SINGLES

Nick Faldo (2 up)	1	Raymond Floyd	0
David Feherty (2 & 1)	1	Payne Stewart	0
Colin Montgomerie	½	Mark Calcavecchia	½
José Maria Olazábal	0	Paul Azinger (2 up)	1
Steven Richardson	0	Corey Pavin (2 & 1)	1
Seve Ballesteros (3 & 2)	1	Wayne Levi	0
Ian Woosnam	0	Chip Beck (3 & 1)	1
Paul Broadhurst (3 & 1)	1	Mark O'Meara	0
Sam Torrance	0	Fred Couples (3 & 2)	1
Mark James	0	Lanny Wadkins (3 & 2)	1
Bernhard Langer	½	Hale Irwin	½
David Gilford		Steve Pate	
(halved, match not played)	½	(injured, halved)	½

1993

THE BELFRY GOLF & COUNTRY CLUB, SUTTON COLDFIELD, ENGLAND

Captains: Tom Watson (USA), Bernard Gallacher (Europe)

USA 15 EUROPE 13

USA		Europe	

FOURSOMES: MORNING

Lanny Wadkins &		Sam Torrance &	
Corey Pavin (4 & 3)	1	Mark James	0

Paul Azinger & Payne Stewart	0	Ian Woosnam & Bernhard Langer (7 & 5)	1
Tom Kite & Davis Love III (2 & 1)	1	Seve Ballesteros & José Maria Olazábal	0
Raymond Floyd & Fred Couples	0	Nick Faldo & Colin Montgomerie (4 & 3)	1

FOUR-BALLS: AFTERNOON

Jim Gallagher Jr. & Lee Janzen	0	Ian Woosnam & Peter Baker (1 up)	1
Lanny Wadkins & Corey Pavin (4 & 2)	1	Bernhard Langer & Barry Lane	0
Paul Azinger & Fred Couples	½	Nick Faldo & Colin Montgomerie	½
Davis Love III & Tom Kite	0	Seve Ballesteros & José Maria Olazábal (4 & 3)	1

FOURSOMES: MORNING

Lanny Wadkins & Corey Pavin	0	Nick Faldo & Colin Montgomerie (3 & 2)	1
Fred Couples & Paul Azinger	0	Bernhard Langer & Ian Woosnam (2 & 1)	1
Raymond Floyd & Payne Stewart (3 & 2)	1	Peter Baker & Barry Lane	0
Davis Love III & Tom Kite	0	Seve Ballesteros & José Maria Olazábal (2 & 1)	1

FOUR-BALLS: AFTERNOON

John Cook & Chip Beck (1 up)	1	Nick Faldo & Colin Montgomerie	0
Corey Pavin & Jim Gallagher Jr. (5 & 4)	1	Mark James & Costantino Rocca	0
Fred Couples & Paul Azinger	0	Ian Woosnam & Peter Baker (6 & 5)	1
Raymond Floyd & Payne Stewart (2 & 1)	1	José Maria Olazábal & Joakim Haeggman	0

SINGLES

Fred Couples	½	Ian Woosnam	½
Chip Beck (1 up)	1	Barry Lane	0

Lee Janzen	0	Colin Montgomerie (1 up)	1
Corey Pavin	0	Peter Baker (2 up)	1
John Cook	0	Joakim Haeggman (1 up)	1
Payne Stewart (3 & 2)	1	Mark James	0
Davis Love III (1 up)	1	Costantino Rocca	0
Jim Gallagher Jr. (3 & 2)	1	Seve Ballesteros	0
Raymond Floyd (2 up)	1	José Maria Olazábal	0
Tom Kite (5 & 3)	1	Bernhard Langer	0
Paul Azinger	½	Nick Faldo	½
Lanny Wadkins		Sam Torrance	
(injured, halved)	½	(halved; match not played)	½

1995

OAK HILL COUNTRY CLUB, ROCHESTER, NEW YORK
Captains: Bernard Gallacher (Europe), Lanny Wadkins (USA)
EUROPE 14½ USA 13½

Europe		USA	
FOURSOMES: MORNING			
Nick Faldo & Colin Montgomerie	0	Corey Pavin & Tom Lehman (1 up)	1
Sam Torrance & Costantino Rocca (3 & 2)	1	Jay Haas & Fred Couples	0
Howard Clark & Mark James	0	Davis Love III & Jeff Maggert (4 & 3)	1
Bernhard Langer & Per-Ulrik Johansson (1 up)	1	Ben Crenshaw & Curtis Strange	0
FOUR-BALLS: AFTERNOON			
David Gilford & Seve Ballesteros (4 & 3)	1	Brad Faxon & Peter Jacobsen	0
Sam Torrance & Costantino Rocca	0	Jeff Maggert & Loren Roberts (6 & 5)	1
Nick Faldo & Colin Montgomerie	0	Fred Couples & Davis Love III (3 & 2)	1
Bernhard Langer & Per-Ulrik Johansson	0	Corey Pavin & Phil Mickelson (6 & 4)	1

FOURSOMES: MORNING

Nick Faldo & Colin Montgomerie (4 & 2)	1	Curtis Strange & Jay Haas	0
Sam Torrance & Costantino Rocca (6 & 5)	1	Davis Love III & Jeff Maggert	0
Ian Woosnam & Philip Walton	0	Loren Roberts & Peter Jacobsen (1 up)	1
Bernhard Langer & David Gilford (4 & 3)	1	Corey Pavin & Tom Lehman	0

FOUR-BALLS: AFTERNOON

Sam Torrance & Colin Montgomerie	0	Brad Faxon & Fred Couples (4 & 2)	1
Ian Woosnam & Costantino Rocca (3 & 2)	1	Davis Love III & Ben Crenshaw	0
Seve Ballesteros & David Gilford	0	Jay Haas & Phil Mickelson (3 & 2)	1
Nick Faldo & Bernhard Langer	0	Corey Pavin & Loren Roberts (1 up)	1

SINGLES

Seve Ballesteros	0	Tom Lehman (4 & 3)	1
Howard Clark (1 up)	1	Peter Jacobsen	0
Mark James (4 & 3)	1	Jeff Maggert	0
Ian Woosnam	½	Fred Couples	½
Costantino Rocca	0	Davis Love III (3 & 2)	1
David Gilford (1 up)	1	Brad Faxon	0
Colin Montgomerie (3 & 1)	1	Ben Crenshaw	0
Nick Faldo (1 up)	1	Curtis Strange	0
Sam Torrance (2 & 1)	1	Loren Roberts	0
Bernhard Langer	0	Corey Pavin (3 & 2)	1
Philip Walton (1 up)	1	Jay Haas	0
Per-Ulrik Johansson	0	Phil Mickelson (2 & 1)	1

1997

VALDERRAMA GC, SOTOGRANDE, SPAIN

Captains: Seve Ballesteros (Europe), Tom Kite (USA)

USA 13½ EUROPE 14½

USA		Europe	
FOURSOMES: MORNING			
Davis Love III & Phil Mickelson	0	José Maria Olazábal & Costantino Rocca (1 up)	1
Fred Couples & Brad Faxon (1 up)	1	Nick Faldo & Lee Westwood	0
Tom Lehman & Jim Furyk	0	Jesper Parnevik & Per-Ulrik Johansson (1 up)	1
Tiger Woods & Mark O'Meara (3 & 2)	1	Colin Montgomerie & Bernhard Langer	0
FOUR-BALLS: AFTERNOON			
Scott Hoch & Lee Janzen (1 up)	1	Costantino Rocca & José Maria Olazábal	0
Mark O'Meara & Tiger Woods	0	Bernhard Langer & Colin Montgomerie (5 & 3)	1
Justin Leonard & Jeff Maggert	0	Nick Faldo & Lee Westwood (3 & 2)	0
Tom Lehman & Phil Mickelson	½	Jesper Parnevik & Ignacio Garrido	½
FOURSOMES: MORNING			
Fred Couples & Davis Love III	0	Colin Montgomerie & Darren Clarke (1 up)	1
Justin Leonard & Brad Faxon	0	Ian Woosnam & Thomas Björn (2 & 1)	1
Tiger Woods & Mark O'Meara	0	Nick Faldo & Lee Westwood (2 & 1)	1
Phil Mickelson & Tom Lehman	½	José Maria Olazábal & Ignacio Garrido	½
FOUR-BALLS: AFTERNOON			
Lee Janzen & Jim Furyk	0	Colin Montgomerie & Bernhard Langer (1 up)	1

Scott Hoch & Jeff Maggert (2 & 1)	1	Nick Faldo & Lee Westwood	0
Justin Leonard & Tiger Woods	½	Jesper Parnevik & Ignacio Garrido	½
Davis Love III & Fred Couples	0	José Maria Olazábal & Costantino Rocca (5 & 4)	1

SINGLES

Fred Couples (8 & 7)	1	Ian Woosnam	0
Davis Love III	0	Per-Ulrik Johansson (3 & 2)	1
Mark O'Meara (5 & 4)	1	Jesper Parnevik	0
Phil Mickelson (2 & 1)	1	Darren Clarke	0
Tiger Woods	0	Costantino Rocca (4 & 2)	1
Justin Leonard	½	Thomas Björn	½
Tom Lehman (7 & 6)	1	Ignacio Garrido	0
Brad Faxon	0	Bernhard Langer (2 & 1)	1
Jeff Maggert (3 & 2)	1	Lee Westwood	0
Lee Janzen (1 up)	1	José Maria Olazábal	0
Jim Furyk (3 & 2)	1	Nick Faldo	0
Scott Hoch	½	Colin Montgomerie	½

1999

THE COUNTRY CLUB, BROOKLINE, MASSACHUSETTS
Captains: Ben Crenshaw (USA), Mark James (Europe)
EUROPE 13½ USA 14½

Europe		USA	

FOURSOMES: MORNING

Paul Lawrie & Colin Montgomerie (3 and 2)	1	David Duval & Phil Mickelson	0
Sergio Garcia & Jesper Parnevik (2 and 1)	1	Tom Lehman & Tiger Woods	0
Miguel Angel Jiménez & Padraig Harrington	½	Davis Love III & Payne Stewart	½
Darren Clarke & Lee Westwood	0	Jeff Maggert & Hal Sutton (3 and 2)	1

FOUR-BALLS: AFTERNOON

Sergio Garcia & Jesper Parnevik (1 up)	1	Jim Furyk & Phil Mickelson	0
Paul Lawrie & Colin Montgomerie	½	Justin Leonard & Davis Love III	½
Miguel Angel Jiménez & José Maria Olazábal (2 and 1)	1	Jeff Maggert & Hal Sutton	0
Darren Clarke & Lee Westwood	1	David Duval & Tiger Woods	0

FOURSOMES: MORNING

Paul Lawrie & Colin Montgomerie	0	Jeff Maggert & Hal Sutton (1 up)	1
Darren Clarke & Lee Westwood (3 and 2)	1	Jim Furyk & Mark O'Meara	0
Miguel Angel Jiménez & Padraig Harrington	0	Steve Pate & Tiger Woods (1 up)	1
Sergio Garcia & Jesper Parnevik (3 and 2)	1	Justin Leonard & Payne Stewart	0

FOUR-BALLS: AFTERNOON

Darren Clarke & Lee Westwood	0	Phil Mickelson & Tom Lehman (2 and 1)	1
Sergio Garcia & Jesper Parnevik	½	Davis Love III & David Duval	½
Miguel Angel Jiménez & José Maria Olazábal	½	Justin Leonard & Hal Sutton	½
Paul Lawrie & Colin Montgomerie (2 and 1)	1	Steve Pate & Tiger Woods	0

SINGLES

Lee Westwood	0	Tom Lehman (3 and 2)	1
Jean Van de Velde	0	Davis Love III (6 and 5)	1
Jarmo Sandelin	0	Phil Mickelson (4 and 3)	1
Darren Clarke	0	Hal Sutton (4 and 2)	1
Jesper Parnevik	0	David Duval (5 and 4)	1
Andrew Coltart	0	Tiger Woods (3 and 2)	1
Miguel Angel Jiménez	0	Steve Pate (2 and 1)	1
Padraig Harrington (1 up)	1	Mark O'Meara	0
Sergio Garcia	0	Jim Furyk (4 and 3)	1

Paul Lawrie (4 and 3)	1	Jeff Maggert	0
José Maria Olazábal	½	Justin Leonard	½
Colin Montgomerie (1 up)	1	Payne Stewart	0

2002

THE BELFRY GOLF & COUNTRY CLUB, SUTTON COLDFIELD, ENGLAND

Captains: Curtis Strange (USA), Sam Torrance (Europe)

USA 12½ EUROPE 15½

USA		Europe	
FOUR-BALLS: MORNING			
Tiger Woods & Paul Azinger	0	Darren Clarke & Thomas Björn (1 up)	1
David Duval & Davis Love III	0	Sergio Garcia & Lee Westwood (4 & 3)	1
Scott Hoch & Jim Furyk	0	Colin Montgomerie & Bernhard Langer (4 & 3)	1
Phil Mickelson & David Toms (1 up)	1	Padraig Harrington & Niclas Fasth	0
FOURSOMES: AFTERNOON			
Hal Sutton & Scott Verplank (2 & 1)	1	Darren Clarke & Thomas Björn	0
Tiger Woods & Mark Calcavecchia	0	Sergio Garcia & Lee Westwood (2 & 1)	1
Phil Mickelson & David Toms	½	Colin Montgomerie & Bernhard Langer	½
Stewart Cink & Jim Furyk (3 & 2)	1	Padraig Harrington & Paul McGinley	0
FOURSOMES: MORNING			
Phil Mickelson & David Toms (2 & 1)	1	Phil Price & Pierre Fulke	0
Stewart Cink & Jim Furyk	0	Sergio Garcia & Lee Westwood (2 & 1)	1
Scott Verplank & Scott Hoch	0	Colin Montgomerie & Bernhard Langer (1 up)	1

Tiger Woods & Davis Love III (4 & 3)	1	Darren Clarke & Thomas Björn	0

FOUR-BALLS: AFTERNOON

Mark Calcavecchia & David Duval (1 up)	1	Niclas Fasth & Jesper Parnevik	0
Phil Mickelson & David Toms	0	Colin Montgomerie & Padraig Harrington (2 & 1)	1
Tiger Woods & Davis Love III (1 up)	1	Sergio Garcia & Lee Westwood	0
Scott Hoch & Jim Furyk	½	Darren Clarke & Paul McGinley	½

SINGLES

Scott Hoch	0	Colin Montgomerie (5 & 4)	1
David Toms (2 & 1)	1	Sergio Garcia	0
David Duval	½	Darren Clarke	½
Hal Sutton	0	Bernhard Langer (4 & 3)	1
Mark Calcavecchia	0	Padraig Harrington (5 & 4)	1
Stewart Cink	0	Thomas Björn (2 & 1)	1
Scott Verplank (2 & 1)	1	Lee Westwood	0
Paul Azinger	½	Niclas Fasth	½
Jim Furyk	½	Paul McGinley	½
Davis Love III	½	Pierre Fulke	½
Phil Mickelson	0	Phil Price (3 & 2)	1
Tiger Woods	½	Jesper Parnevik	½

BIBLIOGRAPHY

In addition to newspaper archives and American and European golf magazines, the following titles assisted with research:

Jarman, Colin M. *The Ryder Cup: The Definitive History of Playing Golf for Pride and Country.* New York: McGraw-Hill Contemporary Books, 1999.

Williams, Michael. *The Official History of the Ryder Cup, 1927–1989.* London: Stanley Paul, 1990.

Concannon, Dale. *The Ryder Cup: Seven Decades of Golfing Glory, Drama, and Controversy.* London: Aurum Press/Pelican Publishing, 2002.

Clavin, Thomas, and Bob Bubka. *The Ryder Cup: Golf's Greatest Event.* New York: Crown, 1999.

Lynch, Michael, and Ben Clingain. *The Ryder Cup Handbook.* Northampton, England: Brooklyn Publishing Group, 1993.